T0340093

Tokyo
JAPAN
CHINA
Kure
Midway
International Dateline
Wake
NORTHERN MARIANA ISLANDS
Saipan
GUAM
MARSHALL ISLANDS
Ratak Chain
Rālik Chain
Kuwajleen
Mājro
Manila
PHILIPPINES
Yap
Chuuk
Pohnpei
Kosrae
PALAU
FEDERATED STATES OF MICRONESIA
Sunday
Saturday
Tarawa
Gilbert Islands
K I R I
NAURU
Banaba
equator
New Ireland
Bougainville
SOLOMON ISLANDS
TUVALU
PAPUA
PAPUA NEW GUINEA
New Britain
Santa Cruz Islands
Guadalcanal
Rotuma
Wallis & Futuna
FIJI
VANUATU
Vanua Levu
Viti Levu
Lau Group
Loyalty Islands
Coral Sea
Makay
NEW CALEDONIA
Queensland
Bundaberg
AUSTRALIA
Brisbane
Norfolk
Sydney
Tasman Sea
Auckland
NEW ZEALAND
160°E
175°E
145°E
130°E
115°E

UNITED STATES

30°N

Los Angeles ⊕

O'ahu

Hawai'i

HAWAI'I

MEXICO

15°N

Mexico City ⊕

North Pacific Ocean

Clipperton .

Kiritimati

Line Islands

0 .　　equator

C O O K

Galapagos
Islands

Marquesas
Islands

F R E N C H

AN
OA

I S L A N D S

Tuamotu Archipelago

P O L Y N E S I A

15°S

Society Islands

Tahiti

Rarotonga .

Austral Islands

Gambier Islands

Pitcairn
Islands

Rapa Nui
(Easter) .

acific Ocean

30 °S

THE PACIFIC ISLANDS

W　E

155°W

140°W

125° W

45 °S

110°W

95°W

God Is Samoan

Pacific Islands Monograph Series 29

God Is Samoan

*Dialogues between Culture
and Theology in the Pacific*

Matt Tomlinson

CENTER FOR PACIFIC ISLANDS STUDIES

School of Pacific and Asian Studies

University of Hawai'i, Mānoa

UNIVERSITY OF HAWAI'I PRESS • Honolulu

25 24 23 22 21 20   6 5 4 3 2 1

Library of Congress Cataloging-in-Publication Data

Names: Tomlinson, Matt, author.

Title: God is Samoan : dialogues between culture and theology in the
   Pacific / Matt Tomlinson.

Other titles: Pacific islands monograph series ; no. 29.

Description: Honolulu : Center for Pacific Island Studies, University of
   Hawaiʻi, Mānoa : University of Hawaiʻi Press, 2020. | Series: Pacific
   islands monograph series ; 29 | Includes bibliographical references and
   index.

Identifiers: LCCN 2019052166 | ISBN 9780824880972 (cloth) | ISBN
   9780824883164 (pdf) | ISBN 9780824883171 (epub) | ISBN 9780824883188
   (kindle edition)

Subjects: LCSH: Christianity—Oceania. | Christianity and culture—Oceania.
   | Theology—Oceania. | Pacific Islanders—Religion.

Classification: LCC BR1490 .T66 2020 | DDC 230.0996—dc23

LC record available at https://lccn.loc.gov/2019052166

ISBN 978-0-8248-8831-2 (pbk.)

Cover art: Wooden carvings of the Holy Family, baby Jesus with Mary and Joseph sitting by a kava bowl at Fatu-o-ʻĀiga (Holy Family) Cathedral, Tafuna, American Sāmoa, May 2016. Photo by author.

✝ Maps by Manoa Mapworks, Inc.

Editor's Note

The drive from Sāmoa's Faleolo International Airport to the capital city, Apia, goes past many villages. In nearly every village, a church building takes center stage, towering above residential houses. With such visibility, you could be forgiven for thinking that you had arrived in God's country or that the Christian God has always been part of Samoan society. It is therefore fitting that Matt Tomlinson titles this book *God Is Samoan: Dialogues between Culture and Theology in the Pacific.*

The prominence of church buildings in Sāmoa illustrates broad and intellectually intriguing issues about Christianity in the Pacific. First, it underscores how Christianity has taken root in Oceania and become an important part of the lives of many Pacific Islanders. Since the first Christian missionaries arrived in the mid-seventeenth century, Christianity has permeated nearly every aspect of most Pacific Island societies.

Second, it shows that Pacific Islanders have agency in this process, rather than simply being passive victims of a global project of Christianization. While it is true that missionization has had some adverse impacts on Pacific Island societies and cultures, it is also true that Pacific Islanders have appropriated and used Christianity and its theology and institutions for their own purposes. In the process, they have indigenized aspects of Christianity and infused it with Pacific Island cultures and worldviews.

Third, it highlights the role that Pacific Islander scholar-theologians, clergy, and church leaders play in shaping church institutions and teachings. While early missionaries were largely Euro-Americans, nowadays there are many Pacific Islander scholar-theologians who have influenced how Christian theology is contextualized to reflect not only Judeo-Christian teachings but also Pacific Island cultures, beliefs, and practices. Many of these scholar-theologians work out of several seminaries and theological colleges in the region, including Malua Theological College and Piula Theological College in Sāmoa, Kanana Fou Theological Seminary in American Sāmoa, and the Pacific Theological College in Fiji. These Pacific Islander scholar-theologians often draw on the land (*vanua* or *fanua*) to shape their societies in ways that foreign theologians cannot.

In *God Is Samoan*, Tomlinson examines the intersections between theology and culture. Informed by his training in anthropology and drawing on a variety of sources, including archival data, scholarly writings (especially from Pacific Islander scholar-theologians), and ethnographic fieldwork, he weaves a captivating and informative account of the infusions of Pacific Island cultures and worldviews into theology. He provides insights into contextual theology and how it is manifested in Oceania. For example, in chapter 4, he refers to how Fiji's iTaukei scholar-theologian, Ilaitia Tuwere, has invoked the Fijian trio of *vanua, lotu* (Christianity), and *matanitū* (government) as foundational to Fijian theology. Rootedness in the *vanua,* he argued, is fundamental to Pasifika theology, or what is sometimes referred to as "Coconut Theology" or "Pacific Way" theology.

Tomlinson focuses on the work of scholar-theologians from Sāmoa, Tonga, Fiji, and Aotearoa/New Zealand, but he locates it within a broader regional context. He also frames it within the disciplines of theology, anthropology, and Pacific Islands studies, providing a refreshing dive into interdisciplinary dialogue, especially among scholars in these fields. Tomlinson's theoretical contribution to scholarship on the Pacific Islands lies in his engagement with the practice and framing of Pasifika theology and his analysis of the ways in which culture is deployed in different disciplinary contexts.

The book's subject matter is particularly important to Pacific Islands studies, as it provides a compelling argument that theology—like anthropology, history, political science, economics, and other such disciplines—should be central to intellectual engagements in Pacific Islands studies. This is especially true given the fact that Christianity has had a profound impact on Pacific Island societies, both at home in the Islands and in the diaspora. While the interdisciplinary nature of Pacific Islands studies is often associated with the interweaving of traditional disciplines, this book provides a convincing case that theology, especially Pasifika theology, is a compelling, contemporary, and crucial topic within Pacific Islands studies.

This volume is masterfully written, and it is an informative and enjoyable read. Tomlinson is able to engage sophisticated anthropological and theological concepts in a way that is highly accessible, and the photographs throughout help illuminate and give life to the various issues he covers. *God Is Samoan* is a valuable contribution to Pacific Islands scholarship. It will make a great course reader in disciplines such as theology, anthropology, Pacific Islands studies, and cultural studies, and it will be useful to anyone interested in these fields or in the Pacific Islands region in general, such as clergy, church leaders, and scholars at seminaries, theological colleges, and other institutions around the world.

TARCISIUS KABUTAULAKA

Contents

Illustrations

Preface

I hope the title of this book will be received in a generous spirit. I am an anthropologist rather than a theologian, and I don't know whether God has a nationality or culture in the regular sense. The title is meant to reflect the key lesson I learned from contextual theologians during my research: that if one wants to understand God, God must be understood in terms that make sense to people within their social situations and life experiences.

The analytic focus of this book is mainline Protestant contextual theology from the central Pacific, especially Fiji, Sāmoa, and Tonga. Because Catholic theologians have had a profound influence on the development of contextual theology with their writings on "inculturation" and Marx-influenced liberation theology, their ideas and words swim through these pages, but most of my textual and ethnographic discussion stays in Protestant waters.

During my research with theologians, I conducted interviews in English, and the theses, dissertations, articles, chapters, and books I quote were written in English. The majority of theological scholarship focused on the central Pacific is written in English, although there are many exceptions. I speak and read Fijian, but not yet Samoan or Tongan, so my discussions of Fijian material likely have more ethnographic traction.

Two notes on terminology are necessary. First, there is no fully agreed-on collective noun for people from Oceania. In an article written to recommend such a collective name, Sitaleki Finau and his coauthors reviewed a range of options including Moanans, Moana Nuians, Oceanians, Pasifikans, Pacificans, South Sea Islanders, Pacific Islanders, and Pacific Peoples (2010, 165–168). They ultimately recommended "Pasifikans," a term used especially in New Zealand and Australia and often in reference to diasporic populations. In this book I use several terms interchangeably—Oceanic, Oceanian, Pacific, Pacific Islander(s)—but recognize that readers may prefer alternatives. Second, I use the term "theologians" for people who have studied at a seminary or theological college. Although there is a vigorous everyday grassroots theology in Oceania—people talking to each other about God at kava sessions or over cold beers—in this book I focus on the work of thinkers who have formally studied and written on God within churches and church-affiliated institutions.

In presenting transcripts of interviews, I have edited texts to remove false starts, repetitions, minor feedback from listeners (including myself) like "mm hmm," and placeholders like "y'know." In some cases I have also corrected minor grammatical matters, such as verb tense, subject-verb agreement, and missing articles. In quoting texts by authors for whom English is not a first language, I have occasionally corrected spelling and punctuation for ease of reading. In all cases, I have aimed to make the text easily readable without altering meanings.

A number of authors have published using several variations of their name. For example, Ilaitia Sevati Tuwere has published as I S Tuwere, Ilaitia Tuwere, Ilaitia Sevati Tuwere, and Sevati Tuwere. In the main text and references list, I standardize the authors' names (in this case, always using Ilaitia Sevati Tuwere), so readers following up on sources should bear in mind that works might be published under lengthened or shortened versions of authors' names.

Acknowledgments

My deepest gratitude goes to the theologians and their families in Fiji, Sāmoa, and New Zealand who showed me such generosity. And not only generosity but also patient teaching in the real matters of life: God, ethics, hope, *loloma*, *alofa*, mana, and, of course, the value of kava drinking for theological thinking. At the Pacific Theological College (PTC) in Suva, my thanks go to the staff members during my time there, including (but not limited to) Principal Feleterika Nokise and his late wife Roselyn, Tevita K Havea, Kafoa Solomone, Cliff Bird, Manfred Ernst, Holger Szesnat, Afereti Uili, and Michael Press. In Sāmoa, the principal of Piula Theological College, Mosese Maʻilo, the registrar, Saunoa Sila, and their staff members made me feel part of their tight-knit community. I owe special thanks to Faʻasalafa Solaese, who took me in as a member of his *ʻauāʻiga* and provided invaluable perspectives based on his experiences in both Sāmoa and Australia. In American Sāmoa, Kanana Fou Theological Seminary President Moreli Niuatoa, Vice President Amaʻamalele Tofaeono, and staff members were welcoming, patient, and supportive at all times. I owe extra gratitude to Harold Eveni and Liusamoa Simolea for taking me on road trips to cover the extent of Tutuila from west to east, giving me an appreciation of an astonishingly beautiful land. When I was a visiting researcher at the University of Auckland (UA) School of Theology, I was given an institutional home and opportunities for wonderful conversation with Elaine Wainwright and her staff members, including Nāsili Vakaʻuta, Stephen Garner, Carolyn Blyth, Helen Bergin, Nick Thompson, and Derek Tovey.

The librarians at all of these sites were gracious with their expertise, advising me on key materials and allowing me to use resources when classes were not in session. Without the help of Nalini Premadish at PTC, Uesile Tupu at Piula, Evelyn Eveni at Kanana Fou, and Mark Hangartner at the UA School of Theology, this book would not even have been started. I am grateful, too, to Andy Connelly for sending me scans of hard-to-find early issues of the *Pacific Journal of Theology (PJT)*.

I also received thoughtful support and guidance from Leāsiolagi Mālama Meleiseā, Penelope Schoeffel, and Dionne Fonoti at the National University of Samoa's Centre for Samoan Studies, where I was fortunate to be a fellow in 2015, and from Latu and Lotu Latai at Malua Theological College, as well as Galumalemana Afeleti Hunkin. At the UA School of Theology, I was grateful that four students, staff members at Malua studying for their doctorates in New Zealand, were willing to share their expertise and insights with me: Vaitusi Nofoaiga, Terry Pouono, Arthur Wulf, and Imoamaua Setefano. I also enjoyed conversations with Christine Dureau and Susanna Trnka, who pushed me (kindly but firmly) to conceptualize more clearly what my project was really about; thanks to those conversations, notes and scribblings began to cohere as a book. And to Apo Aporosa from Hamilton, as always, vinaka vakalevu sara na veitalanoa ena bati ni tānoa. Aporosa's scholarship on kava drinking and indigenous identity is legendary, and his generosity is unmatched.

Many readers offered supportive critical feedback as the manuscript developed. I owe a debt of thanks to Ama'amalele Tofaeono, Ilana Gershon, and the reviewers for the University of Hawai'i Press, Brian T Alofaituli and Philip Fountain, for their engagements with the full manuscript. I am also grateful to PIMS Editor Tarcisius Kabutaulaka and Managing Editor Jan Rensel for receiving my proposal, and then the book manuscript, with a warm and encouraging spirit, and to Candi Steiner for expertly copyediting it. For comments on specific chapters, my thanks to Jessica Hardin, Susanna Trnka, Fepulea'i Micah Van der Ryn, Ma'afu Palu, Brian Howell, and Banu Senay. Parts of the argument were presented in papers delivered at the National University of Samoa's Centre for Samoan Studies, Piula Theological College, the Oceanic Biblical Studies Association (OBSA) conference at the Pacific Theological College, the University of Auckland, Victoria University of Wellington, Academia Sinica, and the Australian National University (ANU). My thanks to the audience members who shared lively insights and suggestions at these events, including Jione Havea at OBSA and Pei-yi Guo at Academia Sinica. In Australia, I have also benefited from the help and advice of friends including Julian Millie, Jeanette Mathews, Debra McDougall, and my valued ANU colleagues, including Andrew Pawley, Alan Rumsey, Francesca Merlan, Assa Doron, Chris Gregory, Margaret Jolly, Katerina Teaiwa, and Carly Schuster. My special thanks also go to Alan Rumsey for inviting me to discuss chapter 2 of this book with his honors students, two of whom, Mitiana Arbon and Alana Tolman, gave especially insightful feedback.

Funding for the research came from the Australian Research Council (ARC). My time at PTC was supported by an ARC Discovery Project grant ("God, Blood, Country," DP0878736), and the work in Sāmoa, American Sāmoa, and New Zealand was supported by a Future Fellowship ("Divine Power in Indigenous Christianity," FT110100524). I am grateful to the council for its willingness to fund research on Christianity in the Pacific and to Monash University and the Australian National University for administering these grants and enabling me to balance research and teaching.

Parts of chapter 3 were published previously as "A Preliminary Historical Survey of the Pacific Journal of Theology" in *PJT* (Tomlinson 2015b). My thanks to the journal and its publisher, the South Pacific Association of Theological Schools, and specifically to Rusiate Tuidrakulu and Tessa Mackenzie, for permission to reuse this material.

Finally, I must thank my family for their love, support, and humor during the years this research and book have come together. My wife Sharon and older son Andrew spent several months with me at PTC; Evan was born later and was able to come with Sharon and Andrew for two visits during my research in New Zealand. Everywhere we have been together, they have contributed to the adventure.

Introduction

For many anthropologists, culture and society ground divinity: divinity is a figure that humans interactively create and transform. No humans, no God. For many theologians, in contrast, divinity grounds culture and society: No God, no humans. Bringing the two disciplines into dialogue, as some anthropologists and theologians have been inclined to do in recent years, is both promising and problematic. Conversation between anthropologists and theologians can move both disciplines forward intellectually, but it can also skew and halt at different understandings of what the terms of engagement are, as well as their stakes.

One reason I have written this book is my observation that theologians in the Pacific Islands have the potential to shape their societies in ways that simply are not possible for theologians in most of Europe, the United States, or Australia. In the Pacific Islands, also known as Oceania and sometimes called the "liquid continent," religion is publicly and privately pervasive. Christian faith plays a foundational role in many people's daily lives and is also part of national constitutions, agendas, and debates. For many historical reasons, Christianity in Oceania is inevitably political—wrapped up in arguments over morality, advocating particular forms of social organization and gender relations, supporting or resisting coups, engaging in processes of reconciliation, and so forth (Tomlinson and McDougall 2013). This thoroughgoing Christianity at the heart of Pacific societies means that in Oceania, theology matters deeply.

In the following chapters, I describe and analyze theologians' use of "culture" as a concept. There are two reasons I take this approach, both of them emerging from observations I have made during research in Fiji, Sāmoa, and New Zealand. First is the simple but crucial fact that many theologians in Oceania use a concept of culture to motivate their arguments. The authors whose work I discuss in the following pages are indigenous intellectuals who situate themselves as such—as having something to say, theologically, partly by virtue of their social grounding as indigenous Fijians, Samoans, or Tongans. Second, in treating culture as an object of analysis that itself grounds analysis, theologians attempt to motivate dialogues of various kinds. The key dialogue is between humanity and God, but others are designed around it: for example, dialogues between readers and texts, between churches and society, and within and between scholarly disciplines.

1

The theologians whose work I discuss in this book are influenced by, or in some cases firmly part of, a field called contextual theology. (In this book, I include biblical studies within theology, although some biblical scholars will object to this classification.) Contextual theology and biblical studies incorporate social context and personal experience at the ground level of interpretation and argument. Culture is treated as central to religious understanding and experience, and eliciting culture is a key step in making theological arguments. In doing such things as defining Christian service in distinctly Samoan terms, framing sacred space in Fijian terms, or developing interpretive strategies in Tongan terms, the theologians in this book address their core concerns in ways marked as self-consciously cultural and specifically indigenous. They might intend their theology to appeal to local audiences or to global ones, but in both cases their scholarship is flagged with an emblematic place of origin that is often anchored in a heroic past such as an Edenic Fiji or Sāmoa as it was brought into being by the god Tagaloa.

The theologians whose work I discuss have distinct perspectives. What unites them is (1) their conviction that cultural distinctions matter theologically and (2) their consistent advocacy of "dialogue" as the best way to make theology meaningful and consequential.

Theology, Anthropologically Speaking

When hearing the word "theology," most non-theologians probably think of what is called "systematic theology," a broad field that includes dogmatics, ethics, and ecclesiology (the study of churches). As Miner Raymond put it more than a century ago, "In dogmatics we discuss doctrines and inquire, What ought we to believe? In ethics we discuss duties and inquire, What ought we to do?" (Raymond 1877–1879, 3:9). Dogmatics includes such disciplines as soteriology (the study of salvation); eschatology (the study of "last things" including death and the end of the world); apologetics (formal argument for Christian truth); and the core, theology itself, which is the study of God—Raymond called it "theology proper" (1877–1879, 1:7). Dogmatics also includes "anthropology," by which systematic theologians do not mean cultural anthropology but rather the biblically based study of universal human nature as seen through a Judeo-Christian lens: humankind is created in God's image but has sinned itself out of paradise.

In this book, I focus on contextual theologians rather than systematic theologians, but it will become apparent that contextual theologians in Oceania often work within the classic systematic categories. For example, many of them are passionate about ecclesiology, but they approach it with a different set of principles and expectations than systematic theologians do. The point is that contextual theologians pay close attention to culture, magnifying and magnetizing it in ways that systematic theologians do not.

In contextual theology, social context and personal experience motivate the questions that are asked and contour the ground of argument. How is Jesus like a Polynesian chief? Can he be symbolized more effectively as the Pig of God rather than the Lamb of God in a place where lambs do not live and pigs are both cherished and sacrificed? What does God's covenant with the earth mean for Islanders facing rising sea levels due to human-caused climate change? Stephen Bevans, a Catholic priest and former missionary whose work is influential in contextual theology, characterized it by writing, "Theology that is contextual realizes that culture, history, contemporary thought forms, and so forth are to be considered, along with scripture and tradition, as valid sources for theological expression" (1992, 2; see also Schreiter 1985). In many ways, the discipline's raison d'être is to "talk back" to mainstream theology, gaining critical purchase as theologians situate encounters with people, texts, and divinity within their own life experiences.

Because from an anthropological perspective all humans are cultural creatures, it might seem to anthropologists that all theology is contextual. How could it not be? Indeed, Bevans has called contextualization "a theological imperative … [and] part of the very nature of theology itself" (1992, 1). But contextual theology is in fact a distinct approach, and "simply saying that all theology is contextual is not the same as it being explicitly contextual" (Garner 2011, 167). As in all disciplines, particular authors' books and articles serve as conceptual landmarks that define the field for both participants and observers. For Pacific contextual theology, they include Bevans's textbook *Models of Contextual Theology* (1992, with a revised edition ten years later);[1] Tongan anthropologist-turned-novelist Epeli Hau'ofa's essay "Our Sea of Islands" (1993b), which called for the region to be seen anew as a vast, interconnected, and expanding space united by the ocean rather than separated by it; and the work of Ilaitia Sevati Tuwere from Fiji, who early on called for the development of a distinctive Oceanic contextual theology and has since shaped the field by focusing on spiritual power and presence in land and sea.[2] Sione 'Amanaki Havea of Tonga is credited with developing the first distinctly Oceanic theology, called "Coconut Theology" (see next section).

Some of the heterogeneity and transgressive potential of contextual theology can be heard in the words of Jenny Te Paa, an Anglican Māori theologian, who has described her background in "feminist, liberation, black, buffalo, Maori, coconut, African, queer, *minjung, dalit* and other such irresistible and compelling identity-based theologies" (Te Paa 2011, 71–72).[3] Te Paa's list calls attention to some of the sources that, marshaled and aligned in various ways, inform contextual theology, including the liberation theology of Gustavo Gutiérrez (1974), second-wave feminism, postcolonialism, and indigenous sovereignty movements—not to mention the popularization of an anthropological concept of culture. But Te Paa has also been critical of contextual theology, especially for the ways indigenous scholars can be pushed into the field as if it were a natural habitat. "It has been my experience," she reflected, "that many of my well-intentioned, white peers...initially endeavored to empower Indigenous and minority students by encouraging, if not mandating, curriculum engagement with *context;* indeed, social location became an almost mandatory feature of every thesis I ever marked from an Indigenous student" (Te Paa 2011, 81; italics in original). Tongan Methodist theologian Jione Havea pushed this point further, observing "an overwhelming expectation that speakers or writers from Tuvalu and Kiribati will address something related to climate change" (2014b, 15; see also J Havea 2011).

In global representations of indigenous, postcolonial, and generically "non-Western" peoples, Oceania does not often feature prominently. Tahitian church leader John Doom once described Oceania as "the forgotten third world" (Doom 1983, 353), and his description seems apt for contextual theology, in which Pacific scholarship is not well represented in global surveys. Consider the popular reader *Voices from the Margin,* edited by R S Sugirtharajah and first published in 1991, with revised editions appearing in 1995 and 2006. The individual chapters offer biblical interpretations from explicitly cultural or national perspectives, such as "The Cornelius Story in the Japanese Cultural Context," "The Rhetorical Hermeneutic of 1 Corinthians 8 and Chinese Ancestor Worship," and "Toward a Post-Apartheid Black Feminist Reading of the Bible." In the original publication from 1991, there was no chapter that focused on the Pacific Islands. In the second edition, one chapter out of thirty-four did so, from Leslie Boseto of Solomon Islands. In the third edition from 2006, Boseto's chapter was dropped, and despite the fact that twenty new contributions appeared, Oceania was absent again. As another case in point, the general editor of the *Global Bible Commentary (GBC)* announced that the book "reflects the fact that almost two-thirds of the readers of the Bible are Christians in Africa, Asia, Latin America, and Oceania"; in recognition of this, "The contributors to the *GBC* are literally from all over the world" (Patte 2004, xxi). Yet its seventy-two chapters contain only one by an author identifying himself as a Pacific Islander, Jione Havea. Havea is also credited as a representative of Australia (his professional home), which is noteworthy, as there are no other authors from Australia. There are also no authors from New Zealand. Eleven are from Argentina.

Within their home societies and church organizations, however, Oceanic contextual theologians can have high profiles and significant authority. For example, Boseto was the first moderator of Melanesian heritage to lead the United Church in Papua New Guinea and Solomon Islands; he also served as chairman of the Pacific Conference of Churches and was a member of the Central Committee of the World Council of Churches. In addition to these positions, he was elected multiple times to the Solomon Islands national parliament (representing his homeland of South Choiseul) and worked for peace and reconciliation in war-torn Bougainville.[4] Tuwere, Fiji's most accomplished Christian theologian, served as president of the Methodist Church in Fiji during a key period between government coups and played a significant role as a peacemaking moderate against hard-line ethnic nationalists calling for Fiji to be declared a Christian state. And in Australia and New Zealand, diasporic "Pasifika" (Pacific Islander) identities are vibrant in many contexts, including churches and public institutions.

Coconut Theology and Its Offshoots

The theologian who developed the first explicitly Oceanic contextual theology, called "Coconut Theology," was Sione 'Amanaki Havea. Havea was a progressive leader of the Free Wesleyan Church of Tonga who served as his church's first Tongan president and was principal of the Pacific Theological College (PTC) in Suva from 1977 to 1981 (Wood-Ellem 2000; Nokise 2015). He pushed for ecumenism in the Pacific, and Feleterika Nokise identified him as one of the " 'founding fathers' of ecumenism" in Oceania, along with Setareki Tuilovoni of Fiji and Vavae Toma of Sāmoa (Nokise 2011, 96; see also Uriam 2005).[5]

Havea described the coconut as a symbol with many meanings relevant to Pacific Christians. It stands for life itself: "Once it bears fruit it continues to bear fruit every year. . . . When the coconut rolls down it rolls down with its many lifegiving possibilities." It stands for *kairos*, or "the fullness of time": "No one can push back the time when it will ripen, nor make it ripen any earlier." It can be seen in terms of Christology, including the Incarnation, Virgin Birth, and Resurrection, as something growing, dying, and being reborn. It also lends itself culturally as a Eucharistic element: "For the people of the Pacific," Havea wrote, "Bread and wine are foreign and very expensive to import. The wheat and the grapes are two separate elements. The coconut has both the drink and the food from the same fruit, like the blood and flesh from the one and the same body of Christ" (see figure 0.1).[6] Beyond these multiple meanings, the key for Havea was that "everyone in the Pacific knows and literally lives on coconut. . . . If Jesus had grown up and lived in the Pacific, He could have added another identification of himself—I am the Coconut of Life" (S Havea 1987, 14–15).

Havea's thinking, as well as his theological influence, seems to have taken shape and gained momentum due to his traveling and talking with others in the 1960s, 1970s, and 1980s rather than from published work. The quotations just offered come from Havea's chapter, "Christianity in the Pacific Context" (1987), in a collection of papers from a conference in Papua New Guinea; the chapter is rarely cited, and the volume does not seem to have circulated widely. Nonetheless, Havea was the figure around whom globally circulating ideas about the value of local contexts and identities coalesced. Through his work, the era's urgent movements for decolonization, national independence, and indigenous rights became united in a single resonant symbol for Christian theology.[7]

Several themes have emerged in Pacific contextual theology since the

FIGURE 0.1. Coconut juice being served for Holy Communion. Photograph by John Taylor, New Caledonia, 1964, World Council of Churches Archives B6841-11; reproduced by permission of the World Council of Churches.

creation of Coconut Theology. In 1992, Tuwere, who succeeded Havea as PTC principal, identified four: (1) "living within the gap" between traditional and modern systems; (2) understanding the history of Oceania in ways both local and expansive ("there must be a direct link between Oceania and Israel, not via Sydney or London or Rome"); (3) focusing on place, both landscape and seascape; and (4) being marginalized, which is a state of "helplessness" but also an opportunity: "How can the church be a community *of* and *for* the marginalised?" (Tuwere 1992, 49, 50, 52, 54; italics in original). Almost two decades later, Catholic priest Philip Gibbs, who has served for more than thirty years in Papua New Guinea, gave the field a fresh evaluation and identified the most inclusive theme in Oceanic theology as "life as a hermeneutical key." He characterized life broadly—"from the cosmic concept of life as found in primal religions, to the struggle for life in the urban and semi-urban settlements of the region"—and argued that attempts to sustain and celebrate life were "behind almost all efforts to do indigenous theology in Oceania" (Gibbs 2010, 35).

Within this wide scope, Gibbs pointed to three main concerns of Pacific theologians. The first is social integration and conflict, a matter of strenuous interest in places like Fiji, with its four military coups since independence, and Bougainville, where more than ten thousand people were killed in the civil war following the takeover of the Panguna copper mine in the late 1980s (Gibbs 2010, 36–37). The second concern is ecology and the environmental crisis, including topics such as nuclear testing and climate change. Indeed, climate change has become something of a regional emblem as international news outlets report on atoll dwellers who fear their homes will soon vanish, becoming part of the liquid continent in a dismayingly literal way. The third concern is local responses to globalization. Attention to this topic is probably found in indigenous scholarship worldwide, not only in theology and not only in Oceania, but it does motivate passionate, energetic work by Pacific contextual theologians who raise questions about the legacies of mission encounters and challenges of appropriate leadership in times of rapid social change.

Coming to Culture

In most contextual theology, discussion eventually focuses on culture. The models of culture used by many Pacific theologians tend to be structural functionalist and cognitivist. Culture is depicted as ordered, stable, and whole, with rules and values joined in an enduring system. For example, in a work of ecological theology ("eco-theology") inspired in part by Samoan creation myths, Ama'amalele Tofaeono drew on definitions of culture that include "the sum total of ways of living built up by a human community and transmitted from one generation to another" and "a plan, consisting of a set of norms, standards and associated notions and beliefs for coping with the various demands of life, shared by a social group, learned by the individual from the society, and organized into a dynamic system of control" (Lesslie Newbigin and Louis J Luzbetak quoted in Tofaeono 2000, 28–29). Tuwere, referring to a report from the World Council of Churches, adopted its definition of culture as "what holds the community together, giving a common framework to meaning," something "preserved in language, thought patterns, ways of life, attitudes, symbols and presuppositions ... [and] celebrated in art, music, drama, literature and the like" (Tuwere 1991, 12). In the work of many contextual theologians from Oceania, then, culture is treated as a way of life, a worldview, and a set of traditions that gets passed from generation to generation. Such definitions turn culture into a stable resource, an identifiable object that can be pulled out for analysis and brought into relation with other objects.[8]

As an example, one goal of much Samoan theology is to arrive at a deeper understanding of *fa'asāmoa*. The term, which can be translated as "the Samoan way of life" or "the Samoan Way" (Milner 1993, 49), is used as an emblem of everything deep, meaningful, beneficial, and enduring about life in Sāmoa. Many Samoan theologians configure *fa'asāmoa* as both the ground and object of analysis. Moreli Niuatoa, the president of Kanana Fou Theological

Seminary in American Sāmoa, wrote that *fa'asāmoa* is "the epistemology of Samoan spirituality... the prism through which the profound and vibrant meaning of spirituality is inherently embedded... the heartbeat of living and practicing of Samoan spirituality" (Niuatoa 2007, 1). "For the people of Samoa," according to Seresese Vaaimamao, "what is regarded as just and right is determined by what communalism and the *fa'asamoa* prescribed for them" (1998, 99). Featuna'i Ben Liuaana, a historian, argued that "*fa'asamoa* was the guiding principle in everything the Samoans accomplished" in their drive to national independence, something that that "gave them pride and identity" in the ideals defining "every aspect of their social, political and religious life" (2004, 294).

Historian Mālama Meleiseā observed wryly that all Samoans consider themselves experts on *fa'asāmoa* "by virtue of being Samoan" (1992, 61–62). Meleiseā's point, which recalls the old idea of culture being carried in the blood, is given humorous ethnographic illustration in Ilana Gershon's description of a Samoan school coordinator in San Francisco who mentioned that her students would put on a dance performance for a visiting official. The students, however, had not grown up in Sāmoa and were thus not likely to be familiar with what was expected of them. When Gershon mentioned that the official's visit was less than a week away and students might not have time to prepare, she was told that "the students didn't need time to rehearse—they were Samoan and would quickly learn any dance" (Gershon 2012, 144; see also Niuatoa 2007, 121; Sakai 2009).

Some Samoan theologians approach the term and concept *fa'asāmoa* cautiously but still emphasize its significance. For example, Anglican biblical scholar Frank Smith observed that *fa'asāmoa* "is not a totalizing code, since... there is a malleable and porous attitude to change allowing flexibility and adaptation. The code I suggest is something which is sought after or pursued rather than adhered to or obeyed, a process of desire rather than a fixed standard of regulation" (Smith 2010, 48).[9] A small minority of scholars have presented sharper critiques (eg, Unasa 2009; see also Wendt 1976a). My point is simply that much of Samoan theology is expressly about Samoan culture, in the deepest possible sense of a quest for an identity meant to be divinely sanctioned and purified. The conviction underlying this theology is that *fa'asāmoa* is "God-given culture" (Sila 2012, 158; see also Kamu 1996, 36; Tuaiaufai 2007, 84n8). To study the Samoan Way is to study God, because God gave Samoans the Samoan Way.

When culture is treated this way, as many anthropologists realize, there is a risk of it being used as a club in both senses of the term: a group you are either inside or outside of and a weapon you can knock people over the head with. I hasten to add that the theologians I describe in this book do not use culture in this aggressive, exploitative way. Instead, many of these theologians are critics of their own societies and churches, and they use the idea of culture to open up different kinds of dialogue. It is important nonetheless to keep in mind the double movement of cultural objectification toward empowerment of self in one direction and disempowerment of others in the other direction (see Linnekin 1990). Many groups in many parts of the world, including the Pacific, defend their ways of life as uniquely God-given and therefore morally superior to the ways of life of other groups.[10] Some men proclaim patriarchal values that justify, even valorize, the oppression of women. In anthropology, older models of culture were used to sort groups hierarchically, with a tendency to laminate skin color, intelligence, language, technology, and existential maturity.

Pacific theologians' deep engagement with context involves a finely balanced movement in which culture is treated as stable enough to serve as a basis of analysis but flexible enough to become the object of critique, something that theology can both work from and speak to. As Tongan Methodist biblical scholar Nāsili Vaka'uta has acknowledged, "There is no pure culture" (2011, 3n8; see also J Havea 2004b)—but his own critical readings of the Bible depend on his self-identified social location as a Tongan commoner, someone already outside his "own" culture yet well enough versed in it to use its tools in significant ways, as I describe in chapter 1. This kind of move requires that there be a recognizable Tongan culture that can both inform critique and be deconstructed by it.

Dialogue and Its Difficulties

The first topic of this book, then, is culture and how theologians from Oceania write about it. The second topic is what they do with it.

I argue that contextual theologians use the concept of culture to motivate dialogues of several kinds. "Dialogue," as an English-language term for conversation in which people anticipate and respond to each other, is a key term in Oceanic contextual theology. It is invoked repeatedly as a method and goal. For example, former Samoan Head of State Tui Atua Tupua Tamasese Ta'isi Tupuola Tufuga Efi, who has written authoritatively about culture and divinity, encouraged "openness to dialogue about the good and bad of our indigenous knowledges," writing that questions such as why "Samoan Christians … might feel the sacredness of God at Mataolemu more than at the Wailing Wall, or whether the God of Christianity and the God of pre-Christian Samoa are one and the same" ought to be part of "intelligent and loving conversation" (2014, 11–12, 39).[11] Samoan Methodist theologian Upolu Lumā Vaai characterized Oceanic theology as a set of dialogues: "Many Oceanic theologians have spread wide the theological mat of reception and [begun] a theological dialogue with past doctrines, with scriptures, with their contexts, and with other contemporary theologians" (2006, 22). Winston Halapua, a Tongan Anglican theologian who proposed his own post–Coconut Theology alternative called "theomoana" (joining Greek *theo-* for "God" with *moana,* a Polynesian term

for the ocean), wrote, "Theomoana is put forward as a new way of doing theology in dialogue with other theologies" (2008a; italics removed). Seforosa
Carroll, a Rotuman feminist theologian living in Australia, described how
experiences of being guest and host "can lead us toward an open dialogue
with other cultures, religions and theories" (2010a, 23). Samoan Methodist
New Testament scholar Mosese Ma'ilo Fuaiva'a argued that biblical interpretation must be a worldwide conversation in which distinct voices contribute
to an ever-richer engagement with an always-hybrid text: for Oceanic scholars, "theological hermeneutics re-signifies our presence, our voices, and our
memories in theological dialogue.... We ... recognize that our hermeneutics
is just part of a global theological dialogue, where nothing is lost but ... gained
in translation" (2011, 51). And for Tongan Methodist theologian Tevita T M
Puloka, the true partner in dialogue for contextual theology is God: "Contextualization as a theological methodology ... is ... a responsive dialogue
between God and God's people" (2005, 16).

   As these statements make clear, dialogue is a luminous ideal. The chapters
that follow explore some of the lines along which contextual theologians in
Oceania draw their plans for dialogue. But there are two facts, easy to overlook, that need attention first. Indeed, they are the warrant for much of the
argument in this book.

   The first is that, in practice, many religious and political speakers speak in
ways that discourage dialogue, presenting their own words as single-voiced
truths or commands that are closed off to challenge. Much religious and
political discourse depends for its force on a fiction of the purity of voice
and the sovereignty of authorship. In the central Pacific, where chiefs and
preachers speak at length in formal oratory without much audience response
and people have strong loyalties to the epic realm of Christian Scripture,
dialogue must always be understood as coexistent with ideals of monologic
(anti-dialogic) ways of speaking.

   The second fact is that getting dialogue started and keeping it going can be
remarkably difficult. As Jione Havea put it, "In our Pacific Islands ... we have
done a lot of talking about needing to talk, we have discussed the importance
and fruits of dialogue, but there is not much evidence of actually doing it.
Now and then when we say that we are having a dialogue, we usually 'talk over'
each other, to the end that some voices go unheard" (1998, 65). As an idealized label, "dialogue" can sometimes be referred to as if that were enough.
These points might seem obvious, but, like many obvious points, they need
to be raised explicitly so their implications can be considered fully.

Authoritative Voices: Monologic Models of Speech from God and Chiefs

Various societies in Oceania and elsewhere feature ideals of monologic
speech. In Fiji, for example, Andrew Arno argued that public speeches in
the Lau Islands are designed to impress rather than persuade and that during

formal discussion chiefs are expected to speak in a style that is "relatively slow, almost halting in some cases. Pauses can be fairly frequent and long, formal openings and closings delineate turn-taking, and there is no overlapping of speakers or competition for the floor. The only interruptions of a speaker's turn are in the form of standardized responses from the audience that indicate assent or encouragement. The pitch register is even and low, and there is no laughter" (Arno 1990, 254; see also Arno 1985; Hocart 1929, 45). Similarly, in Sāmoa, during meetings of titleholders held at moments of crisis or concern, speakers hold the floor and talk for "macroturns," during which interruptions are unusual and unexpected and "predictable responses are elicited from the audience (all of which convey agreement, eg, *mālie!*, 'nicely [said]')" (Duranti 1984, 223).

In Tonga, chiefs usually have their attendants *(matāpule)* speak for them on formal occasions. According to George Marcus (1980b), however, mid-level (non-paramount) chiefs may try to earn authority by acting casual, distancing themselves from their noble status at sessions where the beverage kava is drunk. In other words, chiefs may try to speak more dialogically on these occasions, but they do so, perhaps counterintuitively, in order to legitimate and perpetuate their elite standing and the "feudal-like system of nobility" in Tonga (Marcus 1980b, 438). Yet these attempts can fail when people insist on framing interaction with chiefs according to an authoritative monologic standard:

> Upon entering the kava circle, Noble X takes the central position, but instructs his *matāpule* to forgo the ritual commands by which kava is made and distributed in the presence of a chief. He urges a Government civil servant, visiting his native village, to move and sit beside him, but the man refuses, and the noble lightly ridicules him by asking if the centre of the circle is not good enough for him. The civil servant remains silent and expressionless, his face turned to one side. Another man asks polite questions of the noble about conditions in the capital. The noble answers each question enthusiastically and at length. At the first long break in the conversation, the noble makes detailed comments, in storytelling form, about what he has seen in the village during his visit, but no one responds to his observations in any detail. The kava session lasts three hours, and the noble remains a centre of attention or reference during the entire period. (Marcus 1980b, 447)

The noble's attempts to act casual are thwarted because, as Marcus put it, any titled member of the nobility is a "formal context-marker," someone who changes contexts of interaction by showing up and (intentionally or not) becoming the focus; a titleholder is "isolated by a context-transforming dimension of himself from which he can never be completely dissociated" (1980b, 441). Trying to engage in dialogue with his people, the noble is respectfully pushed away from it by his audience.

This is not to say that in places like Fiji, Sāmoa, and Tonga the rules and expectations are never bent or broken by chiefs, orators, or their audiences or that ritualized speech is inherently effective as a claim to authority (contrary to Maurice Bloch's argument on the restrictiveness of ritualized codes of communication [1975]). Indeed, I have seen a Fijian paramount chief shockingly interrupted during a kava session, and Alessandro Duranti has mentioned that when a speaker delivers a formal oration *(lāuga)* at a Samoan titleholders' meeting, audience members "are hardly listening" because they are focused on what will come later in the meeting (namely, more interactive but still formalized verbal exchange; Duranti 1984, 235). In addition, Marcus provided an example of a noble who acted casually at a kava session more successfully than Noble X, partly because he knew his audience better and partly because his genealogical credentials for nobility were not as strong (1980b, 448–449). I do not mean to imply, either, that a speaker who seems to disregard the possibility of dialogue is necessarily asserting an individualized personal will. As Felix Keesing and Marie Keesing made clear (1956), elite Samoan speakers tend to emphasize group responsibility and balanced power (see also Tomlinson and Makihara 2009). In mentioning these examples from Fiji, Sāmoa, and Tonga, then, I am simply observing that a good general rule in the central Pacific is that when a chief or other high authority figure is speaking formally, there is often an expectation that audience members will largely stay quiet for an extended period of time.[12] This makes theologians' emphasis on dialogue stand out against background assumptions about how speech on important matters from authoritative speakers—including church ministers as well as chiefs—ought to proceed.

Underlying the highly formal public respect for chiefs in places like Fiji, Sāmoa, and Tonga is an expectation that chiefs are chiefs by divine right. In Fijian Christian discourse, Paul's letter to the Romans (which declares that "the powers that be are ordained of God"; Rom 13:1) is sometimes cited as textual proof that chiefs have been placed by God in their positions of authority (see Tomlinson 2013). But while some chiefs may have a quasi-divine aura, it is through the Bible and Christian church ministers that God is supposed to speak—meaning that ministers, like chiefs, are entitled to speak in non-dialogic ways. As it was put by Samoan Congregationalist Tavita Maliko (who received his doctorate in theology at the University of Auckland [UA] shortly before I began my fieldwork there), "The minister is a representative of God.... [Samoan] cultural linguistic resources construct human discourse (the sermon) as words directly from the mouth of God and for this reason, unlike a traditional lauga [speech] where opposing orators negotiate or challenge each other, ministers and their sermons are never challenged because humans simply do not challenge God" (T Maliko 2012, 248). Imoamaua Setefano, another Samoan Congregationalist who studied for the PhD at the UA School of Theology, wrote similarly: "I once held the assumption that [the church minister] was indeed the personification of God. It has been my experience that to many Samoans, such thinking remains a reality. Whatever the [minister] says is taken as the Word of God and whatever he does is God's Will" (Setefano 2008, v; see also Keesing 1934, 409; Koria 1999).

Dialogue's Difficulties: How Do We Start a Conversation and Keep It Going?

Dialogue can be a fragile project, difficult to start and sustain. Kirin Narayan gave a vivid example of dialogue's difficulties in her memoir of growing up in Mumbai. She recalled how elite Indian friends of her family interacted with the "urugs," Western hippies seeking Indian wisdom who flocked to Narayan's mother ("urug" is "guru" spelled backward, a name teasingly invented by Narayan's father).

> Paw's relatives and hangers-on from his office made their way directly to his room with silent, sidelong glances at the urugs. But our downtown Bombay friends— the artists, scientists, writers, filmmakers, and politicians who had been visiting on weekends for years—attempted to make conversation. Somehow, these exchanges never worked. While our Bombay friends wanted to discuss population control, the tragedies of Vietnam, the writings of Günther Grass, or even what Americans might possibly find compelling about *Jonathan Livingston Seagull* [Bach 1970], many urugs tried to guide the conversation back to timeless Indian spiritual truths.
>
> With time, our cosmopolitan Bombay friends started keeping to themselves on urug-free porches, muttering about the "nut cases" overrunning our house. Urugs, on the other hand, could bemoan how "Westernization makes people lose their culture." (Narayan 2007, 129)

One thing Narayan's memoir makes poignantly clear is that the desire to have a conversation does not always find successful expression. Even well-meaning partners in dialogue can end up offering each other competing monologues.

In situations of outright hostility, obviously, dialogue becomes even harder. The Anglican bishop of Malaita in Solomon Islands, Terry Brown, told of his encounter with a group of marijuana-loving religious radicals who formed their own breakaway sect, the "Sabbath-Keeping Anglicans." One of their more notable actions was to place the Reserved Sacrament on the cathedral altar and then light the altar on fire. "Any attempt at theological discussion trying to bring in the New Testament was fruitless," Brown wrote: "It eventually became clear that any theological discussion of changes that took place in New Testament Christianity as it moved...from the Jewish to the Gentile world was irrelevant to these people." All of the mainstream churches in Malaita, he noted, face challenges from groups with "visions, prophecies, syncretistic mixtures of Christianity and *kastom*, neo-*kastom* re-workings, violent conflicts, land and genealogical disputes, illiterate interpretations of written Scripture, literalist interpretations of Scripture, Old Testament interpretations of the New Testament, and economic under-development, not to mention new outside religious groups" (Brown 2005, 19, 25). The Sabbath-Keeping Anglicans were clearly interested in taking up a wide range of ideas and practices from many sources—Brown also mentioned that the forerunner of this group used a kava bowl brought back from Fiji, drinking kava to get spiritual visions (2005, 20–22)—but they seem to have marked traditional Anglicanism as firmly out of bounds. Although they were open to many ideas, they were closed to many others, and Brown found it difficult to get a conversation started with them.

One place where calls for more dialogue are heard, as many readers likely know, is in academic discussions about interdisciplinarity. In the conclusion to this book, I turn from examining how theologians draw on the culture concept to ask what anthropologists might draw from theology. The idea that theology and anthropology can engage productively with each other is neither new nor exclusive to either field (see, eg, Adams and Salamone 2000). Mid-twentieth-century theologians and missiologists such as H Richard Niebuhr, Paul Tillich, and Eugene Nida, whose works predate contextual theology, took culture seriously as a topic of spiritual reflection. Conversely, several histori-cally influential British social anthropologists including E E Evans-Pritchard, Mary Douglas, and Victor Turner were strongly influenced by their religious convictions and interests in Christian theology (Larsen 2014).

My points in the preceding paragraphs have been that in some contexts monologic discourse is considered an ideal rather than a problem and that dialogue is rarely a smooth process and never automatic. These observations frame the chapters that follow, which examine how contextual theologians draw on ideas of culture to propose dialogues of several kinds.

The Field Sites

The following chapters are based on my research in four sites, two of them nondenominational schools and two of them church-run seminaries. My longest stretches of fieldwork were conducted at the ecumenical and multi-ethnic Pacific Theological College in Suva, the capital city of Fiji, and at the UA School of Theology in New Zealand. I spent shorter periods of time at the Kanana Fou Theological Seminary, which is the college of the Congre-gational Christian Church of American Samoa, and the Samoan Methodist Church's Piula Theological College, located between the villages of Lufilufi and Faleapuna on Upolu Island in the independent nation of Sāmoa (see map 1).

I spent eight months at PTC in Fiji, with the majority of research conducted in 2009; six months in New Zealand, with nearly all of that time in Auckland as an academic visitor in the UA School of Theology in 2013 and 2014; and approximately five months in Sāmoa and American Sāmoa, where I was in residence at Kanana Fou for nine weeks in 2015–2016 and Piula for four weeks in 2015. At each site, I talked with teachers and students, read inten-

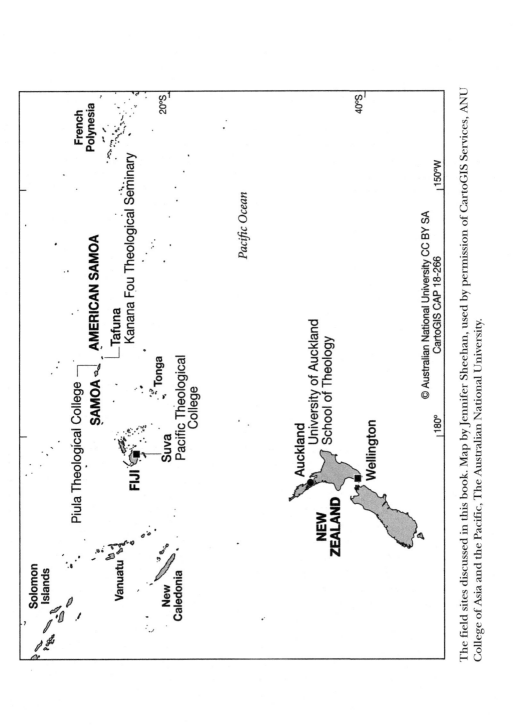

The field sites discussed in this book. Map by Jennifer Sheehan, used by permission of CartoGIS Services, ANU College of Asia and the Pacific, The Australian National University.

sively, and attended some classes. At PTC, most of the time I lived on campus in the student quarters named Bulu House. At Kanana Fou and Piula, I also stayed in campus housing, at Kanana Fou first in the women's fellowship accommodations and then in the residence hall for single students, and at Piula in the guesthouse named Va o Samoa. In Auckland, I lived in a serviced apartment next to campus.

PTC perches in the quiet neighborhood of Veiuto at the tip of Suva's peninsula. PTC is an ecumenical and multicultural institution. It awards degrees for scholarship and does not train students to be ordained as clergy, although many of its students are clergy from mainstream Protestant denominations in Oceania. The creation of a regional theological college was apparently first proposed at a board meeting of the Methodist Overseas Mission in 1944 (Germon 2001, 24; see also Tuilovoni 1948; J A Havea 1956), but the major push for its development came at an ecumenical conference in Malua, Sāmoa, in late April and early May 1961. The chairman of that conference was Sione 'Amanaki Havea, later of Coconut Theology fame. At first, the Anglican, Congregationalist, Presbyterian, Methodist, and Lutheran churches supported the school's establishment; within three years, the number of supporting churches had grown to thirteen; and as of December 2015, twenty different Pacific church organizations were considered the "owners" of PTC (Nokise 2015, 11–12; Germon 1964, 26; Pacific Theological College 2015).

The first students enrolled at PTC in 1966, and the first graduating class, in 1969, saw ten students receive a diploma in theology and six receive the bachelor of divinity (BD)—the first bachelors' degrees awarded in the islands of the South Pacific (Nokise 2015, 13, 24, 25). At the time of my research, the college offered a certificate and a diploma in theological studies, a postgraduate diploma in theology, bachelor's degrees in divinity and theology, the master of theology degree (begun in 1987), and the doctor of philosophy degree (begun in 2004; Nokise 2015, 33, 48–49).[13] The main areas of study are theology and ethics, Church history, ministry, and biblical studies. Nokise, PTC's principal since 2002, has estimated that PTC has graduated more than eight hundred students in its fifty years of existence (2015, 58), although a substantial proportion of these are not higher-degree candidates. He observed that the number of students has been dropping, partly because some Pacific churches have established their own bachelor's programs, as Kanana Fou and Piula have done.

Indeed, PTC has faced two real crises in recent decades. One, according to Nokise, is that many of the college's owners—the various church organizations—have routinely failed to contribute the money they are supposed to (2015, 66–70). As a result, PTC has been short of income for years and has also suffered significant turnover of teaching staff. The other crisis has been Fiji's coups. In 1987, the year of the nation's first two coups, the military demanded that a lecturer from India be deported because his teaching was thought to be "detrimental to the aspirations of the indigenous Fijians";

he left, and as Nokise put it, the event "revealed an unpleasant truth, namely that some students were reporting to the military what went on in the classrooms" (2015, 34). Then came a new coup in 2000, which took place at the new parliamentary complex next to PTC, meaning that coup supporters as well as government troops trying to restore order were buzzing around and through the college's campus. The principal at the time, Jovili Meo, came to feel that the situation was threatening. Students and staff were told to leave, and the college was closed for three months (Nokise 2015, 37–40).

When I conducted research at PTC between 2008 and 2010, the city of Suva faced fresh postcoup problems. Voreqe "Frank" Bainimarama had executed Fiji's fourth coup in December 2006 and went on to become the national prime minister. He acted aggressively to stabilize and maximize his power, for example by having the constitution abrogated and having Methodist Church leaders arrested for supposedly putting politics before religion. PTC was not closed during this time, however, and the campus felt safe. Indeed, it was a welcoming and vibrant place. While there, the ideas that would underlie my research in Auckland, Sāmoa, and American Sāmoa began to develop.

I was continually struck by how students at PTC learned not only to think theologically but also how to represent themselves explicitly in terms of culture. Especially when guests were hosted and fundraisers were held, students and their families were divided into their home groups and encouraged to put on performances displaying emblematic national traditions. In 2009, the main groups were Fijians, Tongans, Samoans, "Melanesians" (as there were not enough students from Papua New Guinea, Solomon Islands, or Vanuatu to form national groups on their own), and the "rainbow" group of French Polynesians plus those of European heritage. On campus, usually in the morning chapel devotions, I heard prayers given in English, French, Samoan, Tongan, Maohi (Tahitian), Tuvaluan, Neo-Melanesian (pidgin), Hano (from Pentecost Island, Vanuatu), and Vella Lavella and Ontong Javanese (both from Solomon Islands). The explicit identification of faculty and students as distinctly cultural subjects both reflects and fosters PTC's academic emphasis on contextual theology (figures 0.2, 0.3, 0.4).

The UA School of Theology, my second field site, existed from 2002 to 2014 (figure 0.5). In 2014 it was folded into the UA School of Humanities. I was officially a visiting researcher there during 2013 and 2014. Like PTC, the School of Theology conferred academic degrees, although because it was part of a public university, it was not supported by any churches. It did have institutional ties with four church schools in Auckland, which enabled the sharing of faculty and student coursework options: the College of St John the Evangelist (St John's Theological College), Trinity Methodist Theological College, the Catholic Institute of Theology, and Carey Baptist College. In its brief life, the school awarded a total of 538 degrees and diplomas, including graduate and postgraduate diplomas in theology and ranging in level from combined bachelor of science or arts and bachelor of theology degrees up to

FIGURE 0.2. Tongan performance at the Pacific Theological College's fundraising bazaar, May 2009. Photo by author.

FIGURE 0.3. Edward Kolohai, a student from Solomon Islands, presents a seminar at the Pacific Theological College, May 2009. Photo by author.

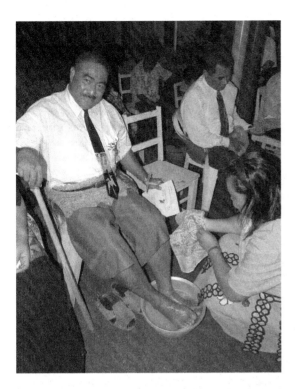

FIGURE 0.4. Ikani Tolu, a student from Tonga, has his feet washed at a Maundy Thursday service at the Pacific Theological College, April 2009. Photo by author.

FIGURE 0.5. Arts 1, the building where the School of Theology at the University of Auckland was based, April 2016. Photo by author.

the doctorate in theology. Of the 538 graduates, 58 received master's degrees and 35 received doctorates by 2014.[14]

For the duration of the UA School of Theology's existence, its professor was noted Australian Catholic feminist scholar Elaine Wainwright, a specialist on the Gospel of Matthew. In her inaugural professorial speech, given in 2003, Wainwright made it clear that a multicultural context was key to her plans for the school, although at the time she spoke of it in terms of "biculturalism," New Zealand shorthand for its plural society with a Māori and Pākehā (European) balance:

> I share with many of the theologians in this school an education within the contexts of globalized theology.... Our globalized theological perspective is often influenced from somewhere else, from North America or from Europe. And so our engagement in theology is in dialogue with our partners from other parts of the world. But also, we can stand in critique of some of that globalized theology from a local context....
>
> At the heart of the School's mission statement is a commitment to bicultural theological education—a commitment whose full meaning is still under exploration in the School.... One thing which this commitment does ... is that it draws our attention in the theological process to the importance of context and to the importance of culture as an element of that context. The Gospel, the theological traditions, and the Church have already shaped the cultures of Maori and their *tangata whenua* [people of the land] as well as those from other more recently arrived groups who teach, research, and who come to learn theology. A bicultural approach to theology will bring to visibility and engage with the complexity of cultures and the embedded theological traditions—the "density of the present" that [Gustavo] Gutiérrez talks about, or the "thickness" of culture which Clifford Geertz speaks about. This will require the development of at least rudimentary skills in the analysis of culture, and this is one of the other directions in which we need to look in theology: we need to look ... in the direction of other disciplines. We need to develop skills in the analysis of culture. (Wainwright 2003; for the published version of this address, see Wainwright 2005)

As part of this commitment to multiculturalism, over the years the UA School of Theology had on its staff several prominent indigenous theologians from the Pacific who were linked through the affiliated church-run schools: Ilaitia Sevati Tuwere, Winston Halapua (who was the principal of St John's Theological College), and, during my time there, Nāsili Vaka'uta, now the principal of Trinity Methodist Theological College.

In addition, the school drew students from around Oceania. Much of my initial research activity in Auckland was simply reading the theses and dissertations from Pacific students who had studied there. And fortunately, a number of Pacific students were pursuing their degrees while I was there, including a group of four PhD candidates who had all been faculty members at Malua Theological College in Sāmoa: Vaitusi Nofoaiga, Arthur Wulf, Terry Pouono, and Imoamaua Setefano. (Pouono ended his association with Malua and chose to stay in Auckland, where he had grown up, after completing his degree; the others had received scholarships from Malua and have since returned there to teach.) In 2013, the school was remarkably collegial, with events held regularly to bring students and staff together. In 2014, the friendly spirit remained, but the school lost its independence by being folded into the School of Humanities as a "disciplinary area."

Having conducted research at PTC and the UA School of Theology, I then wanted to spend time at seminaries to observe theology in action—academic action, to be sure—among candidates for ministry. Kanana Fou (whose name in Samoan is Kolisi Faafaifeau i Kanana Fou), located in Tafuna on the island of Tutuila, American Sāmoa, was my field site for nine weeks in 2015 and 2016. This was a short but intense time, made productive by the generosity of the faculty and students (figures 0.6, 0.7).

Kanana Fou (Samoan for "New Canaan") was founded because of a split between the Congregational Christian Church of American Samoa and its mother church in independent Sāmoa (formerly called Western Sāmoa).[15] In 1960, a missionary from the London Missionary Society "saw the difficulties of carrying out the work of a British L.M.S. mission in an American Territory"

FIGURE 0.6. Kanana Fou Theological Seminary campus, August 2015. Photo by author.

FIGURE 0.7. Student Tulafono Maga leads choir practice at Kanana Fou Theological Seminary, March 2016. Photo by author.

and recommended that American Samoans consider setting up an independent church (Amosa 1991, 23). His ideas were echoed by the territory's governor at the time, H Rex Lee, and were persuasive to many American Samoans, who raised a lot of money for the church only to see that money get used for developments in Western Sāmoa rather than their own home. Plans to request a revision of the church's constitution began to take shape in October 1961, and in May 1962—shortly after the London Missionary Society had given the church in Western Sāmoa its own independence—the American Samoans submitted a resolution to the church's general assembly asking that they be allowed to hold their own general assembly and to use the money they raised for their own daily church expenses (Amosa 1991, 24–25). Their request was ignored. In fact, it was so roundly ignored that it took until 1973 for the mother church to take note of it, and even then they did not make any decision (Amosa 1991, 29; see also Allen 1990, 23). Finally, in 1980 church representatives from American Sāmoa voted strongly for independence, and, after some fruitless last-minute attempts to gain acknowledgment from Western Sāmoa, went ahead and became formally independent in August 1980 (Allen 1990, 23–24; Amosa 1991, 56; see also Ernst 2006, 589–590). Kanana Fou was then established in March 1983 (Kanana Fou Theological Seminary 2014). Key moments in its development include the establishment of the BD program in 1997 (previously there had only been a diploma in theology) and the admission of women to the diploma and bachelor's programs beginning in 2004.[16] The graduating class of bachelor's students in 2016 had eleven students.

My seminary field site in Sāmoa, Piula (Kolisi Faafaifeau Piula), was the place I spent the shortest amount of time. Yet in the unpredictable way of fieldwork, those four weeks were exceptionally fruitful ones that, I have come to realize, were key to how the whole research project worked out. Piula was a welcoming community and also a remarkably coherent one, with a solid structure and regular communal events. The college was founded in 1868, although it was not called Piula, the Samoan form of "Beulah," until 1896 (Fa'alafi 1994, 2005).[17] Like PTC, Piula has suffered through political turbulence, although much longer ago: the school principals' annual reports of 1889 and 1899 both mention "bullets...whizzing" at student preachers who were attempting to foster peace among Samoan warriors (Fa'alafi 1994, 276, 280).

Piula is the ministerial training college of the Samoan Methodist Church and takes its disciplinary standards seriously. Students charged with infractions of any sort are asked to account for themselves at a campus-wide disciplinary meeting each Monday evening. The faculty member who decides on students' punishments also performs a military-style dress-code inspection of the students outside the church after the 7:00 am devotion on Sunday (figure 0.8). The teacher in charge of this during my research, Fa'asalafa Solaese, mentioned that he makes sure students are following such requirements as

FIGURE 0.8. Lecturer Fa'asalafa Solaese conducts a dress-code inspection of students at Piula Theological College, August 2015. Photo by author.

shaving, having a proper haircut (squared off in the back), and, crucially, wearing underpants. I am phrasing this lightly, but the discipline is no joke. In my brief time at Piula a student was expelled for his behavior, and I learned with some surprise that the 2015 senior class of nine students had been nineteen in number four years earlier. Some had been expelled; some had quit. The most common cause for expulsion seems to have been dalliances with women.

An evocative illustration of Piula's regimen and hierarchy comes from the recollections of a first-year student:

> The second night in Piula and my first traditional *"umu"* which involves heating stones till they are red hot and cooking taro, fish and *"palusami,"* which is a delicacy made from taro leaves and coconut cream. After all the food is placed on the hot stones then it is covered up with banana leaves to keep in the steam and heat. All of this took place at approximately two in the morning. Only being in the campus for less than two days I was still unfamiliar with my surroundings. Other students had told me that in this college, the first years have no voice; their place in the college was total obedience, not to ask questions but to run and obey even if you have no idea of what you are doing.
>
> Then it happened, an older student ordered me to get *"laufai laulelei"* for the *"palusami."* I had absolutely no idea of what he was talking about. I nodded my head and ran aimlessly into the night. Eventually I found one of the boys who showed me that *"laufai laulelei"* was the tip of a banana leaf that had not been broken, it was used to hold together the *"palusami"* so the coconut cream would not tip out. It occurred to me that we do the same thing in New Zealand only we use foil paper. I quickly got to the task and went as fast as I could, feeling proud of myself for being able to do something new in my life I ran back to the *"umu"* with banana leaves in hand.
>
> To my dismay I realized that there was no movement around the *"umu"*; everyone was sitting while the older students gave advice. I then realized that the *"umu"* had already been covered and the cooking was complete. I slowly walked towards the kitchen when all of a sudden a second year student who was younger and smaller than I was, had me by the collar. He began to swear at me and questioned why in the world I bothered coming to the college; I had no business in the college because I couldn't do anything. If anything, it made their work harder because they would have to pull up the slack. When I tried to apologize I was pushed aside and told I had no right to speak. At that moment I realized I was in a different world. (Taotua 2011, 135–136; some italics deleted)

The assertion that one does not have a right to speak is, of course, a denial of dialogue: the student was expected to shut up and obey. But the message at Piula, which is echoed at Kanana Fou, is that you will be able to speak eventually, although you will always need to defer to those who are senior to you.

Piula's hierarchy is replicated within the remarkably strong ʻauā ʻiga (pastoral families), groups of students and their wives affiliated with the household of a faculty member. The *'auā'iga* at Piula are core elements in the college's social structure, one of the main ways people's daily responsibilities are organized.[18] At each academic level, students have particular responsibilities within the household as well as on the campus. Internally, they resemble a small Samoan polity, with the faculty member and the senior student in metaphorically chiefly positions. Piula's faculty describe the college itself as a village and see the theological training that students receive not simply as a matter of gaining scriptural knowledge but also as a matter of learning the proper way one should act in a traditional Samoan village—which, after all, is where many graduates will end up as ministers. As ministers, they will be shown extreme deference, and it is felt to be critical that they understand how service works before they become the served (figures 0.9, 0.10).

As church training institutions, Kanana Fou and Piula have several notable features that distinguish them from PTC and the UA School of Theology. The main one is that Kanana Fou and Piula approach education as a balance between academic and physical labor. Being a student at one of these seminaries means that almost every day you will perform such tasks as cooking, cleaning, and maintaining the campus. Having students perform physical labor not only helps keep the schools' appearances fresh without hiring

FIGURE 0.9. The Piula Theological College cricket teams get ready to rumble, August 2015. Photo by author.

FIGURE 0.10. Ploion, Ese, and Faʻaiuga look after the children during a church service at Piula Theological College, August 2015. Photo by author.

professional maintenance staff but is also considered an integral part of students' education.[19] In comparison, students at PTC occasionally participate in "working bees," but the school has professional staff who take care of most maintenance. At the UA School of Theology, some students get part-time jobs (whether within or outside the university) to pay for school and family expenses, but the content of their education does not include physical labor. In addition, students at Kanana Fou and Piula are only allowed to leave campus at scheduled times. If a class is canceled or work is curtailed, students are not free to take off and do their own thing but rather must remain on campus unless given special permission. At PTC and the UA School of Theology, students have more mobility.

There are several other notable differences between the seminaries and the strictly academic institutions. At the seminaries, students in the same year's cohort take the same classes together each year, with no electives. At PTC and the UA School of Theology, in contrast, students have choices of classes to take. In addition, students at PTC and the UA School of Theology might be required to buy books for particular courses, but at the seminaries, reading material is often not purchased but rather made available in the library or distributed in class due to a shortage of resources on the part of both the schools and the students.

There are notable differences between the two seminaries, too. At Kanana Fou, as at PTC and the UA School of Theology, women are allowed to enroll in the BD program, although none were in it during my time there. At Piula, in contrast, women cannot study for the bachelor of divinity.[20] In addition, graduates of Kanana Fou are not guaranteed a job, and to become ministers of congregations, they must be "called" (invited) to serve by those congregations, but graduates of Piula are guaranteed a job of some sort within the national Methodist institution, either as a minister or as a staff member in some part of the organization. Finally, the rules of ordination are different between the institutions. Kanana Fou students must work for the Congregational Christian Church of American Samoa in some capacity for two years after graduation before being ordained. Piula graduates must serve for five years as probationary ministers, being evaluated on their personal conduct and preaching as well as passing a written exam each year, before ordination. In both churches, one must be married to be ordained.

Plan of the Book

As my research project developed over time and across these various sites, I came to appreciate Ghassan Hage's critique of multi-sited ethnography (2005). Hage pointed out that labeling a project "multi-sited" can conceal ethnographic thinness; the deeper one is involved in a community, the more difficult it becomes to "just hop around" (2005, 465). Moreover, scholars sometimes overlook the kinds of movement—existential as well as geographical—that people understand themselves to be making. Hage described how in his research on Lebanese migration he eventually "took [his] site to be the geographically non-contiguous space where a specific transnational familial culture with its enduring social relations was flourishing" (2005, 467). Similarly, I take my site to be a single one, conceptually speaking: the space of cultural analysis conducted by Pacific contextual theologians.

But these theologians, it must be added, do travel between these sites. From Piula's first graduating class of BD students, three went on to do their doctorates, including one (now the college's registrar) who completed his dissertation at the UA School of Theology and one who now lectures at PTC. In 2013, I attended the conference of the Oceanic Biblical Studies Association (OBSA) at PTC along with three of the Samoan students from the UA School of Theology. Two years later, I was unable to attend the OBSA meeting held at Piula, but just before it began, I was at Kanana Fou as some students there were getting ready to attend it. Then in 2016, when a two-person delegation representing the South Pacific Association of Theological Schools came to Kanana Fou to accredit its bachelor's program, one of them was the principal of Piula. I could offer multiple examples of these kinds of dense cross-island and cross-institution weavings, but perhaps the most striking one is that all ten faculty members at Piula in 2015 had earned their master's degrees at PTC.

This book, then, is an anthropological reading of Christian theology in Oceania in an interstitial mode. The four sites are the book's ethnographic lifeblood, but no part of this book is a systematic overview of any of the institutions themselves. Rather, the book offers a set of observations from different places, which I have tried to assemble into a fair representation of the inclusive dynamics among the sites and Oceanic contextual theology in general. The chapters that follow proceed thematically rather than site-by-site. Each chapter addresses a different field of dialogue, which Oceanic contextual theologians set up by drawing on concepts of culture.

The first chapter presents dialogues between scholars and the Bible, asking how the former engage with a text crowned with an aura of sacredness and finality in Pacific societies. I describe how theologians and biblical scholars attempt to reread, reinterpret, and in some cases critically rewrite parts of the Bible. Chapter 2 turns to dialogues within churches and between churches and society. It focuses on three key topics that give theologians intellectual space to discuss social changes: feminist theology, Samoan ideals of service, and models of speaking "prophetically." In chapter 3, I examine three emblems used by contextual theologians to depict national and regional cultural identities. They are *talanoa* (conversation, storytelling); mana (spiritual efficacy); and the narcotic beverage kava, drunk regularly in many parts of the Pacific. I also discuss the pre-Christian spirits that roam theological college campuses. Finally, I examine the role of the *Pacific Journal of Theology* in articulating visions of a unified Pacific Way. The fourth chapter turns to environment and ecology. Some of the most energetic and challenging theology from Oceania is grounded in ideals of sacred seascape and landscape, pursuing the implications of reading the Bible alongside pre-Christian stories from the Pacific. The concluding chapter addresses the question, asked with increasing energy over the past decade, of how anthropology and theology might engage in productive interdisciplinary dialogue.

The following chapters examine the concept of dialogue with critical sympathy. Dialogue is an ideal, treated as both method and goal by contextual theologians. The primary subject of their dialogues, I argue, is culture. But culture's conceptual slipperiness raises additional questions about how dialogue really works and suggests that any investigation of either culture or dialogue must attend to their difficulties and limitations as well as the fresh possibilities they can open up.

Chapter 1
Writing Back at the Bible

When I was a doctoral student in Philadelphia in the mid-1990s, I wanted to begin Fijian language study where I lived. Luckily, a woman from Naitasiri province was living a short distance from me because she had married a former Peace Corps volunteer and they were raising their family in the suburbs. Using Milner's *Fijian Grammar* (1967), Monika began to teach me basic skills in speaking Standard Fijian.

One of the most valuable lessons she taught me was not about speech, however, but about silence. As we sat there one day at her dining room table, Milner's book and my index cards near at hand, Monika told me that in Fiji I would find myself at kava-drinking sessions during which there would be long periods of quiet. I should not rush to fill the silence with words, she said. The silence was not a bad or awkward thing.

She was right, of course, and during fieldwork I grew comfortable with long gaps in which nobody said anything. Late at night in drowsy kava sessions, a pleasant and companionable lack of talk would fill the air. These extended moments of silence occurred in other places, too. One day, I was having a meal with Rev Isikeli Serewai, the Methodist superintendent minister of Kadavu Island in whose house I lived. As we ate, I talked. I don't remember what I said; I probably plinked out a few scattershot questions. But I clearly remember Rev Serewai, poised between politeness and bluntness, telling me that indigenous Fijians preferred not to talk during meals. This was my second lesson about needing to shut up sometimes. I tried my best.

The problem was, once I got better at being quiet, people then wanted me to talk. I spent nearly all of my nights at casual kava-drinking sessions, and the early stages of these sessions often bubbled with energetic conversation and discussion, storytelling, and joking. Things only became quiet later in the evening when everyone got drunk and tired.[1] It was often during these later stretches, when the talk had died back bit by bit and there was now a warm, liquid silence, that someone would eventually say to me, "Talanoa mada!" ("Tell a story, make conversation!"; *mada* makes the command polite).

Talanoa

The Fijian, Tongan, and Samoan languages have the same root term for one genre of talk: *talanoa,* sometimes translated as "storytelling" and connoting an open, interactive style of verbal engagement. *Talanoa* is dialogue. Andrew Arno translated the Fijian *veitalanoa* (*talanoa* with the plural prefix *vei-*) as "exchange of anecdotes" (1985, 129). In Samoan, in which the noun form is given the suffix *-ga* (thus *talanoaga*), the term can be translated as "discussion" in the context of a titleholders' meeting and "chat" or "conversation" in other settings (Duranti 1984, 229). George Marcus translated *talanoa* for Tongan as both "no account talking" and "ordinary conversation" (1980b, 436, 440).

Talanoa is a major speech genre in the central Pacific. It is dialogue because it is conversation, with speakers taking turns and often taking up what has been said previously. It is also dialogic in the sense established by the Russian literary theorist M M Bakhtin (1981, 1984). In Bakhtin's sense, *talanoa* involves a push and pull between centralizing forces (such as rules of speaking and audience expectations) and dispersive ones (such as improvisation and disagreement) that result in "heteroglossia," or the presence of multiple voices and interests, past and present, in any individual utterance.

Some stories in the Bible describe conversations and thus easily lend themselves to interpretation in terms of *talanoa.* For example, in her analysis of Matthew 15:21–28, Valamotu Palu focused on what she called the "Talanoa Session" between Jesus and the woman from Canaan (Palu 2010, 36). In the Bible story, the woman has a demon-possessed daughter and begs Jesus for help. At first, Jesus ignores her, telling his disciples that he was sent only to Israel's lost sheep. But the woman persists, and Jesus tells her that it is wrong "to take the children's bread, and to cast it to dogs." Undeterred by the insult, she says that it is in fact good to do so, as "dogs eat of the crumbs which fall from their masters' table" (Matt 15:26, 27). Jesus praises her faith, and the woman's daughter is instantly healed. Palu compared the woman's actions to the Tongan practice of *fofola e fala,* or "spreading the mat" to sit down and have a discussion. The woman from Canaan "took advantage of the opportunity given to open the dialogue between her, Jesus and the disciples. This was as if she were spreading the mat . . . so that all groups concerned had the opportunity to dialogue" (Palu 2010, 40).

Tongan Methodist biblical scholar Jione Havea wrote that *talanoa* is the conjunction of a story, its telling, and the related conversation. It requires interaction and uptake: "Talanoa is an event in responsibility, in the playful sense that 'responsibility' has to do with response-ability, that is, talanoa has to do with the ability to respond. . . . Not all talanoa are of the holy kind, but they all are of the communion kind!" (J Havea 2010c, 11–15). Evidently a reggae fan, he turned to Bob Marley to suggest *talanoa*'s potential for liberatory readings of the Bible: it emancipates us from mental slavery, it is "one of Oceania's 'songs of freedom'" (J Havea 2014a, 210). Thus *talanoa* can be understood as both subject and method of theology, a kind of microcosm for understanding culture within contextual theology:

> A biblical story is talanoa...drifting in a sea of stories. It thus makes sense to nudge a biblical story out of its textual borders, the context in which it moors and belongs, and that gives it meanings, so that it flows into other stories and other shores. Such is the gifting of talanoa, which will not be too strange to some midrashic, intertextual, and/or contrapuntal readers of biblical stories. I call upon these modes of reading not in order to canonize, or scripturalize, talanoa cultures, or vice versa, but in honor of the rhythms that free me to be native. Talanoa, favored by my migrating ancestors and even in latter-day island communities in diaspora, is neither empty nor innocent. Talanoa moves, links, and grabs, as well as cuts, and releases. It is telling, and interchanging. (J Havea 2014a, 210–211)[2]

The approaches of authors such as Palu and Havea suggest that the practice of *talanoa*—informal, interactive talk—is considered both an ideal object of theological analysis and an effective tool for reading the Bible in Pacific terms. As Havea might put it, you can bring theology to *talanoa*, and *talanoa* can be theology.

As with all forms of dialogue, there are limits to *talanoa* as actually practiced. One speaks differently to different people. Chiefs, church ministers, honored guests, siblings, and cross-cousins cannot all be addressed the same way or included in the same conversations. When I asked one Samoan church authority whether I could interview him, he agreed and suggested we meet in his office rather than around the kava bowl. In his view, the office's formality would help the conversation's flow. As he put it, if we conducted our conversation over kava, other people would be present and there would be "less freedom of expression." Another church authority, the registrar of Piula Theological College, wrote in his dissertation that he had conducted one-on-one interviews for his research because "some participants might feel inferior in the presence of others" (Sila 2012, 19). Thus *talanoa* is not a public sphere of free dialogue detached from political constraints. Rather, it is a form of dialogue open to many participants but not everyone, aesthetically cultivated for many purposes including pleasure and entertainment as well as edification and social planning.[3]

"An All But Magical Finality"

In his introduction to a volume on uses of the Bible cross-culturally, James S Bielo asserted that "a more heteroglossic, polyphonic, or dialogical work is hard to imagine" (Bielo 2009, 1). In the sense of "dialogism" developed by Bakhtin, Bielo was resoundingly right: the Bible is a maximally inclusive text featuring the voices of God, prophets, disciples, angels, demons, and ordinary humans in a collection of genres from epic to lyric, narrative to prophetic, gathered over a long historical period. But many people treat the Bible as a non-dialogic text—something that is final, complete, and cannot be corrected, added to, or reshaped. Indeed, the Book of Revelation declares that anyone who changes its text will suffer plagues and damnation (22:18–19); New Testament scholar Bart Ehrman pointed out that this threat was directed at the early scribes copying the books, who did, in fact, routinely make many errors (2005, 54). Many readers extend the Bible's aura of monologic truth to those who speak its words, who cannot be questioned because they are only animating the words of the ultimate author, God.

In other words, quoting the Bible in Pacific societies often invokes monologic authority. "Christianity is thoroughly embraced and the Bible is taken for granted as the supreme guide by most Samoans," wrote Ama'amalele Tofaeono, who added: "Even though the Bible conveys narratives and traditions written for past generations, the majority of Samoans continue to receive the Christian message through Biblical texts as unquestioned truth, and to apply it to the contemporary conditions of life without question. Most often, there is an absence of awareness that what the Bible says can be problematic and can hardly orient us to face all present-day problems in our particular context" (2000, 148). Tofaeono's observation that the Bible is an ultimate authority for many Samoans recalls Felix Keesing's memorable description of the Bible in Sāmoa and its interpretations as apparently having "an all but magical finality" (Keesing 1934, 409). Similar attitudes toward the Bible are reported throughout the central Pacific, with a fundamentalist reading of the text joined with reverence of the book as a physical object. Nukulaelae Islanders in Tuvalu consider "carrying a Bible to church...a must (a hymnal is optional but desirable)"; because there are often not enough Bibles for each family member to take one, "much good-natured bantering ensues" over who gets a copy to carry (Besnier 1995, 116).

Here are three similar examples, which I quote at length for the way they show the sacralization of the Bible as both meaningful text and powerful object:

From Fiji

Most of our [Methodist] church members [in Fiji] are fundamentalists in their approach to the Bible and from time to time have recourse to it when seeking an answer to their problems, some of which can be easily solved by the local doctor or the development officer or the school teacher. Others regard the Bible as some kind of magic charm that can keep the spirits at bay. It is common in the villages to see the Bible placed in front of the baby's pillow. This is to keep the spirits away from possessing it. In Fijian, the Bible is called Ai Vola Tabu which literally means the prohibited book and so people tend to refrain from handling it and only do so with great care. It is often left alone on top of a shelf or a table, out of the reach of children. This is associated with the belief that the Bible is infested with mana and if it is not handled with care disaster may befall the family. (Ratuvili 1971, 95–96)

From Tonga

In most Tongan families, especially Protestants, the Bible is the only book in their possession, and the only book some people have ever read. It is considered embarrassing not to have a Bible, whether or not one reads it. Regarded by the people as endowed with divine mana (life-sustaining power), the Bible is kept with utmost respect and care. No one is allowed to eat in front of it or to abuse it in any manner or form. Such an act would, according to most, bring a curse upon oneself or one's family. This attitude goes to the extent that people do not welcome a new translation of the Bible that uses vocabularies that are meaningful to the present generation of Tongans....

The Bible in Tonga is also seen as a container of answers to all problems. All issues, political or otherwise, are mostly judged based on biblical insights; or at least on someone's reading of biblical texts. That happened because of the prevalence of Protestant views of the Bible, especially the reformist doctrine of sola scriptura, which gives the Bible the sole authority for life and faith. The Bible offers the first and final word; there is no space for an–other word. (Vaka'uta 2011, 10–11)[4]

From Niue

The organisation of Bible Study Groups for young people is a fairly new thing in Niue—it is only during the last two or three years that young people have been studying together in this way. Many of these young people find it hard to attend these groups as they have had to face opposition from their parents and lack of sympathy as far as many church leaders are concerned. In some villages the pastors and deacons have actively opposed the groups because they believe that the young people are interfering with the old tradition of the church by seeking to introduce many new things. (Tanaki 1964, 23)

The theologians and biblical scholars whose work I discuss below, in writing back at the Bible, are thus writing in part against their societies' conservatism even as they foreground a reverence for culture. Their churches, too, generally remain strongholds of conservatism, as noted by Tevita T M Puloka in his argument that the Free Wesleyan Church of Tonga endorses a decontextualization of the Bible in favor of a "passive pietism" (1998). Scholars who write back at the Bible often do so in adventurous ways that, while opening up the text in dialogic acts of reading-as-reshaping, can also limit the possibilities of dialogue with conservative church members.

Writing Back at the Bible

In his classic discussion of charisma, Max Weber characterized it in terms of a break from a script: the charismatic speaker declares, "It is written, but I say unto you" (Weber 1978, 243). The theologians I discuss in this chapter all follow this charismatic line to some extent, but they do so in order to understand the Bible better: going beyond it, challenging and critiquing standard interpretations, and constructively deforming the text in order to enhance its meaning and relevance.

For example, Joan Alleluia Filemoni-Tofaeono offered a feminist critique in her article "Marthya: Her Meneutic of His Story, A Reflection on Luke 10:38–42."[5] Luke 10:38–42 describes the encounter that two sisters, Mary and Martha, have with Jesus. Mary sits at Jesus's feet and listens to him while Martha serves as host. Martha complains to Jesus, asking him to tell Mary to help her, but Jesus replies that "one thing is needful: and Mary hath chosen that good part, which shall not be taken away from her."

Responding to the story, Filemoni-Tofaeono proposed three exercises for Bible-study groups. First, she listed several questions for discussion, including whether most women identify with Martha or Mary "in your culture...in your church...in your family" and whether Luke 10:38–42 is "life-affirming for both women" (Filemoni-Tofaeono 2002, 75–76). Second, she encouraged readers to invent scenes and role-play the characters before and after Jesus's visit. She offered her own text, "A Possible Dialogue Between Martha and Mary," as an example. It begins in a deliciously casual groove:

Martha: What has got into you?
Mary: Excuse me, what have I done?
Martha: You are asking me that? You know very well what I mean.
Mary: I'm sorry I don't!
Martha: You really think you are something, eh? I was very embarrassed with
         the way you threw yourself at his feet.
Mary: I was not throwing myself at his feet. I was only trying to listen to his
         teachings.
Martha: Since when can you do that here?
Mary: Oh Martha, you are just jealous!
Martha: Jealous? I'm not!
Mary: Who wouldn't be? He is single, available, intelligent, good looking.
         He has all the qualities women usually look for in a man.
Martha: How dare you think like that?!
Mary: I think you have a crush on him. (Filemoni-Tofaeono 2002, 78)

Filemoni-Tofaeono made it clear, in her instructions to readers, that this role-playing should go beyond the biblical text on which it is based. In this sense, she encouraged dialogue of a safe, nonconfrontational kind—Bible fan fiction, as it were.

Her third exercise is more critically engaged. She invented a character, Marthya, "a person neither Martha nor Mary but both" (Filemoni-Tofaeono 2002, 83), and had Marthya compose a letter to Jesus. As in the role-playing scenario, Filemoni-Tofaeono asked readers to go beyond the text of Luke.

In her text, Marthya tells Jesus that "people have interpreted Luke's written account in whatever way they want" and argues that the original account is faulty:

> As our dear friend, you were only trying to warn and remind us not to be torn between ourselves.
>
> Unfortunately, Luke, the Gospel writer, has misrepresented the nature of our last conversation at our house in the way he wrote it all down in the scroll....[6] He was even worse than us. He blew our conversation way out of proportion, putting you as the Kyrios—as the Lord and centre of action. We can understand where he is coming from.... But we were both surprised to read this version of our story. It is not close to what happened. (Filemoni-Tofaeono 2002, 81)

In the fictional letter, Marthya goes on to say that most women have "both Martha and Mary battling away within ourselves"; then the article's conclusion suggests that this story is especially relevant for women of modern Oceania. Pacific women, according to Filemoni-Tofaeono, think they must be Marthas—servants, subordinating themselves. If women have the opportunity to be Marys, decisively pursuing spiritual truth, they can do so only "in a limited sphere" while never escaping the obligation to be Marthas as well. The composite character Marthya is evidently meant to be both biblical and Oceanic, embodying "the 'gut-level' experience of many women" while also serving as "a reflection of my own cultural hermeneutic, as a Pacific Islander, Polynesian, Samoan woman" (Filemoni-Tofaeono 2002, 82, 84, 80; see also Ete-Lima 2013; Uasike 2010, 25–26). Thus a new character is created to reevaluate the biblical text from a markedly cultural standpoint, although Filemoni-Tofaeono kept culture in the analytical frame without explicitly putting it into the fictional texts—that is, the role-playing dialogue and the letter to Jesus do not make direct reference to Sāmoa or Oceania.

Filemoni-Tofaeono's playfully serious criticism of the biblical text, accusing Luke of blowing things out of proportion, resonates with the work of scholars who have analyzed gaps and slippages in missionary translations. For example, in his 2015 master's thesis, Liusamoa Simolea, a faculty member at Kanana Fou Theological Seminary, criticized one particular altered translation in Samoan versions of the Bible (figure 1.1). In 1855, the Bible verse Isaiah 7:14 (which reads in part, "Behold, a young woman shall conceive and bear a son") was translated into Samoan with the word *fafine* used for "woman." Matthew 1:23 refers back to Isaiah, but the English version changes "woman" to "virgin," and many Christians see the birth of Jesus as a fulfilment of Isaiah's prophecy.

When the Samoan biblical text was retranslated in 1877, *fafine* was changed to *taupou* in both verses. *Taupou* is the term for a daughter of a high chief. She is a focus of ceremonial symbolism and traditionally supposed to remain a virgin until marriage. The 1877 retranslation generally elevated the biblical language, replacing ordinary-use terms with markedly respectful ones, and

FIGURE 1.1. Liusamoa Simolea preaches at the "Seven Sayings of Jesus" service, Good Friday 2016, Kanana Fou Theological Seminary. Photo by author.

later retranslations have retained *taupou* and not reinstated *fafine* (Simolea 2015, 24–25). Simolea argued that the term *fafine* is, however, a better translation because *taupou* denotes an aristocratic woman, which Mary was not. Moreover, the term *taupou* itself seems to have been used for "ceremonial virgins" only in the later decades of the nineteenth century (Tcherkézoff 2008, 106); as Simolea (who quoted Serge Tcherkézoff, who acknowledged Aiono Fanaafi Le Tagaloa as his source) put it, "The term *taupou* was created in the 19th century by . . . Samoan translators not only to clarify the [original Hebrew term] *almah* in Isaiah 7:14 but also to depict the virginity of Mary in the Gospel of Matthew 1:23" (Simolea 2015, 64).[7] This clarification, however, was an alteration. Mary was "an ordinary woman, rather than a high-status one," and Simolea urged a reversion to the older use of *fafine,* which would offer "Christian comfort to poor Samoans rather than shoring up the importance of high-status families" (2015, 66; see also Ma'ilo Fuaiva'a 2015, 71).

Challenges of Representation: The Work of Jione Havea, Nāsili Vaka'uta, and Mosese Ma'ilo Fuaiva'a

The most prolific Pacific author to write back at the Bible has been Jione Havea, one of the sons of Sione 'Amanaki Havea, the founder of Coconut

Theology. Born in Tonga and ordained in the Tongan Methodist Church, he earned his doctorate in 2000 from Southern Methodist University in Dallas and has taught at Texas Christian University in Fort Worth, Charles Sturt University in Sydney, Trinity Methodist College in Auckland, and Sia'atoutai Theological College in Tonga. In person and on the page, he has a magnetic personality and an exuberant wit.

In his monograph *Elusions of Control* (2003), Havea examined a single biblical chapter, Numbers 30, in which Moses announces God's laws on vow making. Numbers 30 pays special attention to women's responsibility for the vows they make. In the book's introduction, Havea referred to Jacques Derrida, Frederic Jameson, Paul Ricoeur, and Michel Foucault, but he also took care to situate himself as a specifically Tongan author—even as he playfully undercut his own position in the process of claiming it: "I am Tongan, but Tonga is more than me, and the South Pacific Islands are more than Tonga. In writing as a native I may insult other natives, of Tonga and beyond, for I write as a native and *not* as a native—as an *alter-native*. I read from/at the point where the elusive Other meets, *is*, crosses, the eluding reader. I am both, and not both, Other and reader" (J Havea 2003, 3n10; italics in original). This paradoxical, self-defined situation of being a "native"-who-is-not-a-native has informed Havea's approach to biblical scholarship in both substance and style. He has insisted on destabilization as a strategy and sown doubt about his own claims. At its most poetic, his writing is hypnotic but also dizzying. Even at its most prosaic, it moves shark-quick through interpretive waters. In the nine-page introduction to *Elusions,* readers are greeted by the winking punctuation of "ignor-ances," "(con)fusing," "a_part," "on/to"; meet a great deal of italicization, as if the words themselves are deliriously sliding off the page; and follow the magnetism of homophony, with illusion and elusion, waves and wakes, and rides, writes, and rights all pulling together (J Havea 2003).

Havea described his approach to Numbers 30 as "transtextual," a method and metaphor drawn from ocean waves' combination of pattern and chaos. To read transtextually, he argued, means bouncing around on the waves of texts and falling into their gaps and wakes while giving up the possibility of controlling their interpretation. To read transtextually is both to deconstruct and to offer a "circumreading" (a term Havea said he adapted from Derrida's "circumfession"), in which multiple texts are brought together to both inform and subvert each other. It is a kind of intertextual reading that insists on meaning's partiality and instability even as it resolutely pursues *some* kind of meaning (J Havea 2003, 1–9). (One of the many epigraphs Havea offered in *Elusions,* from John D Caputo's engagement with Derrida, serves as an adequate summary of Havea's own position: "To deconstruct something is not to wreck it but to rewrite it, reformulate it, redo it, remake it; better still, it deconstructs itself, auto-deconstructively" [Caputo 1993 quoted in J Havea 2003, 97].)[8]

Havea juxtaposed Numbers 30 with other biblical texts about vows, especially the stories of a warrior named Jephthah, who unexpectedly has to sacrifice his daughter (Judg 11); the words of Hannah, mother of the prophet Samuel (1 Sam 1–2); and the relationship between Tamar and Judah (Gen 38). In each of these stories, Havea identified a theme of delays. In his readings, Jephthah's daughter delays her sacrifice so that her father might reconsider the vow that will lead to her death. Hannah delays the dedication of her baby to God until after he is weaned, even though she had declared that she would "give him unto the LORD all the days of his life" (1 Sam 1:11). And when Judah sends his widowed daughter-in-law to wait in her father's house until his youngest son can marry her, Tamar exploits the delay by disguising herself, sleeping with her father-in-law, and giving birth to twins, whom Judah has to admit are his own sons. Havea argued that these delays reveal how the authors of Numbers 30 "were blinded" to the deep context of humans' vow making, with its tangled issues of gender relations, will and agency, and possibilities of restoring vows that have been broken (2003, 179–180).

In identifying delays as a key theme for analysis, Havea explained, he was offering an Islander's perspective. "Reading for delays is the stuff of islanders, in and beyond Oceania, who are also known for our laid-back personalities. We are carefree not because we do not care, but because we take advantage of delays (to fish and to kick back!).... We embrace delays for the opportunities they provide." He then pushed this claim in an intriguing direction, recasting Tamar explicitly as an Islander who exploits a delay (J Havea 2003, 159, 160; compare 163n11). This move echoes Filemoni-Tofaeono's creation of "Marthya" as an attempt both to understand and to reshape biblical figures in terms of Pacific values.

Another Tongan scholar who has written back vigorously at the Old Testament is Nāsili Vakaʻuta, at the time of this writing the principal of Trinity Methodist Theological College and an affiliated faculty member at the University of Auckland. He received his PhD from the University of Auckland and was Elaine Wainwright's first student there. Vakaʻuta has pushed culturally contrarian readings of the Bible to a remarkable extent. He has also posed a core question with admirable lucidity: can a specifically Tongan reading of the Bible change biblical scholarship in general? (Vakaʻuta 2011, 3). In other words, and to broaden his question in my own words, can contextual theology transcend its context through dialogue?

An example of Vakaʻuta's delight in transgressive readings is his analysis of the second and sixth chapters of the Book of Joshua (Vakaʻuta 2014). In those chapters, Joshua, an Israelite leader, sends two spies to Jericho in Canaan, which the Israelites intend to claim. They stay at the house of Rahab, who is identified as a harlot—a prostitute. The king of Jericho hears about their arrival and sends men to investigate. Rahab helps the spies by hiding them from the king's emissaries and lying, saying that they had left already. She then asks the spies for help in return. They vow that when they massacre the land's inhabitants they will spare Rahab and her family if she hangs a scarlet cord in her window and keeps all her family members within the house. She does so, and her family is saved.

For Vakaʻuta, the story is almost pornographic—Rahab is a prostitute, she takes the men into her house's hidden recesses (she hides them under flax on the roof), and the men are working to "spread" and "penetrate" Canaan—and his essay invokes Anne McClintock's trope of the "porno-tropics" (Vakaʻuta 2014; McClintock 1995). For him, the biblical account echoes Western writings on Oceanian women, with authors ranging from the most repressed missionaries to the most liberated anthropologists (he names Margaret Mead), who have turned women of the Pacific Islands into icons of sexual promiscuity. This structural resonance, in which women are border-zone figures turned into whores, underlies Vakaʻuta's counterclaim that Rahab is not a prostitute at all, despite the fact that "that is what the Bible says" (2014, 151). She is figuratively turned into a prostitute by God's command to the Israelites in Deuteronomy 7 that they must not enter into any covenants with their conquered enemies or intermarry with them (and more to the point, the Israelites should "smite them, and utterly destroy them" [Deut 7:2]).

In response to the description of Rahab as a harlot, Vakaʻuta introduced readers to a Tongan phrase, ʻa ena ia, which is used "when a person wants to respond to negative remarks by someone else." Rahab "is named and labeled a harlot," he wrote, "but as I have argued, 'harlotry' is a Deuteronomic ploy to justify land acquisition and dispossession of native peoples in their lands. Portraying Rahab as a harlot has no substance. To conclude, I would respond together with Rahab to her story and readers: ʻa ena ia!" (Vakaʻuta 2014, 153–154). In sum, the depiction of Rahab as a whore is a lie and a trick designed to justify the theft of land from indigenous inhabitants, and it should be rejected.[9]

For Vakaʻuta, as for Havea, transgression or "crossing" is an especially effective approach to interpreting the Bible, letting readers contest dominant readings and shape new ones in the act of being faithful Christians. Transgression is intellectually vital. It also seems to be personally significant for Vakaʻuta and Havea, both of whom are Tongan Methodist theologians whose doctoral training and academic careers have been conducted far from Tonga. Havea described how his niece told him he was "'more American than Tongan,' similar to being...a potato, stained and grubby on the skin but white and untainted in the flesh" (Havea 2004, 199). Vakaʻuta explained that he is a tuʻa, a term for the social category often translated as "commoner" (see, eg, Churchward 1959, 515). He pointed out that this translation "is a misnomer, since the meanings tuʻa encompasses... [include] those who are in that class together with slaves and animals, and that is far more dehumanising than being an ordinary person" (Vakaʻuta 2011, 20).

In May 2013, I was in attendance when Vakaʻuta lectured to an undergraduate class (BSTheology 216/316 ["Biblical Texts in Contexts"]) at the University of Auckland and had the following exchange with a female student. For the day's reading, he had assigned an article of his own that had been published in the journal *Concilium* in an issue coedited by Wainwright (Vaka'uta 2010a). In it, he explained his approach to reading "*tu'a*-wise." Speaking to the class, Vaka'uta explained, "For your information, the word *tu'a*, the so-called commoner class in the Tongan religious-social hierarchy, refers to a group of people, or the majority of Tongans, which I am a part of, from the islands of Tonga."

He continued:

Nāsili Vaka'uta: About 95 percent of the population are *tu'a*. And [in] the translation given by early British writers, early colonial writers, they used the word "commoner." But to me, it's a misnomer. That's not a correct translation of the word. *Tu'a*, according to Tongan culture, is much worse than being a commoner in the British context, and I think I explained a bit of that in the article.

So roughly, in Tongan culture, people, places, and things are categorized into two major classes. One is called the *'eiki* class . . . an elite group occupy[ing] the top of the social hierarchy. And according to Tongan culture, only those few have souls. And they are the only ones who are entitled to have an afterlife. The majority of the population, who are *tu'a*, they don't have souls. If they die, they go. There is no afterlife for them. Those at the top, they are descendants of gods. . . . The majority of the population, the *tu'a*, they are the ignorant ones, they are born and destined to serve those at the top. So Tongan society has been like that for thousands of years. And although there are positive influences from outside, and development in other areas within the Tongan society, the way we relate to each other and the way things are operated within Tonga, are still very much dictated by the *tu'a-'eiki* relation.

Some pigs are *'eiki*. Some animals are *'eiki*. Some pieces of land are *'eiki*. So those of us who are in the commoner or the *tu'a* group are not allowed to step over into that space. We are not allowed to speak in some spaces. So the opportunities for *tu'a* in Tongan society are very limited, restricted. And you can find that's why Tongans overseas are much more vocal; they are in a very different space. And the movement for democracy came more from outside Tonga than within Tonga because people have the liberty to voice their opinions.

Female Student: So you're born into class?
Nāsili Vaka'uta: We are born into class. It's—

Female Student: And a pig can be born into the class, too.

Nāsili Vaka'uta: A pig can be born into the class. The *tu'a* class is categorized together with animals, with slaves, and foreigners. And people nowadays are not talking about this categorization, but they still are [using it].

    So, when I came to do my doctoral studies, I struggled to think about a way to develop a hermeneutic. Not only that the trend in hermeneutics was new to me, but I was scared of writing about my own context. And believe me, it's a scary experience, not only to form a framework to read the Bible, but to critique you and your culture at the same time. And without anybody else in the School of Theology doing the same work. I was alone at the time. But I had good support from supervisors and colleagues.[10]

As Vaka'uta made clear in the class and has emphasized in his writings, being a Tongan *tu'a* means one is not really supposed to represent Tonga. Metacultural emphasis on Tongan identity specifically values the chiefly *('eiki)* category as the one worth representing and the one representing worth. Yet he has spoken up as a specifically Tongan *tu'a* theologian, drawing on Tongan categories as both sources of and objects of criticism.

Note Vaka'uta's criticism of the translation of *tu'a* as "commoner" and its perceived slippage in value: being a commoner in English is not so bad, but in Tongan it has a very different shade of meaning. As noted above, some Oceanic theologians who have written back at the Bible have similarly focused on the slippages and misdirections of missionary translations, such as Simolea's argument that the Samoan translation of "woman" as *taupou* in Isaiah 7:14 and Matthew 1:23 has led to an inappropriate reading of Mary as an elite woman. The principal of Piula, Mosese Ma'ilo Fuaiva'a, has made the hybrid nature of biblical translations the focus of his scholarship (figure 1.2). Drawing especially on the work of R S Sugirtharajah and Homi Bhabha, Ma'ilo Fuaiva'a has approached Polynesian Bible translations as hybrid texts in which languages, themes, and content tend toward European rather than Polynesian meanings and power.[11] Reading the Bible critically means retranslating it in ways that reinforce relevant indigenous models and destabilize missionary assumptions about Polynesian linguistic and cultural inadequacy.

For example, Ma'ilo Fuaiva'a observed that the genealogy of Jesus in Matthew 1:1–16 (which begins, "The book of the generation of Jesus Christ, the son of David, the son of Abraham. Abraham begat Isaac; and Isaac begat Jacob; and Jacob begat Judas and his brethren") was first translated into Samoan by Samuel Wilson in 1836, with Matthew 1:1 featuring the terms *upu* for "book" and *tupuga* for "generation" (Wilson 1837; Ma'ilo Fuaiva'a 2016, 19). *'Upu* means "spoken word" and was appropriate for Sāmoa, where genealogies were traditionally recited orally, but in 1846 William Day retranslated Matthew and

Figure 1.2. Piula Theological College Principal Mosese Maʻilo Fuaivaʻa and his wife Terina and baby Mosese Jr attend church, August 2015. Photo by author.

changed the term to *tusi*, "literally 'writing' or 'book,' following the Greek sense of 'record,'" moving away from a resonant Samoan sense of how family records are kept (Maʻilo Fuaivaʻa 2008, 257; 2016, 21). Day also changed *tupuga* (ancestors) to *gafa* (lineage, genealogy), which, Maʻilo Fuaivaʻa noted, was probably meant to make the text more amenable to Samoan understandings of genealogies as sacred forms of knowledge (2008, 259). Jesus's genealogy, as given in the Samoan translation, is a literal equivalent of the King James Version's account with all those "begats"—but the Samoan verb used, *fanaua*, means "give birth" and thus makes no sense when the subjects are men. It would be preferable, Maʻilo Fuaivaʻa argued, to rephrase the text in terms of paternity: "Abraham was the father of Isaac, Isaac was the father of Jacob, and Jacob was the father of Judah and his brothers" (2008, 260).[12] Yet even this new translation would miss the point that genealogies, for Samoans, can include the names of women and their fathers and also convey the sense that "the offspring from a union is . . . a new lineage in itself" (Maʻilo Fuaivaʻa 2008, 262). Putting these principles together, Maʻilo Fuaivaʻa wrote that Matthew 1:2, for example, can be retranslated into Samoan as "Abraham married/united with Sarah the daughter of Tara started the lineage of

Isaac; Isaac united with Rebecca the daughter of Bethuel started the lineage of Jacob; Jacob united with Leah the daughter of Laban started the lineage of Judah and his brothers" (2008, 263).[13] This new version not only keeps the genealogy intact but also fills it out, recognizes women, and even "decolonises the reader's mind," making the text meaningfully Samoan in linguistic and cultural terms (Ma'ilo Fuaiva'a 2008, 263; see also Ma'ilo Fuaiva'a 2013).

The process of translating the Bible is an immense, complex, and always partial effort to align different languages, grammars, registers, concepts, and ideologies. Retranslations can always be accused of failing where previous translations succeeded. In Ma'ilo Fuaiva'a's account, retranslations like Day's do not improve the text and in some ways make it worse.[14] Dissatisfaction with new translations can motivate revivals of the originals, as historian Andrew Thornley and theologian Ilaitia Sevati Tuwere have attempted to do for John Hunt's early Fijian biblical translations (Tomlinson 2014b, 123–124). Such dissatisfaction can also prompt calls for new retranslations of the kind Ma'ilo Fuaiva'a proposed. And, as he concluded in his dissertation, they can also spur new appreciation of Bibles as texts whose hybridity makes them "authentic texts in the global biblical dialogue" (Ma'ilo Fuaiva'a 2008, 297).

The works of Havea, Vaka'uta, and Ma'ilo Fuaiva'a show how contextual biblical studies, drawing on literary theory, positions "culture" differently than much of mainstream contextual theology. In mainstream contextual theology, as I noted in the introduction, culture is often treated in structural-functionalist and cognitive terms as something bounded, stable, and rule-based. In the works of the biblical scholars just discussed, by contrast, culture is treated as necessarily hybrid: a process of making connections, challenges, responses, and reformulations. To be sure, hybridity always depends on a sense that there are discrete referents that can be brought together in the first place: saying that "Tongan culture" is hybrid, for example, still requires a sense that some things count as Tongan and others do not. But in the lively and capacious work of Pacific biblical scholars like Havea, Vaka'uta, and Ma'ilo Fuaiva'a, culture is like an octopus, moving, changing shape, reaching out in all directions.

Erasure and Refusal

One way some translators and theologians have approached the Bible is to suggest that some verses might be strategically omitted to avoid misunderstanding. Describing nineteenth-century Wesleyan missionary William Cross's work at Nuku'alofa, Tonga, Thornley noted that "he took liberties with his free translation from the English text and he deleted some verses, claiming they would not be understood or might be misapplied by the people" (2005, 45).

A recent example of this kind of effort to "deconstruct and reconstruct" biblical texts comes from Samoan Methodist theologian Titimaea Titimaea (2014, 56). In his bachelor of divinity thesis, Titimaea analyzed responses to the 2009 tsunami that hit Sāmoa and American Sāmoa (as well as the Niua island group of Tonga). His thesis was then published and sold as a seventy-four-page booklet. A story that was not heard after the tsunami, Titimaea wrote, was that of Noah and the flood. This was a missed opportunity, he said, because understanding the story of Noah from a Pacific perspective can show how God is "the one who provides warnings and valuable information to Noah about how to survive in such a devastating flood.... The role that God plays... is to warn humans... how to react to such natural disasters" (Titimaea 2014, 58). Natural disasters are caused by natural processes and are well explained by scientists. God does not use floods or tsunamis as weapons. Rather, God guides people in their aftermath. Titimaea criticized Deuteronomic readings of disasters, in which suffering is seen as God's punishment for sin and lack of faith.

To understand the tsunami, then, Titimaea urged a reconnection of Samoans with the Noah story as well as an appreciation of how undersea earthquakes really happen. But reading Noah from a local perspective also requires reshaping it. Titimaea argued that Genesis 6:5–8, 11–13, and 17—passages that describe God's explicit intention to destroy humanity and all life on earth in a flood—are "irrelevant to island reading" and unhelpful reminders of missionaries' denigration of Islanders. He reproduced the New King James Version's text of Genesis 6 and 7 with these lines omitted, and argued that his new version restores "what seems to be an original version" (Titimaea 2014, 56). In other words, Titimaea saw his project not as rewriting but as recovery, identifying an original text in which human sin and God's anger are removed. In doing so, the text becomes an affirmation of God's care for his creation rather than his destruction of it.

The Rejection of Context and the Refusal of Dialogue

At this point, I need to state the obvious but pressing point that many Christians—theologians and others—are skeptical about writing back at the Bible. For example, many nineteenth-century Protestant missionaries did not approve of contextualization of the Gospel. At the fifth annual assembly of Wesleyan Methodists in Sāmoa in September 1862, a resolution was adopted concerning Samoan preaching. "Some of our preachers had a very wild imagination, and often suffered parable to run mad," reported Martin Dyson. "They would use, as similes and illustrations of religious truths, the strangest old legends and tales which their traditions supplied, and often, 'the pure milk of the Word' turned sour in their bowls. To put an end to this, we resolved that all similes and parables which had no foundation in matter of fact, should be forbidden to all our agents in their public preaching" (Dyson 1875, 91–92).[15] An even blunter statement of the position came from an author named Emma Adams, who in 1890 authored a book about Fiji and Sāmoa intended for young readers. There are many problems with her book, including such notable flaws as her indecision about whether the name is "Fiji" or "Figi" and her wildly inaccurate claim that "the natives were mostly atrocious man eaters not twenty years ago" (Adams 1890, 15–16). But at least her prose has the virtue of stating her position as clearly as possible:

> A recent writer upon the Fijians and their customs, says, with an air of great satisfaction: "While the traveler sees, on all sides, traces of the old devil-worship of the islanders, he will yet observe that many of the traditions of heathenism, though dying hard, are fading away, while all that was good in them is being carefully adapted so as to be in harmony with the Christianity now professed." Instantly one is led to ask: Why should the "good things" of devil-worship be engrafted upon Christianity? Is not Christianity, without the slightest admixture of their old heathen worship, the very best thing in the form of religion that can be offered the advancing Fijians? Christianity, with the choicest of their former rites "carefully fitted into it," is no longer Christianity. It is something else. Christianity needs nothing fitted into it to improve it, or to help it make its way. (Adams 1890, 17–18)

The writings of missionaries like Dyson and popular authors like Adams focus on one message, one truth, and one way of expressing it. Any new voices speaking into this relationship are irrelevant at best. This position, which H Richard Niebuhr famously characterized as a "Christ against culture" model (2001), was also adopted by those Christian fundamentalists who began to fetishize a particular kind of literalism beginning in the early twentieth century (Coleman 2006; Crapanzano 2000).

When novel theological interpretations are offered to conservative congregations, questions about the possibilities and limits of dialogue can become clarified. Vaka'uta told me during an interview in Auckland on 21 November 2014 how much he enjoyed sharing his scholarly insights with community members: "The greatest satisfaction for me is when I use my research in my preaching," he said. "People [have] responded positively. It opens up insights from familiar texts that they never thought of before. I got also positive response in courses that I teach at uni[versity], especially the one on Oceanic hermeneutics." He mentioned *pakipaki* Bible discussion groups in which he participates: "*Pakipaki,* it's the word we use for 'breaking bread' in Holy Communion. But instead we use it in this case for a group of men coming together [to] drink kava and at the same time discuss the readings for the following Sunday. . . . I love talking freely with kava drinkers. Most of them are not lay preachers of the Church. They hold no position in the Church. But they are interested in reading the Bible." And yet Vaka'uta acknowledged, too, that because he does not actually work in a parish and is not responsible for a congregation, he has "a privileged position":

Those who are working in congregations, they face the dilemma of either...to offer something different and run the risk of losing their job, or go with the flow. So in my case, I don't have to do that. I have the freedom to preach differently, to do Bible studies differently. But I think the bottom line is to be clear what you're doing, allow the people to get some sense of where you're going, rather than just dropping a bomb that means nothing. I'm encouraged by responses from, especially, women. I've written a lot about women's perspective.

Vaka'uta called attention to the fact that university-based scholars have a freedom of expression, and thus the chance to set up new dialogues, that is not available to pastors who tend to their congregations' needs and depend on their material support.

Coda: Ghost Texts

To finish this chapter in a light spirit, I would like to mention the well-known fact that sometimes the most useful bits of Scripture are the ones that do not actually exist. For example, Brian Malley discussed a British folk remedy for toothaches, in which a text was "worn around the neck, sewn into the clothes, or carried in a pocket" (2009, 201). The verses were said to come from the Bible and described Christ miraculously healing Peter's toothache. In a dialogue published in 1850, a woman called Dame Gray discusses the text with a parson. "I think I know my Bible," the churchman says, "and I don't find any such verse in it." To this, Dame Gray responds: "Yes, your reverence, that is just the charm. It's in the Bible, but you can't find it!" (Malley 2009, 202). Consider also the verses in the Quran that support female genital mutilation. There aren't any, but that doesn't stop some people from referring to them (Walley 1997, 413). Like arrows that create their targets, these ghost texts create the reality they purport to represent (see also Inoue 2006).

Bart Ehrman has popularized the related argument that the earliest Christian texts that would become Scripture were subject to many changes due to the transcribers' self-interest as well as out-and-out mistakes, and whole parts of the New Testament were added after the originals had been composed. For example, consider the story about Jesus's encounter with the "scribes and Pharisees" (religious legalists) who ask him what they should do with a woman caught in adultery. In the story, from the Gospel of John, Jesus cannily avoids giving an answer: saying she should be freed would be to deny the law, but saying she should be punished would be to deny "his own teachings of love, mercy, and forgiveness" (Ehrman 2005, 64). Instead, Jesus writes on the ground and waits for the scribes and Pharisees to leave the scene. When they have all gone, he asks the woman if anyone is left to condemn her, and when she says that no one is, he responds, "Neither do I condemn thee: go, and sin no more" (John 8:11). "It is a brilliant story," Ehrman commented—

and then he added, "As it turns out, it was not originally in the Gospel of John" (nor in the other Gospels, namely Matthew, Mark, and Luke), as proven by the fact that the oldest manuscripts of John do not include it and its style and vocabulary set it apart from the rest of that book (Ehrman 2005, 64–65).

Thus the scribes of early Christianity, engaged in the laborious task of writing out copies of Scripture, were both writing up the Bible—fixing it, with quirks and slips along the way, into its several canonical forms—and also writing back at the Bible even as it took shape, creatively deforming and reforming it again and again. The work of theologians like Havea, Vakaʻuta, Maʻilo Fuaivaʻa, and others discussed in this chapter might seem radical for the way it challenges the Bible as a partial and incomplete text. And this work might seem radical especially within Oceanic Christianity and its pervasive conservatism. But as Ehrman demonstrated, the Bible has always been partial and incomplete. The point of this chapter has been that although Oceanic contextual theologians stick with biblical texts, they do so in decidedly unsticky ways. They seek new ways of discovering surprising meanings, writing back at the Bible from self-consciously cultural perspectives in devout, and sometimes devoutly contrarian, efforts at dialogue.

Chapter 2
Weavers, Servants, and Prophets

"The church in the Pacific is in a truly privileged position," wrote Jesuit priest and historian Francis X Hezel. "Religion has always been an essential element of life for islanders, and the churches are tightly woven into the fabric of these societies. The church enjoys a position of respect and influence which I suspect is unequalled anywhere in the world" (Hezel 1992, 18–19). Such respect and influence is reflected in the high status of ministers as well as the sacrifices in time, labor, and money that people make to churches. It is also reflected in basic statistics, with almost 99 percent of Sāmoa's population and more than 95 percent of Tonga's identifying as Christian (Johnson and Zurlo 2007). In 1996, the most recent time Fiji's government gathered data by ethnic category, more than 99 percent of indigenous Fijians identified as Christians (Fiji Bureau of Statistics 2016; the national population has a significant percentage of Hindus and Muslims). In addition, churches' influence has an inescapably political dimension. Rory Ewins, quoting a Tongan government official who observed that citizens believe the monarchy is "chosen by God," added that "the identification is so close that many Tongans believe that the King is actually head of the Methodist Church" (1998, 215).

The size, prestige, and influence of Pacific churches has two vivid results. One is confidence in Christian identity. In the mid-twentieth century, Felix Keesing and Marie Keesing wrote about Sāmoa:

> Certainly Samoan customs of gift-exchange, reciprocal hospitality, and the like have been fused by now inextricably with the Christian ethic of "brotherly love," "charity," and service, so that the Samoan mental picture of his own people and culture is that they are "the most Christian in the world." A very influential and progressive chief, asked what solutions he had in view for the obviously fast increasing population of Samoans today in relation to quite limited good lands for plantation use, replied: "How do we know that God intends the Samoans to remain only in Samoa; perhaps he is preparing them as his special people, so that when the rest of the world is destroyed by atom warfare they may re-people it as Noah did after the flood." (Keesing and Keesing 1956, 89)

In statements like those recorded by Keesing and Keesing, culture gains a godly aura. "Samoans insist that their culture is of divine origin," observed Methodist theologian Koneferenisi Tuaiaufai. "It is regarded as a gift from god handed down by their ancestors" (Tuaiaufai 2007, 84n8; see also Macpherson and Macpherson 2010).

The other effect of Christianity's prominent social situation in Oceania is, paradoxically, a deep concern about the state of the churches. Because churches are so finely and firmly interwoven with family life, education, and local and national politics, they are inevitably caught up in all kinds of social change. The sociopolitical elite, including church ministers and chiefs, are concerned with their status and authority and can be anxious to shore up perceived bases of their respect. The non-elite criticize elitism but sometimes buy into the system, for example valorizing chiefliness by claiming that most present-day chiefs are not as chiefly as the old chiefs. As Eric Hobsbawm famously argued, concern with formulating and expressing "tradition" intensifies during rapid social change, and modern Oceania is a place of profound transformations (1983). Because Christianity is now so thoroughly identified with what counts as tradition, the explicit and self-conscious values of Pacific Islands as Christian places—indeed, "the most Christian in the world"—are sometimes recast: are we really so Christian these days?

Contextual theology allows intellectuals in Oceania to discuss social change in particular ways through the idiom of culture. In this chapter, I discuss three prominent ways that this happens. One is explicitly feminist. Feminist theologians have argued that women's potential is overlooked or suppressed and that a healthy church and society should resist patriarchal tendencies and allow more women to contribute theologically and pastorally. A second way, prominent in Samoan theology, is to focus on ideals of service: what does it mean to serve, and how does authority depend on demonstrated service? A third is to insist on speaking "prophetically," delivering divinely sanctioned messages that are meant to get churches and societies back onto straight and true Christian paths.

Weavers

In 1989, a regional meeting in Tonga on the topic of women and ministry led to the creation of Weavers, a women's theological collective and "women's advocacy arm" of the South Pacific Association of Theological Schools (Johnson 2003, 12, 19n12). Since its formation, Weavers has produced several collective publications, most notably special issues of the *Pacific Journal of Theology (PJT)* in 1992 and 1996, an edited book in 2003, and an online education course book on "The Church and Violence Against Women" in 2006.[1]

The book from 2003, titled *Weavings: Women Doing Theology in Oceania*, offers chapters by authors from across the region: Solomon Islands, Vanuatu, New Caledonia, Kiribati, Fiji, Tonga, Sāmoa and American Sāmoa, Niue, French Polynesia, and New Zealand. All of the authors are women. Not all of the contributors had academic degrees in theology, but many did, and all addressed significant questions such as whether God should be understood as gendered, whether women should be ordained as church ministers, and how women ought to address the discrimination they face in patriarchal societies. The volume has thematic consistency, but distinct arguments also emerge. For example, Valamotu Palu, an ordained minister in the Free Wesleyan Church of Tonga, offered the strong contextual theological argument that salvation must be culturally ordered and experienced ("To be real to the people, salvation must come as it is defined by Pacific people in their own cultures" [V Palu 2003, 62]), whereas Samoan Congregationalist Mine Pase warned of "people inculturat[ing] the Gospel to suit themselves" (Pase 2003, 76; see also Filemoni-Tofaeono and Johnson 2006). All of the contributors to *Weavings* agreed, however, that women in Oceania can and should make distinct and valuable contributions to theological dialogues.[2]

Several of the authors in *Weavings* described God in explicitly feminine or gender-inclusive terms. Chantelle Khan, a Catholic author from Fiji who spent several years as the director of a Christian nongovernmental organization in Suva, wrote: "If God is all-powerful and all-embracing, and if males and females are made in God's image, then we limit God and do an injustice to God by restricting God to 'He' and almost totally obliterating God's 'She'" (Khan 2003, 189). Similarly, Ilisapeci Meo, a Fijian Methodist who received her master of theology degree from the Pacific Theological College (PTC) and served as the leader of Weavers, described theology as "an engaging reflection on God's self and His/Her reconciling love" (Meo 2003, 156). Two other theologians who received master's degrees from PTC, Michiko Ete-Lima of Sāmoa and Tamara Wete of New Caledonia, characterized God as sister and mother. Ete-Lima invoked the Samoan model of the *feagaiga* ("covenant," including the relationship between a brother and sister; see next section) to argue that God, as our sister, is sacred and deserving of service and loves us with wisdom (Ete-Lima 2003, 29–30). Wete drew on the work of US feminist theologian Sallie McFague to suggest that understanding God as a mother figure "will help women to understand the full potential of their [own] role as mothers" (Wete 2003, 55; see also V Palu 2003, 68; Samate 2003, 168; Faitala 2003, 201).[3]

A key point for many of the authors in *Weavings* is that women of Oceania, living within patriarchal societies, can contribute positively to society and theology through the roles they already occupy as mothers, sisters, birth givers, tapa cloth makers, and, of course, weavers. But besides mentioning these capacities and contributions, several authors also argued that women should be ordained as church ministers. Pase noted that "Samoan churches have yet to embrace the concept of the ordination of women" (2003, 75), and she compared this state of affairs to women's exclusion from royal kava ceremonies. Meo suggested that by failing to ordain women, Christian churches fail at the "prophetic role" of being "the conscience of the society" (2003, 153).[4]

The topics of God's gender and women's ordination offer sharp examples of the limits of potential theological dialogues with a broad public. Biblical verses such as Genesis 1:26–27 and Galatians 3:28, to which many Weavers referred, seem to offer support for theological arguments about God's non-fixed gender and the identity of all people as divinely shaped subjects who can represent and express divine truths. In Genesis 1:26–27, God makes men and women in the divine "image" and "likeness," and in Galatians 3:28, Paul asserts that "there is neither male nor female: for ye are all one in Christ Jesus." But Oceanic societies, as many of the contributors to *Weavings* pointed out, have patriarchal structures and tendencies that resist feminist arguments. Khan told of drinking kava with her choir and asking whether female instead of male terms might be used for God in the upcoming Palm Sunday Mass. She received "a collective chorus of 'Nos' and looks indicating I was close to overstepping some kind of tolerance level." She persisted, asking why God is routinely called "He" when God has no gender, and was met with the stern reply that " 'God has always been He!' " (Khan 2003, 186). When it comes to ordination, the idea that a woman could represent divinity is something that many conservative Christians in Oceania find jarring. As Fineaso Fa'alafi, a Methodist Church historian and former principal of Piula Theological College, put it: "In many village churches, people do not like to hear women from the pulpit and [see them]...conduct an entire service" (1982, 81). Pase, after comparing women's exclusion from church leadership to their exclusion from royal kava ceremonies, suggested that women will soon be ordained in Samoan churches. More than a decade after she published her chapter, it turns out she was correct for the Congregational Christian Church of American Samoa, which not only ordains women but also has an ordained female lecturer at Kanana Fou Theological Seminary, Mafo'e Fa'avae (figure 2.1). However, the Congregationalist and Methodist churches in independent Sāmoa do not ordain women.[5]

The patriarchal systems critiqued by Oceanic theologians can be reproduced within theological institutions. Joan Alleluia Filemoni-Tofaeono and Lydia Johnson stated that PTC, a site of progressive thought within Fiji, is itself a place where "violence against women continues unabated" (2006, 123). I did not personally witness signs of violence against women while I was there, but Filemoni-Tofaeono and Johnson, with their deeper knowledge of the institution, presented a sobering array of cases of abuse, harassment, and discrimination: a student beats his wife repeatedly and is never disci-

FIGURE 2.1. Mafo'e Fa'avae, lecturer in New Testament and women's studies at Kanana Fou Theological Seminary, March 2016. Photo by author.

plined; another student beats his wife, gets drunk, visits prostitutes, and is never disciplined; yet another flirts so aggressively with a woman (married to a different student) that she avoids him whenever possible and begins to feel sick from the stress (2006, 119, 124–138). The well-known observation that biblical texts can be lined up to support opposing arguments is strongly relevant here. Whereas members of Weavers often pointed to Genesis 1:26–27 and Galatians 3:28 as passages that emphasize human unity, Filemoni-Tofaeono and Johnson noted that there are also "a few selected texts which have been used most frequently in Oceanian churches to justify the subjugation of women—and thus, indirectly, violence against women": Genesis 2:4b–3:24, the second creation story, in which Eve is made from Adam's rib, and 1 Corinthians 11:2–16 and Ephesians 5:21–24, in which Paul emphasizes that just as God is the head of Christ and Christ is the head of the church and men, so husbands are the heads of wives (Filemoni-Tofaeono and Johnson 2006, 96–102; see also Casimira 2008, 138–143; Tone 1986).

Weavers is not the only feminist theological group effort in the Pacific. For example, Manahine Pasefika was formed in New Zealand in 2006 to bring together women of Oceania, including those in diaspora (Carroll 2008). Sia'atoutai Theological College, the Methodist seminary in Tonga, developed a "curriculum to substantiate God's call for women['s] discipleship within the Church" in the late 1990s or early 2000s, with funding from the World Council of Churches (Fuka-Tu'itupou 2001, 10). The process resulted in the publication of an edited book that examines Tongan women's roles in various professions—development, health, finance, policing—from a theological standpoint and also considers more purely theological issues such as the meaning of discipleship and the nature of God's wisdom (Fuka-Tu'itupou 2001; see also Ah Siu-Maliko 2010, a volume produced by women at Piula).

The problem with social change, from a feminist contextual-theological perspective, is that modern society has not changed enough. Sometimes this claim is counterposed by another, that in truly traditional Pacific societies women had higher standing than they do now: "a growing number of women are all saying that... if one were to go back and really understand tradition, one would find that [women] were given respect and significant places and roles in society" (Uriam 1999, 157; compare Te Paa 2007). In sum, Oceanic cultures, despite their patriarchal tendencies in the modern era, are thought to have latitude for increased appreciation of divinity's feminine aspects and women's potential to contribute to theology and pastoral care.

Servants

Whereas the topics of women's ordination and God's gender have been raised by authors from many Pacific societies, the topic of "service" is of special interest in Sāmoa. Before turning to this major theme in Samoan contextual theology, I describe the wider network of discourse in which it is enmeshed.

Sāmoa has produced many theologians who have criticized the state of Samoan Christianity. They have put enormous effort into diagnosing and analyzing perceived problems in their churches and society in order to fix things: to revitalize the Church, to keep youth in the fold, and to find the best path for Sāmoa and Samoans in the modern world. As noted in the introduction, the answer has often been a turn to culture—specifically, an emphasis on *fa'asāmoa*, the Samoan way of life, seen as the core of identity in a spiritual and cultural sense. But different authors have identified different elements within it as foundational or atomic. For example, a former head of state referred to *fa'asāmoa* as being "founded on *alofa*," or love (Efi 2009a, 52).

Two key terms that are often mentioned are *fa'aaloalo* and *feagaiga*. *Fa'aaloalo* is generally translated as "respect" (eg, Milner 1993, 16). A Methodist theologian teaching at PTC, Upolu Lumā Vaai, described *fa'aaloalo* as "a symbol that shapes the whole of Samoan existence... [and] defines relationship[s] between persons, between a person and creation and between a person and God" (Vaai 2006, 58; emphasis deleted). He developed a distinct theology of the Trinity centered on the term, arguing that God can be understood as "Being-in-*Faaaloalo*" (Vaai 2006, 187–191; see also Faleali'i 2002, 17–19; Koria 1999; Kupa 2006; Ta'avao 2003; Tuaiaufai 2007, 84).[6] The second term, *feagaiga*, often translated as "covenant," denotes various relationships, including that between a sister and brother and their respective descendants as well as that between high chiefs and their orators (Pratt 1862, 118; see also Gershon 2012, 118–123; Macpherson and Macpherson 2010, 107–108; Schoeffel 1995; Tapuai 1972). The word is based on *feagai*, meaning "opposition" in a complementary rather than an antagonistic sense, "persons or parties being of reciprocal and mutual status and valuation" (Latai 2015, 93). *Feagaiga* is used to denote the relationship between a Protestant minister *(faife'au)* and his congregation (see Milner 1993, 8). In other words, a minister and his congregation should take care of each other the way a sister and brother are supposed to take care of each other, with the minister symbolically filling the female role and the chiefs and village filling the male role. It is also used for "testament": the Old Testament is called the Feagaiga Tuai, and the New Testament is called the Feagaiga Fou.

As a crucial part of their covenant, Samoan church ministers are supposed to attend only to spiritual matters and not participate in village politics (Kamu 1996, 145–146; Latai 2015, 96–97). The minister is supposed to be set apart and exalted: "To a Samoan, a pastor is the embodiment of the covenant between God and people. He is God's ambassador, agent, emissary, intermediary and representative on earth" (Koria 1999, 10). But some Samoans criticize ministers for consuming too much and sharing too little, tipping the relationship off balance (see, eg, Gershon 2006 and Hardin 2015 on evangelicals' criticism of mainline Christian pastors). Moreover, as God's representative, the minister is supposed to be able to curse those who oppose him, just as a sister is supposed to be able to curse her brother (Latai 2015; see also Efi 2009b, 110–111; T Maliko 2012, 260).[7] My point is that for a number of theologians, and also some anthropologists (eg, Shore 1976, 283), terms and concepts like *fa'aaloalo* and *feagaiga,* respect and covenant, show how the Samoan Way is supposed to work. By extension, they point to people's ideal relationship with God. Showing respect and honoring relationships as covenants are considered essential practices for maintaining proper social and spiritual order.

It is the concept of service or being a servant (the term for both is *tautua*) that gets the most attention in Samoan theology. Many student theses make a point of quoting the proverb "O le ala i le pule o le tautua," meaning "The way to authority is through service" (figure 2.2).[8] Uesile Tupu mentioned that of the forty-one sermon texts he analyzed from services held in Samoan Methodist churches on Father's Day in 2009, seven used the saying "O le ala i le pule o le tautua" to interpret the lectionary's text for the day, Matthew 25:14–30 (the "parable of the talents"). This is a remarkable figure considering that more than half of the sermons had "nothing to say about the Samoan

Figure 2.2. The Congregational Christian Church of American Samoa administration building features a sign with the famous Samoan saying "O le ala i le pule o le tautua" (The way to authority is through service), Kanana Fou Theological Seminary, August 2015. Photo by author.

culture," even as all were preached in the Samoan language (Tupu 2010, 33, 41n23, 42). In other words, of the sermons that did address Samoan culture as a topic, at least one-third turned to the well-known saying.

The point of this maxim is that a person has to serve a leader now in order to become a leader later. Obedience leads to authority. The rule applies to future church ministers just as it applies to future chiefs. At Piula, I saw vividly how students are expected to carry out a great deal of physical labor and remain as quiet as possible, especially in their earlier years, in order to appreciate the necessity of serving obediently before achieving honored positions as church ministers. But even when they become ministers, they are supposed to defer to elder ministers (Tuivanu 2013, 1), and a supposedly paramount authority—such as the principal of a theological college—may find himself expected to keep quiet in meetings in which senior authorities make decisions about his workplace without seeking his input. The general social ideal, for both ministers and chiefs, is that they will be served by their communities and serve their communities in turn. That is, ministers and chiefs can expect to receive a lot of service but should be willing to give back to the people who support them. As I discuss in this section, however, some critics doubt this actually happens.[9]

The principal of Piula, Mosese Ma'ilo Fuaiva'a, observed that the translation of "servant" as *tautua* caused a problem for early Samoan Bible translators. In a family, a *tautua* is a member who, having served appropriately, will eventually become a titleholder—the chief, the served—which is a different model of servitude than that in the Bible, in which slavery is a norm. Accordingly, except in the case of Matthew 20:27 ("and whoever would be first among you must be your slave"), "the missionaries created the term *auauna* to depict the biblical notion of servant" (Ma'ilo Fuaiva'a 2008, 233; see also Tutuila 2009). The term *tautua* now flourishes in Samoan contextual theology (and *auauna* does not), and authors have identified several varieties of traditional service.

For example, Methodist theologian Tevita Amituana'i described three kinds: *tautua 'upu,* or service through words, in which one knows how to speak in a polite and poetic manner; *tautua matavela,* or "service which burns [or cooks] the eyes," in which one provides titleholders with food; and *tautua toto,* blood service, in which one is a warrior or a bodyguard for a titleholder (Amituana'i 1979, 71–74; see also Fonoti 2011, 28–34). Other modifiers can be added after *tautua* to specify how one is supposed to serve or who the object of service is. Congregationalist Gataivai Nepo wrote about *tautua tuavae,* an everyday, ready-to-go kind of service from an untitled man to his chief; the term "describes figuratively the alertness and readiness to act immediately whenever one is called for" (Nepo 1990, 12). Peletisala Lima mentioned that there is also a negative category of service, *tautua pa'o,* meaning service given noisily and resentfully. He noted that Jesus himself might be seen in terms of *tautua pa'o* because he told potential followers, "If any one comes to me and does not hate his own father and mother and wife and children and brothers and sisters, yes, and even his own life, he cannot be my disciple" (Luke 14:26). Lima argued, however, that although "Jesus is not following the conventional cultural script" in Samoan terms, his "purpose is not to devalue the conventional family; instead, he is uplifting and enriching a far more important institution, the kingdom of God" (Lima 2012, 311–312).

And it is Jesus to whom theologians turn as the model of perfect service, a divine figure who began in abject humility and became—but actually always was—the real titleholder of the whole world. For Frank Smith, Jesus was in blood service *(tautua toto)* when he washed his disciples' feet (John 13), because he served them even as he knew one of them would betray him (Smith 2010, 216–227; see also Taule'ale'ausumai 1994, 119–121). "The life of Christ," wrote Ama'amalele Tofaeono, "is identified as a life in service" (2000, 256; see also Allen 1990). Tofaeono went on to explore various dimensions of this service, describing Christ as, among other things, a *tautua 'āiga* (one providing service to a family—but for Tofaeono, "family" expands to the whole interconnected universe of creation; see chapter 4) and a *tautua mana e tapu* (a term that is difficult to translate but might be glossed as giving "powerful, holy service").[10] Here, my point is simply to observe that at the heart of his theological vision of expansive interconnectedness, Tofaeono placed Jesus as a servant—a *tautua*.

While many authors agree that proper service is essential to the Samoan Way, there are several points at which discussions of *tautua* as a term and concept take a critically engaged turn. One key critique concerns the link between service and money. A complaint of Samoan social commentators is that those who earn money nowadays expect to be treated like chiefs ("many...wage-earners go back to their communities with a new sense of power and a feeling almost of equality with their elders") and that chiefs try to gain wealth from their positions (Nepo 1990, 33, 38). Nepo observed the effect of new economic ideologies on what happens inside churches:

> With the change of values in the life of Samoa, money prevails as the dominant means by which one can serve his family, his matai, his village and his church. Hence, the possession of money guarantees one's eligibility to become a good servant. Even the Church is dependent on money for its administration and development. The growth of the Church is measured in terms of money. With this idea portrayed and advocated in the Church, it is not difficult to observe the trend in which money becomes the means by which tautua is practiced. In the Church in Samoa today, when the message goes out from the pulpit, "Offer your whole self for the sake of the Gospel," underneath is the real message "Give money to the Church." (Nepo 1990, 29; emphases deleted)

Giving money, then, is now considered a key form of service to the church (or *tautua lotu;* see also Elisaia 2008 for Samoan Methodism). It is sometimes described as "sacrificial giving," based on a "theology which legitimises... 'giving all you have' because Christ has given up... his life to redeem humanity" (Tuivanu 2013, 21–22; see also Hardin 2016; Macpherson and Macpherson 2010, 136–142; Vaai 2001). Because the minister represents God, when you give him anything, you are directly honoring God. For Amituana'i, service and worship are essentially the same thing (1979).[11] Nepo and others have pointed out the uncomfortable fact that service is now often defined by giving money. No theologian from Oceania, I believe, would take the logical next step of saying that money is the heart of worship. In fact, they would probably find the idea repellent. But the belief that some churches tend to handle money more appropriately than others is, in fact, a major issue in Pacific Christianity. Service is considered the core of being a good Christian for many Samoans. But disagreement persists over what constitutes proper service and how in serving God one should either suffer sacrificially or be set free.

Another point of critique concerns service to titleholders or chiefs *(matai)*. Many authors have mentioned how church ministers, during the mission era, were granted high status by Samoan chiefs. Indeed, ministers became like chiefs themselves in some ways—and, in other ways, were even more highly honored than traditional authorities. As Keesing and Keesing put it, Christian ministers and catechists "have assumed in some degree the traditional mantle of the old-time priestly adept, are counted supreme in matters that touch the spiritual and the ethical, and also usually exercise strong secular influence.... Age and influence gives them a status much like that of a *matai*" (1956, 63). With their high status, they are receivers of deferential service. But the mechanics of the relationship between ministers and chiefs are subtle. As mentioned earlier in this section, a minister is supposed to attend only to his congregation's spiritual life and not participate in village politics. In theory, chiefs should then let the minister handle all the affairs of the church, although this does not always happen, and in cases of families leaving one denomination for another and thereby splitting a village's religious identity, the lines between sacred and secular authority tangle. Indeed, a "situation of conflict between chiefs and pastors is very common in Samoa," as Gustav Allen put it (1990, 85; see also Tupu 2012).

Historian Mālama Meleiseā pointed to a crucial distinction in Sāmoa between honor and power that is relevant to this discussion. Pastors are respected but are supposed to keep out of politics. Sisters are highly valued but, marrying out to other villages, cannot exercise family authority as often as their brothers. High chiefs *(ali'i)* are more honored than orators *(tulāfale)*, but the latter have more authority in the day-to-day politics of villages (Meleiseā 1992, 24; see also Meleiseā 1987b; Duranti 1994; Sala 1980). Similarly, Feleterika Nokise, the PTC principal, observed that Samoan chiefs can shape the church but church leaders cannot shape the chiefly system. Evidently referring to the Congregational Church in Sāmoa, Nokise wrote:

Serving ("tautua") in the practical sense is, to Samoans, the only way to a position of authority, personified in the office of "matai." In church offices, the same prerequisite applies. Ironically however, those who [have] succeeded in becoming chiefs have virtually bought their ticket for holding a church office. Thus, in village churches, one finds that apart from the position of pastor, virtually all important positions (deacons) in the Samoan church are held by chiefs, who in reality control both the politics of the village and the church.

The authority of the pastor in relation to that of the matais is limited. Although he occupies the most prestigious position in the village, he is in many ways at the mercy of the matais, in that the latter group has the power to call a pastor and the power to remove him. The latter power, though rarely exercised, is a reminder to the pastor and the church that both of them are under the "fa'asamoa." (Nokise 1978, 21–22; see also Deverell 1966)

Thus, as I have argued for Fijian Methodism (Tomlinson 2009), a system in which church authority and chiefly authority seem to be balanced and parallel is, practically speaking, tipped in favor of chiefs. Being a servant in this context is something of recognized value but vexed practice, as signaled by the repeated references Samoan theologians and preachers make to the saying that the way to authority is through service: O le ala i le pule o le tautua.[12]

Prophets

In June 2013, not long after I began my research at the University of Auckland's School of Theology, PhD student Terry Pouono gave a seminar presentation in which he examined theological dimensions of the Samoan phrase *teu le vā*. In the published version of his paper, Pouono described how *vā* means "'space' or 'interval,'" that *teu* is "to 'preserve' or 'keep' something," and that for Samoans, the phrase "*teu le va* is commonly understood as preserving harmony in relations" (Pouono 2013, 90). In other words, *teu le vā* is an ideal of negotiating interpersonal spaces respectfully (see also Anae 2010; Duranti 1997; Koria 1999; and Shore 1982, 136, who translated the phrase as "take care of the relationship").

After Pouono's Auckland presentation, his supervisor, Stephen Garner, pointed out that the paper's abstract had mentioned how observing *teu le vā* could increase imbalance in social relations. As Pouono had written, "The concept and practice adversely promotes increasing social, economic and political imbalance between the 'haves and the have nots' in the Samoan community" in New Zealand. Maintaining a conservative ideology of harmony means that, as the cliché has it, the rich get richer and the poor get poorer. Garner asked for clarification, and Pouono responded:

Terry Pouono: Maybe something that comes to mind—I didn't want to
                  raise it because some of the issues are really quite dramatic.
                  And I don't want to give a negative sense [or] impression
                  of Samoan Christian identity. But just out of the top of my
                  head, two of our families from my old church lost their
                  houses, lost their estates over the last six months. And [in]
                  this church, there's a lot of giving, lot of giving, and their
                  belief is that's their relationship with God....I wanted to
                  mention that a lot of the common people of our church
                  are struggling, socially, economically. And it's maintaining
                  that *vā* [relationship].
Stephen Garner: Yeah.
Terry Pouono: They don't—they can't do anything about it.
Stephen Garner: Without breaking from—
Terry Pouono: Without breaking—
Stephen Garner: The *fa'asāmoa.*
Terry Pouono: Breaking, breaking from the *fa'asāmoa.* They haven't—
Stephen Garner: Yeah. So I just wanted—that's, I mean, that's what you're
                  hinting at.... If you put it in the [paper] abstract, someone
                  is going to be looking for it.
Terry Pouono: OK. Yeah. Thank you.
Stephen Garner: So.
Terry Pouono: I was a bit afraid to put it—to forward it, but I—
Stephen Garner: Well if you're going to be prophetic and bold, you've gotta,
                  you've gotta strip naked while you're doing it. [*general
                  laughter*]
Terry Pouono: But yeah. But definitely there's a lot of issues that really hurt
                  us. In my family alone, we nearly lost our house based on a
                  lot of the practices that are carried out in our church. And
                  it really hurts.

As Pouono made clear, treating money as the heart of service can wound families, but talking about the issue is dangerous in its own way. Garner responded that if one is going to bring an urgent message to get the church on the right path—that is, to be prophetic—one needs the courage of explicitness.

According to religious historian Garry Trompf, the definition of a "prophet" has been complicated by anthropological research. "A hundred years ago," he wrote, "most scholars would have quoted from the relevant parts of the Old Testament and sown [*sic*] up the matter from there; today the great wealth of ethnographic commentary makes the task of definition so much harder" (Trompf 1977, 1). His own definition is almost circular: prophets are the people who deliver prophecies, and prophecies are, among other things, messages "confirmed as decisively important by the earnestness of their bearer(s)"—in other words, they gain their significance because they are delivered by prophets. His next move was to say what prophets are not: they are not augurs (who look at "omens and entrails" to understand fate); they are not fortune-tellers; they are not diviners. He then offered a more fruitful understanding of prophets by calling attention to three related characteristics: (1) they express divine will publicly; (2) they do so in unexpected ways; and (3) they aim at "the procuring of a just society by warning about the future consequences of unrighteousness" (Trompf 1977, 1).

Of Trompf's three criteria, many contextual theologians from Oceania fulfill the first and third ones. They express divine will as they understand it publicly, although the audiences for many of their forms of expression—theses, dissertations, articles, books, seminars, and conference presentations—are often a modest group of fellow theologians. They criticize a present situation, warning people of continuing on the present course. Trompf's second criterion, that prophets act in unexpected ways (or, as he put it, a prophet engages in "often unexpected oracular activity, his declarations of divine will not being confined within formal consultations or observances" [1997, 1]) does not fit most Pacific theologians quite as well. Because the process of developing an academic argument (theological or otherwise) is so highly regularized, and the themes of contextual theology are so standardized (despite their grounding in a positive evaluation of diversity), there is a remarkable regularity to being prophetic.

Trompf acknowledged that "in our day many of us are inclined to call great social critics by the name prophet, just because they demand change for the better and lament the perpetuation of existing human ills" (1977, 1). Despite Trompf's doubts, this is probably the most useful definition of being "prophetic" in the sense articulated by Oceanic contextual theologians, with the qualification that to act prophetically is to express social criticism that is thought to be divinely sanctioned. When I began my research, I did not intend to study "prophets" per se. But over the course of fieldwork, as I heard and read references to prophetic voices and the need to be prophetic, I gradually realized that being prophetic is an ideal for many contextual theologians. Being a social critic is one thing. Being a social critic who can bring (or try to bring) one's church, society, or the whole earth in line with God's plans is another—a calling, clarified and intensified.

Prophets make difficult partners in dialogue. If they express the divine will, they are expressing a theoretically uncontestable truth, but they do so with the knowledge that their message is out of tune with the song most people are singing. To put it in a convoluted but, I think, irreducible way: prophets have to bring the dialogues shaping their churches and societies into a new dialogue—but the object of that new dialogue is essentially a monologue, something that is not supposed to be taken up critically (and thereby potentially reshaped) but rather affirmed and carried out.

The term "prophecy" is sometimes used in English-language texts to describe the moment when a spirit *(aitu)* or goddess named Nafanua foretold the arrival of Christianity in Sāmoa. In the western part of Sāmoa's largest island, Savai'i, Nafanua fought and won a war known as *"A'ea i Sasa'e ma le A'ea i Sisifo* (conquest of the hills to the east and to the west)" (Meleiseā 1992, 20). In her victory, she granted ruling authority to A'ana district and its supporters. Sāmoa's future paramount leader, Malietoa Vainu'upo, from Sapapali'i village (which is not in A'ana), asked Nafanua to grant him authority, too. In response, she said, "*'Tali i lagi se ao o lou malo'* ('Wait for a head/title of your kingdom from heaven')" (Leaupepe 2013, 39). When John Williams of the London Missionary Society came with eastern Polynesian missionaries to Sāmoa in 1830, he arrived at Sapapali'i and left the Polynesian evangelists there, seeming to fulfill the prophecy.[13]

Nafanua's prophecy raises the question of whether prophets are expected to make successful predictions or only to warn "about the future consequences of unrighteousness," as Trompf put it (Trompf 1977, 1), in order to avoid those consequences. In other words, a really successful Christian prophet should theoretically shape events so that his or her vision does not come true. When prophecy is taken primarily in the sense of prediction, as many scholars know, it is likely to fail. Sekaia T Loaniceva, the founder of a Fijian Christian sect called the Church of the Poor, predicted in the late 1960s that Fiji would become the "head of the world" in 1991 (Rokotuiviwa 1975). In 1991, however, Fiji was fresh off its first coups and struggling just to shore up its own government.[14]

But contextual theologians in Oceania who refer to the prophetic are emphasizing critique, not prediction. And, I must add, they never identify themselves as prophets, although they might apply the label to others.[15] Being prophetic, in Oceanic contextual theology, especially means calling for church leaders to act prophetically themselves. For example, Tofaeono argued that in relation to the global environmental crisis:

> The church in Samoa needs to develop a prophetic voice concerning all issues that threaten life.... On the political scene, the church in Samoa should actively address adverse government policies and unsustainable development projects which work to exploit not only people but life-supporting ecosystems. Moreover, it should insist that the seas not be open for drift-net fishing or to be dumping grounds for any nuclear or chemical wastes of foreign powers. For the church to be prophetic, it must cherish the land and the sea by resisting any threats to these precious God-given gifts of life. (Tofaeono 1993, 114–115)

A prophetic church, Tofaeono suggested, does not yet exist in Sāmoa. Theological writing might be seen from this perspective as part of a double movement: a prophetic call to church leaders, and the church as an institution, to become prophetic—to be boldly critical, to challenge and change current thinking in order to align more closely with divine purposes.

Other theologians have echoed Tofaeono in arguing that Christianity in Oceania is not prophetic at the present time. In an article lamenting the decline of ecumenism in Oceania, Nokise suggested that a prophetic spirit has been lost. In the 1960s, 1970s, and 1980s, he wrote, churches in the Pacific worked across denominational lines, especially on three issues: nuclear testing, political autonomy, and church autonomy (Nokise 2011, 101; see also Uriam 2005). In the 1990s, however, this ecumenical impulse weakened, and as part of this decline, some churches stopped supporting PTC financially (they stopped paying agreed-on fees) and in terms of personnel (they did not send staff or students). Nokise declared that the financial situation had become dire for PTC as well as for the South Pacific Association of Theological Schools (SPATS, the regional accreditation body) and the Pacific Conference of Churches (PCC). Indeed, "there are now serious questions concerning the sustainability of each especially when they are competing for declining funds from basically the same sources" (Nokise 2011, 110). He proposed a solution, but it was one of cutting losses and consolidating what remains, integrating PTC, SPATS, and PCC more tightly and forming an ecumenical council to oversee them.

Nokise identified two key problems that are both caused by and reflected in the decline of Pacific ecumenism. One of them is an increasing difficulty with engaging in dialogue. Describing the current situation of PTC's governing council as a "tragic picture" of ineffectiveness, he reported:

> In the beginning, leaders of the member churches attended Council meetings as required in its constitution. Their presence offered some guarantee that discussions, debates and decisions were conducted with a certain air of authority and officialdom. In recent years however, only a [handful] of leaders have been attending and for those who could not attend, proxies were sent.... Discussions tended to be dominated by a few. Decisions have a fragile nature about them with much uncertainty about commitment and support of envisaged actions. Many of the issues that demanded firm decisions tend to meander somewhat aimlessly because most of the proxies felt they did not have the authority to commit the support of their churches. (Nokise 2011, 120)

Dialogue is ineffective, Nokise suggested, if the participants are not authorized or committed to it. He almost seemed to hint at the model of a chiefly council meeting, a setting with "a certain air of authority and officialdom" in which the main representatives show up and decisions are consequential. But even if my reading is a fair one, Nokise was decidedly not advocating a return to an idealized past of traditional authority, because "prophetic faith" undercuts conservatism. Here he turned to the second key problem:

> How is God understood by our churches? What is the basis of such understanding? Some of our churches are favouring a theocratic understanding of God that empha-

sises male domination and control. Others tend to understand God as demanding relatively little. Both positions compromise the biblical and historical evidence of the kind of God we are dealing with. In so doing, our churches conveniently omit the crucial place prophetic faith has in understanding the nature of God.

Prophetic faith perceives God as a God of justice, mercy and truth. Therefore there is a call to address social injustices as well as a conversion of social systems to ensure that God's will is done on earth. There is also a call to the oppressive elites to repent and do justice. (Nokise 2011, 115)

In Nokise's vision, being prophetic requires ecumenism and motivates dialogue, but since the 1990s, the three legs of this triangle have crumpled; the prophetic spirit has been lost.

Nokise's perspective on this loss of the prophetic spirit is given a different shading by those who have argued that in conservative Polynesian societies, being prophetic—always a difficult business—is *really* difficult business, as chiefs and churches stand at the top of their own sacralized social orders. As Bernard Thorogood, a British missionary who served for eighteen years in the Cook Islands and Kiribati, put it, "A church born into a chiefly society and itself imitating that society is poorly equipped to challenge the *status quo*.... What then happens to the prophetic note of the gospel? It is muted, domesticated." He pointed to local corruption, foreign economic domination, violence against women, and sexual diseases as subjects on which "the Polynesian churches have largely been silent and have offered little leadership" (Thorogood 1995, 7; see also Thorogood 1967, 2014; Knuth 2012, 62; Szesnat 2010, 42).[16]

Challenges of Dialogue

I have written of contextual theologians in Oceania as weavers, servants, and prophets because their writings demonstrate that these roles are considered both attractive and demanding. Theologians who see themselves as weavers, servants, and prophets are passionate about the well-being of their churches and societies and are often concerned about perceived decline. This leads them into various textual projects based on, among other things, the critique of tradition as well as the valorization of it, criticism of modern social relations, and advocacy for different kinds of change.

As I discussed in the previous chapter, there is an obvious difficulty in taking contextual theology public. If an adventurous reading of the Bible is not likely to please staid church elders, saying that those elders are ruining the church through elitism and greed is probably even less likely to do so. And here, ironically, it is the invocation of "culture" that sometimes frustrates contextual theologians, who ground their claims in an appreciation of culture in the first place. For example, Filemoni-Tofaeono and Johnson referred to

Pacific cultures' "captivity to patriarchy" and commented: "All too often we have heard Oceanian women's efforts to question aspects of cultural and theological patriarchy, in the supposedly safe haven of the theological school, brushed off by their male counterparts' standard reply: 'But that's our culture!'" (2006, 170).

I was told, too, that church elders are not likely to read academic theses and dissertations. Consider the situation: students are chosen by their institutions for advanced study, sometimes going overseas on church scholarships. When they do so, they are encouraged to be culturally contextual and contextually cultural—to write theology as Fijians, as Samoans, as Tongans—but also to be critical. Accordingly, students interested in topics like ministry, ethics, and church history write theses and dissertations that focus on the problems of their churches and societies. These texts are the products of dialogues with students' supervisors, other scholars, and the church members' students routinely interview for their research projects. But the most potentially consequential partners in these dialogues—church leaders—are not, I was told by more than one theologian, inclined to read these theses and dissertations.[17]

Here, again, is the partiality and difficulty of dialogue. What could be more dialogic than a dissertation that pulls in sources from different cultures, languages, and academic disciplines to engage critically with an institution in transformation? And yet these theses and dissertations are not necessarily going to be taken up by those who could respond most effectively to their arguments and recommendations. Moreover, students themselves might come to discard their own scholarly recommendations when they make the transition from being student-theologians to becoming practicing ministers:

> Many pastors (including the author) during their preparatory theological training critique the pastorate system as being stagnant, having short-sighted and parochial visions, and always being piously condensed [on] spiritual matters. At the same time, they are also aware of a kind of materialism that is oppressive to the religio-cultural lifeway. Although aware of the irregularities of the contemporary system, many who are called into parish work easily lapse into the operative system and eventually become the energizers of the same system, with little or no effort expended in providing appropriate changes. (Tofaeono 2000, 137n31)

In other words, writing a thesis or dissertation in contextual theology is not, in itself, sufficient to motivate dialogue or make change happen. One can argue as a student that the system needs to be changed, but joining the system as a professional makes it harder to voice that critique. If one takes a challenging or even radical message public, one might well be ignored or shut down. One can, of course, become a teacher at a theological college and continue the dialogue in a chain of academic transmission. This might seem to turn contextual theology into a rarefied domain of dialogue that moves mostly inward, engaged primarily with other contextual theologians. Yet the clear urge behind the work of weavers, servants, and prophets is to make a bigger difference, to take the social power of Christianity in Oceanic societies and use theological insights to make church and society work together in newly dynamic and durable ways.

Chapter 3
Coconut Theology and the Cultivation of a Pacific Way

When Sione 'Amanaki Havea sought a meaningful symbol to join Christian theology and Pacific identity, he chose the coconut. As I mentioned in the introduction to this book, he identified the coconut with life, time, growth, and Christology, writing, "If Jesus had grown up and lived in the Pacific, He could have added another identification of himself—I am the Coconut of Life" (S Havea 1987, 14). In doing so, Havea established a referent that other Oceanic contextual theologians could use to begin developing a discipline.

As mentioned earlier, not all scholars have embraced this symbolism; I discuss the work of one critic later in this chapter. But perhaps some of the critics have taken Havea's model, with its lightness of touch, more seriously than he meant. His son Jione Havea noted that Coconut Theology is tinged with humor. Recalling that in 1976, John Guise, then governor general of Papua New Guinea, had told delegates to the Pacific Conference of Churches assembly in Port Moresby that it was time to find a "Pacific Christ," the younger Havea remarked: "Our church leaders responded with a host of contextual theologies and so Pacific theologians joined the ranks of leaders in contextual theology. But what they did was to put brown masks over white theologies, and so they were like coconuts: brown on the outside but white in the inside. (Sione 'A Havea did not address this coconut characteristic in his Coconut Theology, but he often spoke about it in jest)" (J Havea 2012, 5; see also Koria 1999, 3, 11n1; Wright and Fugui 1986). The joke is that sometimes contextual theology might only be husk deep—and the elder Havea was in on the joke.

It is crucial to note that Havea's foundational published statement on Coconut Theology, besides offering the coconut as a symbol, also offers the claim that Pacific theology should be one of *celebration*. He mentioned that the luminaries of twentieth-century systematic theology—Dietrich Bonhoeffer, Paul Tillich, Karl Barth, Emil Brunner—had been "victims of war, and their theological perspectives were based on crisis backgrounds." In contrast, he wrote, Pacific Islanders' perspectives "are deeply involved in celebrations" (S Havea 1987, 11). He compared the legendary origin of the royal kava ceremony in Tonga to the Eucharist, implying that the kava ceremony, like the Eucharist, is a celebratory offering (see Kamu 1996, 100, for a similar claim about kava in Sāmoa; compare Pase 2003). Havea invoked several cherished ideals of Pacific communal life—"the cooperation of the community, the inclusiveness of the extended family, the sharing and caring for the old folks"—to suggest that a Pacific theology ought to be grounded not in crisis but in celebration (S Havea 1987, 13). However, most theologians who have taken up Havea's work have focused on the symbol of the coconut rather than his call to reshape theology through an understanding of celebration.

In this chapter, I discuss several symbols that contextual theologians have used to define a broader Pacific contribution to regional and global theological dialogues. I begin by looking at emblems that are recognized beyond national borders: *talanoa* (conversation, storytelling); mana (spiritual efficacy); and the beverage kava. I then turn to a topic that is not often the subject of explicit discussion but is a common feature of Pacific societies: the continuing existence and activities of indigenous spirits. Finally, I consider the role of the *Pacific Journal of Theology* in disseminating ideas about a regional identity often referred to as "the Pacific Way." This chapter, in short, is about dialogues within and across islands in which a broader regional identity is articulated.

Emblems of Pacific Christianity

When looking at Pacific contextual theology, several emblems stand out. By "emblems," I mean symbols that are invoked, elaborated, and emphasized in projects of defining local and regional identities. Such symbols are thought to have special significance, to be extra meaningful, akin to "key symbols" as theorized by Sherry Ortner (1973). Kambati Uriam mentioned "the canoe, the outrigger, the pandanus, the ta'ovala [Tongan dress mat], the kava, the sea, the land, the gap, grassroots, migration, celebration, and many others" as emblems used by Pacific theologians (2005, 308). Here, I focus on three closely related symbols: *talanoa,* mana, and kava.

Talanoa

As I described in chapter 1, *talanoa* is dialogue. It means conversation and storytelling. Many Pacific scholars (not only theologians) have identified *talanoa* as an emblematic regional practice, an icon of how people in Oceania interact: "Pacific island societies have throughout their histories relied upon the talanoa process" (S Halapua 2015, 1); "Story-telling is central to the Pacific thinking and understanding of reality" (Samate 2011, 72); *talanoa* "is an Oceanic gift and contribution to the whole quest for more listening and dialogue" (W Halapua 2008b, 54). Understood as dialogue that is both sympathetic and effective, *talanoa* has been adopted as a kind of institutional methodology. Sitiveni Halapua, an economist and former director of the Pacific Islands Development Program at the East-West Center in Honolulu, developed a *talanoa*-centered process of political reconciliation that he first applied in the Cook Islands in 1996 and later adapted for postcoup Fiji, civil war–wracked Solomon Islands, and then his native Tonga as it struggled to negotiate loyalty to the monarchy with demands for democracy (see the summary in W Halapua 2008b, 56–61). In 2008, Tongan Methodists Jione Havea and Nāsili Vakaʻuta began leading a series of annual academic conferences based on the organizing theme of *talanoa*, characterizing it as a gift and something that "can help redefine who we are" (J Havea 2010b, 180; see also J Havea 2010a, 2010c). *Talanoa*, in these political and academic approaches, is a type of especially therapeutic conversation, something that brings people together and defines their interactive space in Pacific terms (see also Clery 2014; Goundar 2005; Rogers 2008).[1]

Real-life *talanoa*, like all dialogue, can be unequal, fractious, and competitive in practice (Brenneis 1984; Silverstein 2013). In his contribution to the *Global Bible Commentary* on the Book of Numbers, Havea observed that "Island storytelling is not so much about forming conclusions as about responding, redirecting, transgressing, engaging, disagreeing, teasing, angering, crossing, challenging, and letting go" (J Havea 2004a, 50). Vakaʻuta cautioned that *talanoa* could, in fact, be monologic, although he then proposed a different Tongan term *(tālanga)*, which he characterized in the way most other authors characterize *talanoa:* "a dialogical process that involves both the acts of speaking and listening, and they must always go together" (Vakaʻuta 2010b, 153).

Tongan Anglican Archbishop Winston Halapua discussed *talanoa* in several of his publications, including his book *Waves of God's Embrace*, published the same year that he served as chaplain to the Lambeth Conference (2008b). In the book, he suggested that *talanoa* is both distinctive to Oceania and useful to all of humanity, a Pacific way of talking from which the rest of the world can learn. Agreeing with Havea that *talanoa* is a gift the Pacific Islands can share with the rest of the world, Halapua defined *talanoa* as "to tell stories within a community that is open and receptive" (W Halapua 2008b, 55).[2] He discussed his brother Sitiveni's work on political reconciliation across the Pacific and suggested that *talanoa* is a historical product of crew members' need to listen to each other and respect each other's responsibilities as they sailed ocean-going canoes (W Halapua 2008b, 65). Indeed, he identified this seafaring heritage as the basis of a unified Oceanic identity, writing that "the impact of life relationships from within the world of the *vaka* [canoe] formed the cradle of the emerging culture and world view of the early Oceanic people," and he saw evidence of this heritage in the intense look on the face of his young son as he paddled on a piece of driftwood (W Halapua 2008b, 44–45, 15–16). Halapua described how he felt "compelled" to express his Oceanic heritage and the way it connects him to God so that the rest of the world could learn from it: "I write because I believe that concepts and values from Oceania have a wider relevance. Theology has in a sense been landlocked—I write using metaphors arising from the different aspects and waves of the ocean" (2008b, 3). *Talanoa,* in Halapua's poetic unfolding of it, offers a kind of freedom in connection.

The idea that the world needs more dialogue and less monologue is, I suggest, hardly limited to Oceania or theology. Calls for dialogue resonate through so much political and civil discourse that it can seem to have "something of a holy status…held up as the summit of human encounter" (Peters 1999, 33). But theologians such as Havea and Vaka'uta have called attention to the fact that *talanoa* does not always resolve matters or unify people and that the question of which words will be taken up and receive responses remains an open one.

Mana

A counterpart to *talanoa* is "mana," the term generally associated with spiritual efficacy, found across much of Oceania and now beyond the Pacific as well (Golub and Peterson 2016; Morgain 2016; Tomlinson and Tengan 2016; Meylan 2017). Mana was considered by many early social theorists of religion to be a human category of supernatural power; contextual theologians have cultivated the fertile ground of mana's relevance to both pre-Christian indigenous spiritualities and Christianity.

Mana forms a conceptual pair with *talanoa* because they both require an act of recognition, an interactive acknowledgment or affirmation that something is a token of a particular type (Keane 1997). To recognize something is both to identify it according to preexisting criteria and to establish a new relationship with it. Just as *talanoa* requires a responsive audience, so too does mana. As various scholars have noted, mana, like charisma, is not only an extraordinary quality displayed by a person or object but also an audience's recognition or attribution of such extraordinariness. That power might, of course, be associated with gods. Valerio Valeri wrote of Hawaiian divinity, "The real locus of mana is in the reciprocal but hierarchical relation between the gods whose actions demonstrate efficacy and the men who, by recognizing that efficacy, increase and fully actualize it" (1985, 104). Mana can also be associated with a secular state, as Alexander Mawyer has shown (2016).[3]

Mana's remarkable features—its lexical presence in many Oceanic languages, its grammatical versatility, its frequent associations with divinity and spiritual action—make it a valuable resource for Oceanic contextual theologians, something many find useful in exploring regional connections as well as universal truths. It is a dynamic concept, subject to authors' variably balanced interpretations. For example, some Fijian Methodist theologians have equated mana with "blessings" (Meo 1996, 109) and have characterized it as "something wholesome and good" (Raitiqa 2000, 53), but it is often spoken of as a pair with *sau,* which Ilisapeci Meo translated as "a curse" (1996, 109). Suspending the question of ethics, mana and *sau* can be described as "joined…in a great power that exists (sema tu…kei na dua na kaukaua levu e jiko)" (Apete Toko quoted in Tomlinson and Bigitibau 2016, 250). Theologian and deaconess Lesila Raitiqa, who called Jesus "the True Mana of the Vanua [land and people]," presented mana as a beneficent, encompassing power and aesthetic:

> *Mana* is a whole new dimension of spirituality, that which is in harmony with both the spirit world and the physical world. It is a dynamic living phenomenon which is invisible yet present and at work in the community of the living. *Mana* is seen in the extraordinary strength of a person, in the quiet dignity of a chief or royal person, in the sacredness of a ritual, in the beauty of kinship, and in the survival of persons against all odds. It is seen in the *sautu* or "abundance" of the *vanua*, of land and sea, and the health and wealth and happiness of the populace. *Mana* is the peace of the land. (Raitiqa 2000, 52–53)

Such a vision of mana makes it both intensely local—in this case distinctly Fijian, suffusing systems of kinship, ritual, and chiefliness belonging to that place—and also expansive, something that can go beyond the local to pervade any Christian community that seeks peace and prosperity (see also Vaaimamao 1990).

The most accomplished theologian of mana is Fijian Methodist Ilaitia Sevati Tuwere. In *Vanua,* his 2002 monograph based on his 1992 dissertation, Tuwere described different aspects of mana from a theological perspective. Mana is blessing and power, but it is also the powerlessness manifest in Jesus's humility and despair. It is linked to forms of social control such as the authority of chiefs, but Christ as "the source of all life-giving mana" also offers ultimate freedom. Mana is integral to the wicked effectiveness of sorcerers ("The important elements necessary for the attainment of *mana* are part and parcel of the nature and function of sorcery"), but it is also what Christ offers to the whole world for healing and unity. For Tuwere, land *(vanua)* is taboo because it grounds the gods, and the gods provide "life and the power of life," which is "the fundamental orientation of... [the] meaning" of mana (2002, 164, 161, 142).[4]

From this brief discussion of mana centered on Fijian Methodism, it should be evident that the concept of mana is tremendously appealing for theologians and also not entirely stable. It is something whose significance is paradoxically reflected in the fact that it is hard to pin down semantically. One does not, however, need to go as far as Claude Lévi-Strauss did in his famous characterization of it as floating signifier, a pure symbol that can soak up any meaning (Lévi-Strauss 1987). Mana can mean many things, but, within Oceanic contexts at least, it cannot mean just anything, loaded as it is by now with Christian freighting and the political weight of indigenous sovereignty movements. Tuwere acknowledged that "*mana* poses an immediate problem for a sustained theological reflection because of its ambiguity" and added that its meaning is "arbitrary"; yet he went on to say that mana "does not exhaust the nature of God but it is the only meaningful way of describing God and what his power may mean in the Fijian context" (2002, 135, 165). Similarly, Samoan Congregationalist Amaʻamalele Tofaeono, whose critical use of the term "mana" to make sense of polytheism I discuss in chapter 4, defined it as "a divine life-giving power" but also argued that it "belongs to those terms that cannot be clearly explained in words, but must be experienced" (Tofaeono 2000, 67, 169).[5]

One of the liveliest explorations of mana's complex meanings and practical force comes from Aram Oroi, an Anglican priest, theologian, and educator from Makira, Solomon Islands. In a chapter on the theology of mana in his homeland, he observed how priests—himself included—were asked to press a metaphorical button that will activate mana. The reasons people want mana activated are not always benign. One woman came to Oroi to ask him to make her estranged husband have "a big sickness, a heart attack" so that he would return to her (Oroi 2016, 187). Another man, widely suspected of sorcery, invited his own punishment by challenging a priest from the Melanesian Brotherhood to make him die if he were really practicing evil magic. The priest tossed his walking stick in the air above a chapel pew, where it hung in place; three months later, the suspected sorcerer collapsed and died, his tongue reportedly unrolling from his mouth to a meter long, eerie evidence that he had lied (Oroi 2016, 190–191). Oroi explained that "*mana* at work in the church comes from God," and laypeople believe they gain "access to *mana*" when they are baptized (2016, 185, 194)—but not all of the buttons that are pressed are pressed within the church, and sorcerers and ancestral spirits work their mana, too. Mana can be recognized in distinctly non-Christian characters and events, but it still has been taken up as a useful symbol for Christian theological consideration by many authors.

Kava

If mana and *talanoa* are related as acts and products of interactive recognition, the beverage kava is the third leg of the triangle. Kava is called *yaqona* in Fijian and *'ava* in Samoan; the Tongan term is "kava," which has become the English standard. It brings people together in conversation and is itself mana, linked to ancestral spirits and sanctified by its central role in chiefs' rituals. As Vincent Lebot, Mark Merlin, and Lamont Lindstrom made clear in their comprehensive summary (1992), kava is associated with life, death, sexuality, social order, and spiritual efficacy in many parts of Oceania, its significance reflected in origin myths and present-day drinking practices. In places like Fiji and Tonga, it is drunk most days by men as long as they are not members of evangelical churches that ban it; in Fiji, I often saw women drinking it as well, although there is a long history of saying that this did not happen in the old days (figures 3.1–3.4). For many Pacific Islanders residing overseas, too, kava is an icon of tradition (Aporosa 2015).

FIGURE 3.1. Casual *talanoa* at a kava-drinking session, Kadavu, Fiji, January 2010. Photo by author.

FIGURE 3.2. A Tongan-style kava session at the Pacific Theological College, May 2009. Photo by author.

FIGURE 3.3. Samoan kava bowl featuring Christian iconography at the Immaculate Conception Cathedral's chapel in Apia, April 2015. Photo by author.

FIGURE 3.4. Wooden carvings of the Holy Family, baby Jesus with Mary and Joseph sitting by a kava bowl at Fatu-o-'Āiga (Holy Family) Cathedral, Tafuna, American Sāmoa, May 2016. Photo by author.

Even as it is consumed regularly and often quite casually, kava retains a vibrant spiritual aura because of its associations with sacrifice and spiritual inspiration (Lebot, Merlin, and Lindstrom 1992; see also Leach 1972; Turner 1986). "Kava-drinking is associated with ancestral *mana* and the power of God," Christina Toren has observed for Fiji; "it is always hedged about by ceremony" (1988, 706). In Sāmoa, the practice of offering dropfuls of one's first cup to God is something that I saw and that was well described by Lalomilo Kamu: there is a "prayer where each recipient pours a few drops from his cup on the mat while saying something like: 'This is your *'ava*, God, thank you for this day, help us,' then he takes his drink" (1996, 117).

Because of these dense links between kava drinking, communal gathering, sacrifice, and spiritual presence, I used to wonder why I had never seen or heard of kava being used instead of wine or red fruit juice during Communion at the many Fijian Methodist services I had attended. When I began research at the Pacific Theological College (PTC), I learned that there had indeed been experiments at using kava in Communion there in the 1970s but that the project did not succeed in the long term. Kava's association with pre-Christian tradition is too strong.

Some places outside of Fiji have taken up the experiment of using indigenous substances as Communion elements, although they usually shy away from using kava.[6] In a master's thesis written at PTC, Tele'a Faleali'i pointed out that bread and wine are foreign to Sāmoa, and he asked why the "veneration and supplication of God" seen in kava ceremonies is not "capitalize[d] on" in the Eucharist (Faleali'i 1998, 133). Rather than insist that kava replace wine in Communion, he suggested that taro could be used instead of bread and coconut juice instead of wine as more appropriate elements (1998, 134). Hemisemidemiquaver Fa'aeafaleupolu reported that this has indeed taken place, with some Samoan Congregationalist services featuring taro, yam, or breadfruit instead of bread and coconut juice instead of wine (2004, 14; see also Taofinu'u 1995; Bargatzky 1997; compare Meo, Dale, and Dale 1985, 19, on a suggestion within Fiji's Methodist Church).[7]

In French Polynesia, the use of indigenous substances has led to controversy and a church schism, as Gwendoline Malogne-Fer described for the Papetoai (Mo'orea) branch of the Maohi Protestant Church (2016). On Christmas night in 1996, a church deacon informed the pastor during the service that, instead of bread and wine, they would now be using the flesh and juice of the coconut for Communion.[8] Congregants who did not like this innovation began attending Communion services at the neighboring church, which stuck to standard liturgy. The next pastor at Papetoai tried to appease both sides in the conflict, offering bread and wine to those who wanted it and breadfruit and coconut juice to those who wanted that instead. But his attempt at reconciliation only highlighted the church's internal theological division and prompted an official schism. Later, having lost half of its members in this attempt to bring contextual theology into tangible practice—to drink contextual theology, as it were—the church alienated some of its remaining members by introducing Polynesian dance during the Communion service.[9]

Even though kava is rarely used in Holy Communion, its symbolism has proven to be a great resource for Oceanic theologians. Liona Le'i Thompson compared the Christian Eucharist and Samoan kava ceremony for their power to produce unity: in consuming bread and wine in Communion, "Christians profess the significance of oneness with Christ. Likewise in the [kava] ceremony, when the hosting village and visitors sit together and drink from that one cup, [it] is a symbol of oneness. It is a sign of celebration of love and harmony, peace and unity; it is a token of thanking god Tagaloa for a safe journey" (2007, 83). Urima Fa'asi'i observed a parallel between Christ's suffering and the crushing of kava in preparation for its drinking: "The *ava* drink is produced from the crushed solid pieces of the *ava* or *kava* plant. The pounded *ava* can be interpreted as a symbol of the Christ who was crushed on the cross. From the cross His blood (the liquid *ava*) was poured out to redeem, reconcile and unify the world as God's people" (1993, 63). Faleali'i argued that kava is a resonant symbol of baptism when understood in reference to the installation of chiefs. When a person becomes a chief, he or she is ritually transformed through kava's sacramental nature as both a leader of people and a servant of God (Faleali'i 1998, 108–109). Although a chief is not literally baptized in kava, Faleali'i considered the role of kava in ritually transforming a new chief's identity to be like the role of baptism in initiating a new "belonging" (1998, 109; see also Taofinu'u 1995; Taule'ale'ausumai 1994).[10]

The examples in the preceding paragraph are all from Sāmoa, but authors from elsewhere in Oceania have also taken up kava as a theological symbol (see, eg, Vaka'uta 1991; Vuetanavanua 2009; W Halapua 1998, 27). Kava, in short, is a potent regional emblem of Pacific Christianity and its indigenous theological resources. It joins mana and *talanoa* as a symbol that theologians have thought and written about productively. It must be mentioned, however, that there are significant regional differences in practices of kava drinking that should not be glossed over too quickly. For example, writing of Tanna in Vanuatu, Lindstrom described how when men gather at the drinking grounds at dusk, each man takes his cupful to the edge of the meeting place, drinks it quickly, and then spits, which "establishes contact with the supernatural world and precedes a prayer, request or demand whispered to one's ancestors who are present in the surrounding dusk.... After drinking, men sit silently on the periphery... 'listening' *(-aregi)* to their kava. Men maintain... that any speech or noise disturbs their kava" (1982, 428). This kind of overt appeal to ancestors and dismissal of human conversation would be considered deeply problematic in Fiji. Although many indigenous Fijians would concede that kava can put you in touch with the ancestors, they would not approve of anyone openly trying to do this. Moreover, human sociability, especially conversation, is what gives many Fijian kava sessions their satisfying energy. To speak of Tannese kava drinking at dusk as a kind of *talanoa* makes sense only if one considers ancestral spirits and the kava itself to be proper conversation partners, and Lindstrom acknowledged that the kind of kava consumption seen on Tanna, as well as the style of drunkenness that results, "differs from the more noisy, garrulous kava ceremony and festivities elsewhere in the Pacific" (1982, 428).

Excursus: Lively Spirits

I have suggested that *talanoa,* mana, and kava form a triangle. Each term intersects conceptually with the others. But another dimension needs to be added to this simple model because pre-Christian spirits are fully implicated in ideas of mana and the efficacy of kava, whether or not they are thought of as partners in *talanoa* in the usual sense. In chapter 4 I discuss the great Samoan deity Tagaloa and his presence in Christian theology, but in this chapter I am referring specifically to spirits that are not deities: ancestral spirits and the restless dead we might provisionally call ghosts. Even though Oceanic contextual theology does not tend to emphasize the usefulness of thinking about these kinds of spirits (but see Talapusi 1976), I must discuss them briefly because, as I learned in Sāmoa and American Sāmoa, they can be vibrant presences on theological college campuses.

When I was at PTC in Suva, I heard a story about an enchanted cave pool in Sāmoa. The freshwater pool, called Fatumea, is at the edge of the sea on the campus of the Piula Theological College (figure 3.5). As I recall the *talanoa* from Suva, a PTC staff member said, in a lighthearted way, that an indigenous Fijian scholar had visited Piula for a conference, done something at the pool that must have offended the local spiritual powers, and died shortly thereafter. When I went to Sāmoa several years later and wound up conducting short-term fieldwork at Piula in July and August 2015, I asked about the pool's reputation. (I also swam in it. It is bracingly cold and brilliantly clear.) At an informal kava-drinking session one night, I asked a teacher about taboos on the pool, mentioning that I had heard a story about this in Fiji.[11] The teacher immediately identified the story and said he did not know what had really happened; perhaps the Fijian man had already been sick when he visited the pool. But he did mention that it is guarded by female spirits who take care of the place.

The cave pool is a significant source of income for the college because tourists visit it and pay a fee. For this reason, the women of Piula regularly clean the area of the cave pool, including the visitors' restrooms. A few weeks earlier, the teacher told me, a student and his wife had been left in charge of the campus while everyone else was away. The wife was cleaning the restroom area by the pool, but there was a problem. I do not recall the specifics; I think the water or electricity might have been turned off. In any case, she had to go up the hill to fix the problem, and while she was up there, she heard banging from the restrooms. She called to her husband but received no reply. When

Figure 3.5. Fatumea,
the Piula Theological
College Cave Pool,
August 2015. Photo
by author.

she came back down, the place was clean. The job was done. Thinking that
the water bucket was empty just as she had left it, she tossed it to the side and
then realized it was full of water. But it had not been her husband who had
done the work, as he was just then walking down the hill.

The cave pool, then, is a classic taboo site. Respect it and it respects you.
Violate it and you will suffer. The teacher mentioned another story about
some men who had come to the pool, did not pay the entry fee, drank alcohol
against the rules, and later, driving home, had a car wreck that killed two of
them. Another day, when I asked the teacher whether any students had written their bachelor of divinity (BD) theses on the cave pool, he said no and
joked that maybe they were too scared—but this was one of those jokes that
did not seem to be entirely a joke.[12]

Near the end of my stay at Piula, I asked the principal, Mosese Maʻilo
Fuaivaʻa, for his theological reflections on the cave pool and its guardian
spirits. I quote his response at length for its detail, theological nuance, and
poetic force:

Well, this place has been here for many years before us. And when we came here
as students, we were—the story was passed on to us by other students and lecturers
about this place. And we ourselves have experienced the presence of our ancestral
spirits. I will call [them] our ancestral spirits, not evil spirits or bad spirits, I just

call them ancestral spirits. And I think this is universal: spirits are always with us, OK? Spirits of our loved ones, spirits of people who... have died a long time ago.

But I believe, what I'm saying is, this is my own personal experience and my own personal view of things, because there have been incidences where we have witnessed that in this theological college. And what I'm saying, I'm not saying we worship them. It's totally different. We worship God. But we also believe we have the spirits of our ancestors around us. And we are so comfortable that we have our ancestors around, OK?

We Samoans believe that wisdom—the *tōfā mamao*, the *tōfā* is the deepest form of wisdom, to judge and to make decisions—so I still believe in that, that they can help us with that, you know. Whatever way, where they whisper, or where they influence the way we think, whatever. But... we appreciate that. Some people may [say]...we worship idols. But we don't. We worship God. But we also believe we have helpers around us. And they can be harmless, and they can also be harmful.

It all depends on what we do. If we please them or if we do something that they think is wrong, we don't know that, because we can't directly communicate with them, but we feel it, we feel it. Even myself as a principal. I feel it. I sit in my office sometimes, and I feel it, that they are somewhere around here. Maybe they are here, listening to us.

So we give them our utmost respect. But we don't want them to tell us what to do, if you understand the paradox of what I am saying. We don't want them to tell us what to do, but there are some things where they can help us.

I will tell you one incident. You may not believe it; it's up to you. But we went to the synod, so everyone went to the synod, only one couple stayed back [on campus]. But they had a lot of things to do, to clean up the pool, because it's believed that the pool is the dwelling place of those spirits. To clean up the bathroom for the pool, and to pick up the rubbish all over the community. And this couple, when they came down to clean the toilets for the pool, it's already done. Perfectly done....And they were afraid. They were scared.

So when we came back, they told me the story, and I just told them, just don't say anything, just say "thank you." That's all.

But that is the latest. It was in June this year. So, yeah. But a lot of things like that have happened, for many years now.

Are they helping us? We don't know. Are they scaring us? We don't know. What we know is that spirits of our ancestors are always with us. We don't worship it, but we appreciate their presence, and we thank God to have our ancestors around us, for allowing them to—if you read the Bible, Jesus has allowed the spirits to roam around....The only thing Jesus didn't want them to do is to possess people. (Ma'ilo Fuaiva'a, interview, 14 Aug 2015)

The cave pool, in the principal's view, is an indigenous spiritual site that must be respected by Christians, especially Samoans who look for wisdom in connection with the ancestral past. Its taboo aura apparently keeps students from looking too closely at it in their theological theses, but it is not inherently frightening, just powerful.

I expect that many mainstream Christian theologians in Oceania would agree with Maʻilo Fuaivaʻa's warning that ancestral spirits are to be respected but not worshipped. His reference to Jesus not wanting spirits to possess people leads to the story of another campus spirit, however, that does afflict people in this way. Unlike the Piula cave pool, whose legend is widely known but about which I have not been able to find any written reports, the spirit on the campus of the Kanana Fou Theological Seminary in American Sāmoa has been mentioned in a dissertation written by the president of Kanana Fou, Moreli Niuatoa.

Niuatoa recalled how when he was a student at Kanana Fou, his wife had become possessed by Tui Atua, a famous Samoan spirit who is "fond of beautiful women" (Niuatoa 2007, 267n31; see also Mageo 1998, 180–182). He explained:

> I was saddened. I didn't believe this happened in a seminary, a place that was supposedly a "holy ground" for the training of future Samoan church leaders. So we took her to a Samoan healer. . . . Caught up with this worrisome experience, I felt sadness towards God for allowing this to happen to my wife. But my wife kept saying that I should not blame God for what happened to her. She said she would be okay. Faʻa-Samoa [the Samoan Way] has ways to deal with the *maʻi aitu* (ghostly possessed). (Niuatoa 2007, 267–268; see also Goodman 1971)

After a high chief called Ulufale chanted and prayed for the possessed woman, she became well again. Key to the story is that Ulufale is considered to be related to Tui Atua.

When I was conducting research at Kanana Fou, I encountered Tui Atua in an indirect and unexpected way. On 15 March 2016, I reported in my field notes: "A few students in the library were buzzing about pictures being displayed on a cell phone." They had been taken at an evening service four days earlier that had been part of a global event called the "World Day of Prayer," meant to bring together women who conduct services on a designated theme and country. In 2016, the country was Cuba, and the women of Kanana Fou dressed in cheerful outfits reflecting their vision of Caribbean chic.

I was shown the photos on the student's cell phone. Especially in one of the images, it looked like there was a face reflected in the glass behind one of the women performing at the front of the church. It was a hazy but striking image, blurry and off-kilter but resembling a face. One student dismissed the image as just a reflection, but one lecturer said it was "spooky." Later, another teacher mentioned it to me and said Samoans believe that when there is a dance—in context, I took him to mean a celebration in general—the dead would come to it (author's field notes, 28 March 2016). He mused that maybe this was what had happened, as the service at which the photographs had been taken had featured the women in their colorful costumes.

I spoke with the man whose phone held the ghostly images, and he explained that one of his children had taken the photo. And—here is the key part—his family is part of Ulufale's line, related to Tui Atua. So his phone was not just enchanted technology: his family was in the right genealogical position to have this kind of vision—although, as Niuatoa's dissertation points out, an encounter with Tui Atua does not necessarily depend on such kinship. The student seemed inclined to believe that it could be a real spiritual presence in the photo. He said he had seen people possessed before and recalled how his grandfather had healed people possessed by Tui Atua; he indicated that his grandfather's healing method had consisted of words spoken respectfully. The college's librarian was humorously blunt when I spoke with her later, saying that in all her time on campus she had never seen anything odd. But, I must add, Tui Atua is not the only spiritual figure associated with Kanana Fou. One teacher mentioned to me the belief that spirits *(aitu)* are "incarnated especially in dogs," of which the campus has a few. An Australian student at the college told me of an eerie ghost encounter he had inside one of the *pulega* (district) houses on campus. There is also a legend about an invisible path, cutting across the field in the middle of campus, traversing the lands of the living and the dead.[13]

I did not hear of spirits hovering about my field sites in Suva or Auckland, although the theology faculty at the University of Auckland School of Theology became involved in a publication project about spirit possession. In 2006, a barrister representing the George Sainsbury Foundation asked the school whether its members "could conduct research into spirit possession"; the foundation had been established to promote research on spirit possession's link to mental illness (Wainwright 2010, vi). The school agreed. It accepted a grant from the foundation and produced an edited volume (Wainwright, Culbertson, and Smith 2010), one of whose chapters is by Winston Halapua. Two of the volume's coeditors offered a concluding chapter in which their main recommendation is, perhaps not surprisingly, that what is needed is dialogue: dialogue between Christians about spirit possession and dialogue between academic disciplines with different perspectives on religious experience (Culbertson and Smith 2010).

I conclude this excursus with a Samoan proverb: "E mana'o i le vao 'ae fefe i le aitu" (There is a need for the bush, but there is fear of ghosts). Ama'amalele Tofaeono interpreted this to mean that "the human will desires, but the body is weak," and "there is danger in the face of uncontrolled desires" (Tofaeono 2000, 103n49; see also Meleiseā 1980). The proverb puts ghosts in the bush. Yet they clearly belong on theological college campuses as well, living as pre-Christian presences in the heart of Christian institutional spaces. Their lively existence in *talanoa,* and their associations with mana and kava (whose consumption can set up a channel of communication with them), means that spirits keep moving, ambiguous beings with resolute significance.

Articulating the Pacific Way

Emblems of Pacific Christianity represent connections across island groups. Fiji, Sāmoa, and Tonga are very different places when examined up close, but from an analytical distance, they can be seen to share a great deal. The recognition of shared elements, values, and styles across Oceania is sometimes referred to with the phrase "the Pacific Way."

Fiji's first prime minister, Ratu Sir Kamisese Mara, took credit for coining this phrase, which he used in a speech to the United Nations General Assembly in 1970 (Mara 1997, xvi, 237–241). In his speech, he pointed to the smooth paths to independence taken by Fiji, Sāmoa, Tonga, the Cook Islands, and Nauru, implying that the Pacific Way is fundamentally one of peaceful interaction. The era's indigenous scholars took up the term avidly. Epeli Hauʻofa recalled that when he arrived at the University of the South Pacific in 1975, "the campus was abuzz with creativity and wide-ranging discussions generated by the emergence of the Pacific Way. Whatever one may say about it the Pacific Way was a large and an encompassing idea that became the ideology of its time, perfectly suited to the immediate postcolonial euphoria and expectations of the 1970s" (1993a, 126; see also Meleiseā 1987a, 145).[14] Bruce J Deverell, in a dissertation reflecting on his time teaching at PTC in Suva, wrote that "the discovery of the common Austronesian language and cultural roots is often exciting for students, the sense of finding out what it is to belong to the Pacific Way—what is common in the diversity" (1986, 157).

Oceanic contextual theologians have participated energetically in crafting discourse about the Pacific Way—whether or not they have used that specific term—and they have done so especially in the pages of the *Pacific Journal of Theology (PJT)*.[15] The journal's first issue was published in 1961, a sign of growing interest in developing indigenous-run institutions as the era of Pacific independence drew near. Such interest also led, during the decade, to the establishment of PTC, the University of the South Pacific, and the South Pacific Association of Theological Schools (SPATS), which publishes *PJT*.[16] From 1961 until 1966, the journal was published in Sāmoa; since 1967, it has been published in Suva, Fiji. Series 1 ran from 1961 to 1970, during which time the editors struggled to get enough articles submitted, and, perhaps due to production problems, subscriptions fell "from 563 in 1962 to 175 in 1963"; attempts to begin publishing again in 1973 and 1977 were unsuccessful (Forman 1986, 33). However, after an almost two-decade hiatus, series 2 began in 1989 and continues to the present.[17]

To understand the journal's focus and scope and how it has evolved over the decades, I undertook a historical survey, taking notes on all the issues in the journal's history from number 1 of the first series (1961) through number 47 of the second series (2012). As I moved through more than five thousand pages, I focused on scholarly articles, reports, substantial news items, and testimonies; here, I refer to these major contributions as "articles" for simplicity's sake. I tallied 520 articles in all. I did not take notes on shorter items such as editors' introductions, letters to the editor, notices, book reviews, quizzes, questionnaires, Bible studies, prayers, poems, brief research progress reports, or lists of theses.

Especially as the journal developed over the 1990s and 2000s, it became notably inclusive in its authorship. Many articles were written by theologians, but some have come from scholars with doctoral degrees in anthropology, chemistry, demography, history, education, public policy, and religion, as well as from nonacademics. In addition, *PJT* has often published speeches from public officials at events related to churches or nongovernmental organizations. Most authors whose religious affiliation is identified have been mainline Protestants—which is to say, not evangelicals, Pentecostals, or Mormons; Catholics are also well represented. Nearly all articles have been published in English. Fourteen have appeared in French, most of these with an English translation.

One of the questions motivating my survey, spurring me on through all those pages, was: who gets written about? That is, what social and geographical entities have been most well represented in *PJT*? I do not mean authors' ethnicities; I mean the topics of articles. I had noticed during research at PTC that some places are written about a lot, while others are rarely mentioned. This is partly related to student demographics: students from Sāmoa tend to write theses about Sāmoa, Tongans about Tonga, and so on, and a comparatively small place like Tokelau is not likely to be well represented textually (and it isn't).[18] But Oceania as a unified place was rarely the topic of student work.[19] Authors contributing to *PJT* over the decades, in contrast, have foregrounded Oceania. Of the 520 articles on which I took notes, 242 treated the Pacific Islands as a meaningful unit in some way.[20] Not all of the articles I listed as having an Oceanic focus make much of it, and some do so only by virtue of institutional reference, such as items related to the Pacific Conference of Churches. Nevertheless, Oceania emerges in the pages of *PJT* as a focal site, a place worth paying attention to and writing about. As a result, the Pacific Way takes shape in theological form in the pages of the journal.

When the journal began publishing again in 1989 after a two-decade hiatus, Tuwere declared in the first issue:

> Never has there been a time like the present period when we have been drawn so closely together in the region; a time in our history when we in a very real sense become one vanua [land and people] both historically and ideologically; a time when so much attention by the superpowers is turned on us. What happens in one

island can no longer be ignored by others. Events that happen in Kanaky [New Caledonia] or Maohi Nui [French Polynesia] or Fiji affect us all, for we belong to the same body, the same womb. Denial of justice and peace in one area is the denial of the same in other areas. But there is a new sense of community that is growing, a quest for regional identity. The Pacific people are not only entitled to, but obliged to be actively involved to the fullest possible extent in shaping their own future. (Tuwere 1989, 12)

Oceania's dominance of the journal might seem to make obvious sense. After all, on the first page of the first issue, Vavae Toma wrote in a foreword that *PJT*'s "underlying theme will be the theological foundation of the life, witness and current problems of the Church in the Pacific" (1961)—a statement noteworthy for its inclusiveness combined with definiteness: the foundation, the life, the Church, the Pacific. On the other hand, the way Oceania has been represented has changed between series 1 and series 2. In series 1, from the 1960s, much of the discussion about Oceania has an anticipatory air. It is fed by excitement about regional institutional developments: the Conference of Churches and Missions in the Pacific at Malua in 1961 and its decision to create PTC; the Pacific Islands Christian Education Curriculum consultation in Suva in 1963; the subsequent creation of the college in the middle of the decade (its council first met in 1964, the foundation stone was laid in 1965, and the school was formally opened in 1966);[21] and the creation of the Pacific Conference of Churches and its first meeting at Lifou, New Caledonia, in 1966. Many of the early articles that focus on Oceania attend to these developments. Some articles in series 1 begin to develop the kind of intellectual vision that would become familiar in series 2, with an emphasis on contextualization (such as Lale Ieremia's article from 1967 on "The Indigenisation of Worship") and how Oceanic theology might fit into global theology (such as Cyril Germon's article from 1963, which asks how Pacific scholars might develop a "Theology of Community, for which the rest of the world is groping" [5]). Overall, however, Oceania is represented in the first series as a place that is coming together institutionally (with some late-colonial input) and is freshly facing the future. In series 2, the representation of Oceania shifts in the direction charted most poetically by Hauʻofa as an expansive and inclusive place, inherently interconnected and globally distinct.

One of the strongest themes in *PJT* has been the sacredness of land and sea, the subject of chapter 4. Feminist theology has also been well represented in series 2, especially in the work of Weavers, the theological collective discussed in chapter 2 (see also Lamb 1964). Weavers edited issue 30 of series 2, and earlier issues focused on the themes of "Women in Church and Society in the Pacific" (number 7, 1992) and "Women's Theology–Pacific Perspectives" (number 15, 1996, which included articles based on presentations from a Weavers meeting the year before). In addition to the work of Tongan Catholic Keiti Ann Kanongataʻa, who put forth a "Theology of Birthing and

Liberation" in *PJT* in 1992, the journal has featured noteworthy work such as Fijian Methodist Ilisapeci Meo's writings on women's silencing and the politics of romanticizing culture (Meo 1990, 1992, 1994, 1997, 2012) and Seforosa Carroll's work on the experience of diaspora (Carroll 2010a, 2010b). Not all feminist articles have been written by women; for example, in 1999, Malua Theological College's principal, Otele Perelini, published on "The Emancipation of Church Women" in light of Luke 13:10–17, a passage in which Jesus heals a sick woman and defends himself against criticism for having done so on the Sabbath.

Themes in the journal have been shaped by current events. For example, twelve of the thirteen articles that discuss Bougainville were published between 1990 and 1998, and most of them focused on the crisis unfolding there and attempts at reconciliation. The coups in Fiji received comparatively little attention, however, presumably because of the concerns of publishing analysis and critique with a political edge in a Fiji-based journal.

PJT is heavily influenced by contextual theology. Several issues in series 2 have been devoted to contextual work.[22] The three main theological emblems discussed above—*talanoa*, mana, and kava—have all received attention in *PJT*. For example, in an article on gender and hermeneutics, 'Asinate Fuakautu'u Samate argued that *talanoa* should "be promoted as a source of empowerment by telling, sharing and listening to the stories, especially those of the marginalized and disadvantaged in society" (2011, 72). Cliff Bird wrote of mana as "grace," and Here J Hoiore offered a devotion in which he identified mana as "Jesus' Name" (Bird 2009; Hoiore 2011). Kava is both celebrated as a Tongan and Samoan Eucharistic element and derided as "the No. 1 enemy of the church" in Fijian Methodism because of how much is drunk (Vaka'uta 1991; Fa'asi'i 1993; I Meo 1994). Here, then, is one key way ideas about the Pacific Way have lived on since their heyday in the 1970s. Despite the fact that *PJT* was not published during the 1970s, it has consistently built on that era's understandings by offering and extending visions of what it means to be Pacific and Christian.

I have spent the preceding section arguing that much of the dialogue in *PJT* concerns Oceania itself, framed by contextual theologians as the ground or seascape whereupon Pacific Islanders can understand God. As Upolu Lumā Vaai wrote, in *PJT* (among other places), "the theological mat of reception" has been unrolled and laid out as a place to "begin a theological dialogue with past doctrines, with scriptures, with their contexts, and with other contemporary theologians" (Vaai 2006, 22). But I must mention, too, that criticism of contextual theology has also been published in the journal.

A vigorous critic of contextual theology has been Ma'afu Palu. In a series of articles in *PJT*, he launched an attack on what he saw as the field's flawed principles, taking special aim at Coconut Theology as formulated by fellow Tongan Methodist Sione 'Amanaki Havea (M Palu 2002, 2003, 2005, 2006). Palu made five core criticisms. The first is that "culture" should only matter if one asks about the cultural context of Jesus's actions and the history of the Bible. For Palu, it is reasonable to ask about Jesus's Jewishness or what Paul was "actually saying to the Ephesians," but asking "what if Jesus was a Tongan" is not, because Jesus was not Tongan. Indeed, Palu argued that Christ is both culturally and "ontologically" distinct from representations of him as a Pacific Islander (2002, 31; 2005, 39; see also Etuale Lealofi quoted in PCC, PTC, and SPATS 1986). Gaps in cultural understanding do not matter, according to Palu, because God's message is universal. Counterintuitively, he accused contextual theologians of edging into Docetism, a heresy in which Jesus's full humanity is denied, because making Jesus into a Pacific Christ "disregards" his historical humanity and individuality (M Palu 2003, 38).

Palu's second criticism relates to his first: theologians who foreground Pacific identity limit the ways they can talk to non-Pacific Islanders as Christians. As he put it, "We have no message to proclaim to people with a different cultural orientation" (M Palu 2002, 38). His third criticism, also related, is that contextual theology becomes an uncritically self-referential system in which Pacific scholars read Oceanic cultural and natural contexts *into* the Gospel and then read them back *as* Gospel (M Palu 2002, 38; 2003, 32–33). Palu took issue with the idea (which I discuss in chapter 4 in relation to Tofaeono's work) that Christianity preceded the arrival of Western missionaries in Oceania; as Tofaeono put it, the "spirit of Christ" was first present in the Samoan deity Tagaloa (2000). For Palu, in contrast, early Tonga was definitely not a Christian place, and "there was no good news at all with us" until the missionaries showed up (2002, 39). His fourth core criticism is that Oceanic contextual theology does not pay enough attention to sin, and his fifth is to note that coconuts, as a metaphor, are partial truths open to subversive readings: "Why speak about the theological implication of the mature coconut but leave unmentioned the fact that the juice of immature coconuts tastes better than that of mature ones?" (Palu 2002, 37, 40).

As I read them, Palu's theological arguments are tinged with frustration that contextual theology has become central in the intellectual life of Oceanic Christianity. His first critique in *PJT* is dedicated to the memory of Sione 'Amanaki Havea, but it is a curious memorial, as it expresses regret at Havea's influence. Referring to an article published by the Tongan Catholic theologian Kafoa Solomone in *PJT* (Solomone 2000), Palu wrote:

> The pervasive influence of Dr. Havea's thinking in contextualization is largely felt in many ways in the Pacific today. In a more recent issue of the *Pacific Journal of Theology* one contributor says that with respect to the theological enterprise we are only starting to yield the fruit of the past effort to steer our theological boat towards contextualization. He indicates the fruit as theological topics such as "theology of the coconut, the theology of kava, Christ the perfect pig, the Pacific Christ" as well as the contextualized worship practices in the Pacific Theological College where the Eucharist is celebrated with taro and coconut juice instead of the more tradi-

tional elements. Now, apart from the reference to Christ being the "perfect pig," the rest of these contextualized theological formulations can trace their origin to Dr. Havea's thinking. (M Palu 2002, 35)

Palu added that in 2001, at a meeting of Methodist leaders in Sāmoa: "Banners were hoisted all over the venue for the meeting with 'coconut theology' written on them. Even young coconuts were scattered around the venue of the meeting. This suggests that coconut theology has become the distinctive identity of Christianity in the Pacific context. In a very real sense, therefore, Dr. Havea's conception of 'coconut theology' can be ranked as the most distinctive formulation of Pacific theology" (M Palu 2002, 35).

For Palu, this distinctive formulation must be critiqued, not embraced. God is beyond culture. Contextual theology, in his view, threatens to cease being theology and turn into "religious anthropology"; theology should concern itself with "the *logos* about the *theos*," but Oceanic theologians have turned their attention instead to "the *logos* about *anthropos*" (2002, 36–37; 2003, 49).

Palu acknowledged that Havea did not speak of Christ as the perfect Pig of God, but other authors have, and they have been able to do so because of the intellectual space that Havea's Coconut Theology opened up. The image and concept of Christ as a pig rather than a lamb has evidently been discussed informally at least since the 1970s (Callick 1977, 260; see also Fugui 1986; Solomone 2000, 98–99; Toap 1998). An article by Ama'amalele Tofaeono published in *PJT* in 2005 offers the most effective elaboration of the metaphor's theological significance, however. Tofaeono, of Samoan heritage, focused his discussion on Melanesia, where people have a "sacred attachment" to their pigs—cherishing them but also sacrificing them to restore community harmony. Because of their reconciling and restorative power in Melanesian societies, according to Tofaeono, pigs offer "a channel for a 'Christic-spark' or a 'Christ-emanating light' that moves the hearts and persons of communities to mend relationships and to embrace and appreciate the gifts of others" (Tofaeono 2005, 94). He concluded his article by echoing Havea, who closed his own foundational statement on Coconut Theology by declaring, "I am convinced that if Christ had grown up and lived in the Pacific, He would have used the coconut to represent the body which was bruised and crushed, and the juice for the blood as elements of the Holy Eucharist" (S Havea 1987, 15). Tofaeono, in turn, finished his argument about pigs being Christ-like by declaring (following John 1:29), "If John the Baptist had lived in one of the islands in Oceania 2000 years ago, and had encountered the Christ walking by, he would surely have exclaimed, 'Behold, the Pig of God that takes away the sins of the world'" (Tofaeono 2005, 98).

Palu's counterargument—made before Tofaeono's article was published, but relevant for the discussion here—is that culture has little or nothing to do with the sacred meaning of Christ as sacrifice. "For Jesus to be the 'perfect pig' is extremely different from Jesus as 'the Lamb of God,'" Palu argued.

His identification as the lamb "was not taken simply from the cultural environment of Palestine to illustrate the mission of Jesus but was used to confirm Jesus' continuity with the Passover meal or even the sacrifices in the day of atonement *(yom kippur)* in the Old Testament. It is in those religious rites and not... the cultural milieu of Palestine that one can find the true meaning of Jesus being the Lamb of God" (M Palu 2002, 49n41). Note that Palu's criticism depends on a separation of human-designed culture from divinely ordered ritual.

Palu sharply posed the question of divinity's relationship to culture, but I am not aware of his work being taken up to any significant extent by other theologians. He has continued to publish his criticisms (now in venues other than *PJT;* see M Palu 2012, 2016, 2017), but contextual theology retains its vibrant presence and influence in Oceania. For Palu, a focus on culture limits Christianity: it is a closing down. For contextual theology's strongest proponents, many of whom have written in the pages of *PJT,* it is an opening up: the cultures of Oceania give their inheritors unique ways of understanding God in and through the Pacific Way.

Chapter 4
Sea and Earth

Much Oceanic contextual theology can be summarized in six words: *the sea and land are life.*

The most prominent scholars in the discipline have pressed this claim, including Ilaitia Sevati Tuwere, Winston Halapua, Leslie Boseto, and Ama'amalele Tofaeono. And they have expanded on it: All of life and creation is interconnected. The people of Oceania, with a heritage of traveling the sea over vast distances and cultivating the lands they settled, are historically and geographically positioned to appreciate the spiritual power of physical place. I refer to the eco-theological approaches discussed in this chapter as "totalizing holism" for the way they pull everything into themselves. The position was elegantly stated by John Muir over a century ago: "When we try to pick out anything by itself, we find it hitched to everything else in the universe." (1911, 211). Psychoanalytically, it is Sigmund Freud's "oceanic feeling," a sense of universal oneness (1961).

As an example of Muir-style environmentalism given a theological stamp, or the oceanic feeling applied to Oceania, consider a polemic Boseto published in the *Pacific Journal of Theology (PJT)* in 1995. In the piece, titled "Do Not Separate Us from Our Land and Sea," he put forth two claims that run through most of the works discussed in this chapter. First, Boseto presented a totalizing holistic image of existence, declaring that all of creation is God's and thus that "the more we love Christ, the more we love the earth and the more we love the earth the more we suffer together with the whole creation as one body of Christ." He compared the Pacific Islands generally, and Solomon Islands forests specifically, to the garden of Eden. For Boseto, global capitalism does the worst possible thing: it attempts to separate indigenous peoples from their ancestrally owned lands and sea. It does so by using the law as a weapon. He observed that the Solomon Islands government owns the trees as well as mineral rights six feet below the ground's surface. The act of dividing things up this way—this is mine, that is yours, and the twain shall meet only in court—is an act of murder: "Our land and sea are us and we are them. Do not separate us, if you do so, you are murdering us!" (Boseto 1995, 71, 69–70).

While seeing all existence as fundamentally interconnected, Boseto also made the claim that God has given particular peoples responsibility for particular places. After making the world, "God peopled every part of it and allocated them land and sea. People on their ancestral allocations of land

and sea are to cultivate and guard their given places" (Boseto 1995, 69). He referred at this point to Genesis 2:15: "And the LORD God took the man, and put him into the garden of Eden to dress it and to keep it." Resources belong to indigenous groups by divine authority and blessing. The problem, obviously, is that governments and transnational corporations do not respect claims of godly inheritance, and local people in places like the Solomons have a hard time challenging the forces determined to cut up the earth for profit. In the conclusion of his article, Boseto turned from denunciation to appeal, evidently assuming (correctly, I expect) that readers of *PJT* would be on his side. He asked readers to be in solidarity with his people, not only for earthly justice but also for heavenly reward, and finished by asking God to "bless you who read this article" (Boseto 1995, 72).

Environmentalism has been around for decades, and many readers will be familiar with its principles: that the earth is a living web, that harming part of it will have effects on other parts of it and perhaps everywhere, and that we are currently in a dire situation around the globe with metastasizing problems of pollution, species loss, and climate change. This understanding motivates arguments with different tones. The classic work often hailed as the beginning of the environmental movement, Rachel Carson's *Silent Spring* (1962), is relentlessly downbeat—for good reason; she was writing primarily about DDT and other pesticides. But Stewart Brand's hippie classic *The Whole Earth Catalogue* is entirely pragmatic: it offers "access to tools," giving information on products readers can buy to improve their lives, from books to yarn and from snowshoes to tongue-in-groove bricks. To justify this wholehearted embrace of shopping in the age of Aquarius, the editor offered a distinctly theological opening statement: "We *are* as gods and might as well get good at it" (Portola Institute 1972, 1). Oceanic contextual theologians are joining a long-running conversation on humanity's relationship with the natural world, adding contributions based on their lamination of culture and place.

A Disturbed Sea

In the early 1990s, when *PJT* began to be published again after almost twenty years' hibernation, Tuwere made several key contributions toward developing new themes for Oceanic contextual theology. His first major statement came in an article based on a sermon he had given in the Pacific Theological College (PTC) chapel in September 1987. In the published version, Tuwere offered "thoughts for a Pacific Ocean theology," identifying three notable "avenues which might be useful for...discussion." The first is to recognize that because the sea is central to Pacific Islanders' lives, it can be thought of as a mother: mother sea. The second is that missionaries who came from distant lands opened up new paths across the sea for Islanders, who were then able to move beyond their own reefs in new ways. In discussing how Islander missionaries evangelized other Islanders, Tuwere wrote, "Sailing to other islands to bring a new *mana* (power) through peace and *loloma* (love) marks a significant period in the history of the islands." The third avenue for discussion, however, is a darker one: afflicted by the greed of "the rich and powerful nations of the world," the Pacific Ocean is now "a disturbed sea" (Tuwere 1990, 5–6; see also Vaka'uta 2015).

The disturbed sea is now a globally resonant theme as scholars and policy makers around the world express intense concern with climate change and rising sea levels. Islands are sinking. People will lose ancestral homes and ways of life. The future, for many Islanders, seems to be located in only two places: overseas or underwater.

Some churches in Oceania are not especially concerned with these issues, due in part to what Cecilie Rubow and Cliff Bird have called "the Noah controversy" (2016, 158), the expectation that rising sea levels will not matter much because God promised Noah that he would never again destroy the earth in a flood (Gen 9:11). Colette Mortreux and Jon Barnett reported that in the forty interviews they conducted in Funafuti, Tuvalu, in 2007, "around half [of the respondents] raised religion in response to climate change. These people believed that climate change was not an issue of concern due to the special relationship Tuvalu shares with God and due to the promises God made to Noah in the Bible" (2009, 109).[1] Taking a more nuanced view, theologian Teatu Fusi argued that Tuvaluans will eventually need to leave Tuvalu because of climate change but that because of their relationship with God, they can continue to prosper and be blessed, becoming "landed, even in a foreign land" (2005, 44). Drawing in part on Walter Brueggemann's work on Israel's "landedness" and "landlessness" (1977), Fusi argued: "The God of Israel is also the God of Tuvalu; the God who promised a land for Israel must also promise a land for Tuvalu. We are indeed treasuring and enjoying the land, or what is left of it, that God gave to our ancestors. But the fact remains that nature [will] eventually take control over the vulnerable islands of the Pacific and elsewhere" (2005, 43).

The disturbed sea became a theological topic in the aftermath of the tsunami that hit Sāmoa, American Sāmoa, and northern Tonga in 2009. In chapter 1, I describe how Methodist theologian Titimaea Titimaea, in response to popular views of the tsunami as God's punishment, urged a reconstruction of the biblical story of Noah and the flood that would emphasize God's goodness. Many other Samoan theologians contributed their interpretations as well. Moreli Niuatoa, the president of Kanana Fou Theological Seminary, wrote a paper shortly after the tsunami in which he criticized the "perpetual fog" of the "'wrath of God' theory promoted by the [Christian] conservatives and fundamentalists." Describing commentary on the disaster "from my personal discussion with people and heard through the media," he offered nine illustrative quotes in Samoan with English translations. Their dominant theme is that the tsunami was "the will of God," punishment for wayward people, some referred to in general ("we are living a life contrary to [God's] purpose"; "the nation has so many sins") and some referred to specifically ("too much corruption in the government"). One comment addresses the destruction of a particular building by noting that people were playing bingo there "but not attending church services." Against such interpretations, Niuatoa argued that God is not evil and that the scientific explanation of how the tsunami came about should be accepted, with God's role in the event seen as one of "consolation" (Niuatoa 2009, 2, 3, 8).

The topic also came up when I interviewed three PhD students in theology at the University of Auckland—Vaitusi Nofoaiga, Arthur Wulf, and Imoamaua Setefano—in July 2013:

Imoamaua Setefano: Everything in Samoan culture, or as a Samoan, is given a theological tag, eh? We see things, that God is talking to us, or relating to us, through things that happen. So things like the tsunami, and things that—we always look for a theological answer, even though the answer is maybe a geological one.

Matt Tomlinson: But what would have been some of the prominent explanations of the tsunami? Was God angry at Sāmoa? Or at that particular place where it hit the worst? Sorry, I don't mean to be offensive, I'm just curious, what were some of the interpretations?

Arthur Wulf: Yeah, that's one of [them], because this is one of the most popular areas for tourists, and, so, like, they opened their hotels and stuff on Sunday, the beaches on Sunday. And when the tsunami struck, they're seeing it as a punishment from God. Because of the—not respecting the Sunday and the Sabbath. And, like I said, that portrays for us . . . we saw, like, our belief in God portrays our God as a judge, judging the people, cursing and blessing the people. So that image is a bit problematic for me.

Vaitusi Nofoaiga: And that's one of the challenges that we have as *faife'au*s [pastors], is to preach the Word of God in accordance with the reality of what is happening. Like what happened [with] the tsunami. 'Cause the main question that people asked us—where was God when this thing happened? Particularly when children were killed, you know, in the tsunami. So we have to come up with an explanation.

The destructiveness of the sea, in short, became a theological challenge that many Samoan theologians and ministers knew they needed to address. As in Clifford Geertz's 1974 classic discussion (via Max Weber and Susanne Langer) of the problem of meaning, suffering does not need to be alleviated, but it needs to be made comprehensible. Whatever the tsunami was, it was not meaningless. Many lay Samoans saw it as punishment, but some theologians urged a reinterpretation of it that would emphasize God's care for humanity.

Despite theological attention to rising sea levels and the destructiveness of tsunamis, the ocean, in Oceanic contextual theology, is often presented as a benign and unifying force. Tongan Anglican theologian and archbishop Winston Halapua has written the most sustained treatment of this kind, labeling his approach "theomoana" (W Halapua 2008b). In Halapua's view, the key feature of the ocean is its essential interconnectedness to all things. The oceans of the world flow into each other as waves dance endlessly. He acknowledged that places like Tuvalu suffer from climate change and that tsunamis can strike, but the tone of Halapua's book is buoyant, with metaphors ever expanding as the ocean is described as path, womb, gift-giver, embrace, love, an expression of eternity, and, ultimately, God. The ocean, for Halapua, is the ultimate manifestation of totalizing holistic oneness.

In fact, his use of the ocean as a theological concept is so all-inclusive that it embraces life on land. He described sea, islands, and sky as linked in "triune interconnectedness"—a holy trinity—and declared that "experience of the land and the ocean cannot be separated" in the Pacific (W Halapua 2008b, 5, 7). But he also presented theomoana as a way of going beyond a land-centered perspective:

> I write because I believe that concepts and values from Oceania have a wider relevance. Theology has in a sense been landlocked—I write using metaphors arising from the different aspects and waves of the ocean. I write with a deep oceanic sense of interconnectedness with creation, with others and with the mystery of the God who calls into being all things....
>
> We, as people of Oceania, are an integral part of the world. Although we may be perceived as people far distant and isolated in islands scattered in a vast ocean....I contend that we speak not as people of the land but people who have been nurtured by the vastness of the ocean and the huge importance in human relationships of life-giving space. (W Halapua 2008b, 3, 54)

In distinguishing his approach from a land-centered one, Halapua might have been responding to the way land-focused political claims in Fiji have led to violence (see W Halapua 2003), or he might have been politely critiquing the work of his former colleague at St John's Theological College in Auckland, Tuwere, which I discuss in the next section. But in an affirmative sense, he was taking up the project articulated by Epeli Hau'ofa in "Our Sea of Islands," reimagining Oceania as an expansive place connected by the sea rather than separated by it (Hau'ofa 1993b).[2] For Halapua, as for Hau'ofa, the ocean is an integral space in all senses. In this kind of contextual theology, the Spirit of God continues to move across the face of the waters.

Land as Community

If Sione 'Amanaki Havea's call to develop Coconut Theology was a charismatic spark for Oceanic contextual theologians, Tuwere routinized it. Here I am following the Weberian parallel (Weber 1978) because, like Paul following Jesus, Tuwere has set standards and defined paths, establishing contextual theology in Oceania as something structured and generative. Tuwere published several foundational articles in *PJT,* offering his vision of a united Pacific theology and explaining how contextualization is a vital way to think about God here and now (Tuwere 1989, 1990, 1991, 1992, 1995). For his scholarship on Fiji specifically, a key development was his turn to focus on the land rather than the ocean.

Tuwere's landmark publication is his monograph *Vanua: Towards a Fijian Theology of Place* (2002), based on his dissertation from the Melbourne College of Divinity ten years earlier. The book is a sustained investigation of the Fijian term and concept *vanua* in Trinitarian terms. It draws on several key theological sources, including Walter Brueggemann's *The Land* (1977), Sallie McFague's *Models of God* (1987), and Jürgen Moltmann's *God in Creation* (1985), but its focus is distinctly Fijian.

The core meaning of *vanua* is "place," but it also means dry land as opposed to water, a specific territory under the authority of a chief, and "practically everything" in that territory, including people (Tuwere 2002, 33). Because *vanua* includes land and people within a chiefdom, it becomes an emotionally resonant symbol of one's true home and of "tradition" writ large. "Land, its settlement, ownership, usage and distribution," according to Tuwere, "cannot be divorced from the people who live on it. They are united together in a living memory of common descent of which the chief was the visible symbol" (2002, 28). Even more expansively, Tuwere described *vanua* as a source of life, the location of time itself, a site of ancestral memory, and the basis of identity. He mentioned how the term is often used in alignment with *lotu* (Christianity) and *matanitū* (government), the three presented as the interlocking bases of indigenous Fijian life (see also Niukula 1994; Tomlinson 2009; Ryle 2010). For Tuwere, a key theological task is to understand how the *vanua* and Christianity must go together but must also be distinguished, especially as Fiji has suffered from conflict between indigenous and nonindigenous citizens, most notably Indo-Fijians—citizens whose ancestors came from South Asia during the early colonial era as laborers, many of whom are Hindus and Muslims. The core of Tuwere's argument is that the *vanua* and Christianity must remain inextricably joined but that Christianity rather than the *vanua* should define the terms of the relationship: "The distinction between *vanua* and *lotu* must be made, not to abrogate their unity, but to redefine their mutual immanence within each other in the light of the incarnation. There is an inescapable imperative under present circumstances to remove the *lotu* [the Church] under the garb of the *vanua* from its normative position and allow Christ the incarnate Word of God to become the norm" (2002, 104). In other words, the *vanua,* including the chiefly system, has reshaped Fijian Christianity in ways that have helped lead to the nation's roiling social and political crises, with rising poverty, ethnic and religious tensions, and four coups since independence. For Tuwere, the *vanua* and the Church must go together, but it is time for the Church to reform the *vanua.*

Tuwere acknowledged that *vanua*-as-landscape can include the sea. His own emphasis is decidedly terrestrial, however. His core symbol for God's relationship with humanity is the garden, which has divine associations in pre-Christian Fijian myth and the account of creation in Genesis. For Tuwere, God is a gardener, and the garden is in God. Humanity also works in gardens, whether in the story of Adam and Eve or in traditional Fijian agricultural practices and their mythic links with the Fijian fertility god and ancestor Ratumaibula (also known as Ratumaibulu). Tuwere observed that many languages in Oceania have the same word for land and womb or placenta, such as Samoan *fanua* and Tongan *fonua* (although this linguistic equation is not found in Fijian), so the *vanua* has a feminine aspect. He acknowledged, however, that because landownership is such a contentious and anxiety-provoking issue in Fiji, "the *vanua* is understood in terms of the masculine" when it comes to politics (Tuwere 2002, 107; see also Tomlinson 2015a).[3] Ultimately, land is a divine gift to humanity, but not one that humanity is free to reject or neglect. "One does not own the land," Tuwere declared, "the land owns him. Man and land are one" (2002, 49; see also Tuwere 2006, 2007, 2010).

Tuwere's theological exploration of the *vanua* touches on ecology and humanity's responsibility toward all of creation. As I have quoted Muir on the interconnectedness of the whole universe, so Tuwere quoted L Charles Birch's claim about the "physical unity of the universe.... The little flower participates in the universal activity of God. If we could know that participation, we would know what God is" (Birch 1965, 113, quoted in Tuwere 2002, 89; the "little flower" is a reference to Alfred, Lord Tennyson's 1863 poem "Flower in the Crannied Wall"). But because *vanua* means people as well as place, his ultimate theological framing of the *vanua* places as much emphasis on social terms as environmental ones:

> The central issue [in understanding *vanua* theologically] is *community:* the community of living and dying in a given place. It is the will and persistence of the human spirit to be rooted in a particular locality. This is of course universal. Every human being possesses it. We all yearn for rootage, for home. We all want to have a place and a home and the longing is as old as humanity.... The central idea is belonging.... Belonging begets meaning. One will never receive the same depth of

meaning away from home. What is conceptualised in the *vanua* is life that acquires its meaning when lived in community with others—not only with other human beings but also with ancestors, with seasons and festivals, plants and animals, land and sea and everything on it.

Community is an ambiguous term which means different things to different people and cultures. For the *vanua*, community means life lived close to the soil. (Tuwere 2002, 69–70; emphasis in original)

For Tuwere, this community of the *vanua* must be related to the Trinity of Father, Son, and Holy Spirit. Whereas Halapua rhetorically extended the trinitarian model to sea, islands, and sky, Tuwere invoked the Fijian trio of *vanua*, Christianity, and government (but see also Tuwere 2002, 143). Quoting historian John Garrett's description of these three elements having a "trinitarian solemnity" (1982, 114), Tuwere described his book as "an attempt to move this 'trinitarian solemnity' from centre stage" in Fiji (2002, 79). As I understand him, he was arguing that Father, Son, and Holy Spirit must be the core community for all existence and that indigenous Fijians must continue to come together for God in the *vanua*, both *vanua*-as-community and *vanua*-as-sacred foundation. Land, people, and history are united in projects of both creation and salvation (Tuwere 2002, 82).[4]

Intriguingly, despite his focus on holistic interconnection and its responsibilities, Tuwere did not conclude by advocating more dialogue, as so many contextual theologians (and other scholars) have done. Rather, observing that Fijian rituals feature reverential silence, Tuwere implied that listening is a sacred act, a way of drawing closer to God and fellow humans: silence as community (2002, 73, 204–206). Yet pragmatically, his book is evidently offered as a contribution to a specific kind of dialogue: a discussion of how Fijian society can be made more Christian, more tolerant, more communal. In other words, although Tuwere drew on global theological scholarship and would surely not mind being read outside of Fiji, his monograph *Vanua* can be understood as a work addressed to Fiji's citizens, urging them to think about God, place, community, and identity. In this regard, his work differs sharply from that of Halapua, who has positioned his work as Oceanic in order to speak to a global readership.

The Gospel according to Tagaloa

"We have to draw a very clear line between Gospel and Christianity," Ama'amalele Tofaeono instructed his third-year students in Theology 340 ("Gospel and Culture") at Kanana Fou on 23 March 2016. I scribbled the line in my notebook and wondered how many students were ready to be as bold as Tofaeono was challenging them to be.

His statement, which would startle a systematic theologian, points to a key claim in his own work: as he went on to say, "The Gospel was already in Sāmoa, way before" Christian missionaries showed up. For Tofaeono, the "spirit of Christ" (and thus the Gospel) was in Sāmoa long before missionaries brought news about the life of Jesus. The spirit of Christ pervades all of creation. In his book, he elaborated:

> Armed with the glorious blessings of the Gospel, the early missionaries were con-
> vinced that, in and through their work, they were bringing Christ and salvation
> to the savage nations. Although this was partially true, what the majority of mis-
> sionaries overlooked was the fact that the spirit of Christ was already present in
> Samoa and had been worshipped throughout many ages. Christ cannot simply be
> wrapped up and transported in suitcases from a knowledgeable to an unknowl-
> edgeable place; otherwise, the spirit of Christ would have no freedom of its own.
> (Tofaeono 2000, 127)

Pre-Christian Samoans may not have had the Bible, then, but they did have their own "myths, rituals and oral traditions" that "were living witnesses to this ever-living presence of the divine" (Tofaeono 2000, 128).[5]

The key figure in Tofaeono's understanding of the pre-Christian Gospel in Sāmoa is Tagaloa. Tagaloa (short for Tagaloalagi) is Sāmoa's "Creator God" (Tofaeono 2000, 32), with variations of the deity's character found in closely related societies such as Hawai'i, where the name is Kanaloa.[6] Tofae-ono quoted a German author's characterization of Tagaloa as "the unbound one, not constrained by space or time, and thus the almighty, the absolute, the sovereign, the highest, the master of everything, as he is not bound by any taboo."[7] Crucially, Tagaloa was not separate from creation, but part of it, even while shaping it: "There was an intermarriage of the earthly preex-istent materials, from which issued *Eleele* (soil or land). This was followed by the marriage of the heavenly materials, which gave birth to [Tagaloa], the ever-living being of the heavens" (Tofaeono 2000, 170n76; compare Sah-lins 1985 and Gell 1995 on Eastern Polynesian creation and cosmology). The birth of the universe, in this account, was "a self-contained creation" (Tofaeono 2000, 170).

There are multiple stories from different parts of Sāmoa about Tagaloa's role in creating the world. Tofaeono made a useful distinction between east-ern and western versions. In the eastern Samoan version of creation, from Manu'a in what is now American Sāmoa, creation is said to have taken place from above and somewhat resembles the account of Jehovah's creation of the world in Genesis. In the western Samoan version of creation, from Upolu and Savai'i in what is now independent Sāmoa, creation takes place from below. To give the stories equivalent weight, I present Tofaeono's rendition of them side by side.[8]

Eastern Samoan versions of creation

The Supreme Being of the Universe, Tagaloa, dwelt in the highest heavens. Being alone in such an expanse, Tagaloa envisioned the creation of all things through his intelligence while wandering the Universe. There was then no sky, no seas, no land. Other things were not created and, accordingly, on the place where Tagaloa stood, *papa* (rocks) sprang up. Then Tagaloa spoke to *papa* to split up, and there emerged *papataoto* (spreading rocks), followed by other different kinds of rocks which existed after each divine spoken word. The Creator-God turned the other direction, spoke to the rocks and then smashed the rocks with the right hand. The rocks were split into pieces and spread [in] the other direction. Out of this mighty act, the earth, sea and all the universe was formed....

One other version of the creation myth starts with *Leai* (nothingness or endlessness). There was only nothingness, into which *Nanamu* (smell), *Efuefu/Eleele* (dust or soil), *Ao* (clouds), *Savili* (wind), and *Asu* (smoke) all emerged and filled the vacuum. Smoke turned into clouds, while earth became rocks. The clouds and the winds interacted and produced *Puao* (vapors). As Creator-God was covered by the clouds, *Masina* (moon), *La* (sun), *Sami* (sea) and *Vai* ([fresh]water) were created. After a devastating catastrophe, the moon and the sun escaped to the heavens, while rocks endured to revolt against the sea. Through the splashing of the sea waters against the rocks, a fire

Western Samoan versions of creation

Mythical versions of the western islands acknowledge Tagaloa as the Creator and Giver of life. This creative principle who was inhabiting the underworld was active in shaping the earth and other forms of life. The underworld Gods created the world by pushing up materials from the bottom of the deep ocean to form the whole cosmos. For instance, one creation myth features the existence of Samoa as a product of the mighty action of the God Fee (Octopus), the ruler of the underworld. Fee, upon the command of Tagaloa to fulfil Tuli's request for a resting place under the heavens,[9] pulled up a huge rock from the bottom of the ocean. The rock was crushed by the waves of the sea and gradually divided into pieces, forming the group of islands of Samoa.

Werner von Bülow presents another version that was told by an old Samoan chief who resided on the island of Savaii. The narrative begins with the birth of Tagaloa from eternal or pre-existent materials ([Ger] *Urstoffe*). Tagaloa had a child, and both were recognized to have authority over all the earth. Creator-God and the child one day engaged themselves in bonito fishing. While Tagaloa was advancing from a distance, God heard the child calling that a fish had eaten his fishhook.[10] Tagaloa ordered him to hook it up. The object was declared as a newly found homeland, which was considered as the whole world....

The founding of the homeland was followed by the formation of the whole cosmos through a sequence of

Eastern Samoan versions of creation
(continued)

broke out. And through an intimate relationship of the waters and fire, the land, Samoa, came into existence. (Tofaeono 2000, 176–178)

Western Samoan versions of creation
(continued)

forceful interactions between...rocks of various sorts. As a result of the conflicts between different types of rocks, *eleele* (soil) existed, which was...defeated by *maa talanoa* (talking rock) that was covered by *mutia* (grass). The process continued with the growth of trees and plants, followed by the existence of animals and sea creatures. The existence of other parts of the created order was without divine command. The natural laws became effectively in action after the incidental act of the divine when the fish was hooked up. (Tofaeono 2000, 178–179)

The different versions resonate with each other but, as Tofaeono observed, take different perspectives on the metaphorical movement of creation. The eastern myths have a "vertical dimension," and God/Tagaloa acts individually to create; the western myths, in comparison, focus on "the lateral dimension and creation from below," with "underworld" deities (in the example quoted, the octopus god) acting in relationship with Tagaloa as part of creation (Tofaeono 2000, 177–178).

Tofaeono acknowledged that the Samoan myths have probably been influenced by Judeo-Christian ones (2000, 231). But he emphasized points of distinction, too, such as the fact that Tagaloa did not speak the world into existence but instead "natural laws...brought forth the order of everything" and that, whereas Genesis describes God creating order out of chaos, in Samoan myth, "chaos itself worked out/arranged order from within itself" (2000, 231; italics removed). Other points of distinction are less abstract, such as the fact that the first humans, in Samoan myth, were not humans like Adam and Eve but rather two earthworms or maggots (2000, 180, 232).[11]

In Tofaeono's understanding, Sāmoa before Christianity was literally Edenic: there was a "centrality of a reverence for and sustainability of nature. The climate was generally healthy and comfortable, and the natural rhythm of life was harmoniously woven into a pattern that perpetuated, restored and sustained the balance of life-supporting systems. The way in which Samoans viewed, experienced and related to the world could be seen as an equivalent of Eden before the Fall of humankind." Sāmoa cannot make this claim alone, however. As Tofaeono went on to argue, Eden is "the place where we find life in and with God in its fullness," and thus can be anywhere (2000, 90, 293). But Tofaeono's writing, while cultivating images of Oceania as a violated Eden, is not garden-variety romanticism. A decade after the publication of his book, his commitment to ecological holism led him to critique a statement on climate change authored by Pacific church leaders, the Moana Declaration (World Council of Churches 2009). The Moana Declaration lists twelve points needing urgent attention, most of them related to plans for resettling affected people. Tofaeono's critique is that the document is anthropocentric, focusing on human rights and needs, but "human rights... [should be] considered equal to the rights of any living species" (2010, 81).[12]

The historical irony for Sāmoa, as Tofaeono presented it, is that an inherently unified place was conceptually and practically broken up by those who should have been most committed to unity—namely, Christian missionaries. In Tofaeono's view, the missionaries acted as they did for two reasons. First, they believed in a sovereign Jehovah who was distinct from any Samoan deity or deities. Second, they viewed natural resources as commodifiable private property (2000, 122). For Tofaeono, then, the legacy of Christian missionaries' work in Sāmoa includes an overemphasis on salvation at the expense of creation, an image of God as a male figure who is existentially separate from His creation, an altered social order with destructive new ideas about the natural order, and resulting land alienation, pollution, and other violations of the seascape and landscape (see also White 1967). In his view, Christian missionaries made Sāmoa less Christian. Before the missionaries arrived, Samoans already knew the Gospel, already knew the spirit of Christ, and revered creation.

This critique, which would discomfit most systematic theologians, is nonetheless a deeply Christian one. Tofaeono's understanding of Christ is based on a "cosmic Christ" model, in which, as Jaroslav Pelikan put it, Christ is "the foundation for the very structure of the universe and the belief that 'the Logos of God is in the whole universe'.... The Creator could be described as 'the one who is...,' while creatures had their being by derivation from the Creator and participation in the Creator and they could not 'be of themselves' " (Pelikan 1985, 66).[13] For Tofaeono, the Trinity is grounded not in masculine Fatherhood but in relationality itself. His point, as I understand it, is that God-as-Trinity does not relate only to a three-part Godself but to everything in the universe.[14]

Tofaeono used two Samoan terms and concepts to pull everything together—to argue that the universe is a self-creating, unified ecological network and that pre-Christian Samoans got some things resoundingly right that European missionaries got disturbingly wrong. One is ʻāiga. Its usual definition is "a family and a household community in blood, close or distant relations.... Each family unit is a self-sustaining economic group... [working] for the common good of the whole family" (Tofaeono 2000, 30–31). For Tofaeono, the family and household are intrinsically connected to the whole universe: "*aiga* constitutes the wholeness of Samoan life. It has bonded the divine and the ordinary into a synthesis of existence.... In [an]... extensive sense, *aiga* incorporates the communal ties with the Gods, the ancestors, as well as the divine heritages, the sea, land, and the sky" (2000, 30–31). To echo Muir, Tofaeono picked out family and found it hitched to everything: divinity, ancestry, community, and all the natural world. In the ancient Samoan world as Tofaeono interpreted it, everything was in kinship with everything. He connected the idea of a triune God with a Samoan phrase, "'Āiga o Atua ma le Atua o 'Āiga," which he translated as "Household of God and God of the Household," with the household being the whole universe and the distinction between God's immanence and transcendence collapsed (Tofaeono 2000, 235–251).

The second Samoan term that lends its conceptual gravity to Tofaeono's argument is *mana,* which I discuss in chapter 3 as an emblem of Oceanic spiritual power. Tofaeono wrote of an inexhaustible "energy which is known as Christ, the *mana* of God," a description echoed by Tuwere and by Seresese Vaaimamao (Tofaeono 2000, 253; Tuwere 2002, 158–169; Vaaimamao 1990). But recall that for Tofaeono, Christ is not limited to Jesus. Tagaloa embodies divine mana as well. Indeed, in pre-Christian Sāmoa, "the possessor of all mana was Tagaloa," who shared it with other beings, including humans (notably, chiefs) as well as "trees, stones, animals and fish" that had divine associations (Tofaeono 2000, 170). Tagaloa is thus connected to the whole universe in a way that Jesus, understood as a human male individual, is not. This is why it is crucial, in order to understand Tofaeono's theology, to bear in mind what he told his class at Kanana Fou: "We have to draw a very clear line between Gospel and Christianity."[15]

I have spent many paragraphs discussing Tofaeono's work because I find it among the most stimulating in Pacific contextual theology, especially for the way it directly confronts the question of indigenous divinity.[16] But it must be noted that Tofaeono is not the only Samoan theologian to have written about Tagaloa in order to develop a Christian theology. Methodist Lalomilo Kamu said he was convinced that Tagaloa and Jehovah are "essentially the same" (Kamu 1996, 31; see also Efi 2014). Tele'a Faleali'i, whose symbolic connection of kava to both Eucharist and baptism I discuss in chapter 3, asserted: "God has been present in Samoa from the dawn of its history.... So if God's revelation is through creation, and culture is his means of communicating with his people, it logically follows... that God could communicate with the Samoan people through the medium of the [kava] ceremony" (Faleali'i 1998, 2–3). The God recognizable to pre-Christian Samoans, he pointed out, was Tagaloa. Thus a truly Christian exploration of Christ and culture, and creation and salvation, should lead Samoans on the ritual path of kava ceremonies to take them back to an original apprehension of God's spirit as Tagaloa.

Conclusion
Culture, Dialogue, and the Divine

Tongan Catholic theologian Keiti Ann Kanongata'a once told a funny story about trying to buy bananas in Germany. The tale came at the beginning of a talk, later published in the *Pacific Journal of Theology*, on why contextual theology matters:

> When I told the lady at the shop what I wanted, green bananas, she replied, "One does not buy green bananas." I told her that I want to buy the green bananas because I eat them. She then quickly replied, "One does not eat green bananas." She then picked up a ripe banana to show me that this is the banana to eat, not green bananas! I did not want to give up as I really wanted to eat green bananas so with the best German sentence I could put together, I said, "Ich komme aus dem land die Banane" [I come from the land of bananas] but the German lady...dismissed me saying, "das macht nichts" [It makes no difference]! One does not eat green bananas! (Kanongata'a 2002, 21–22)

From Coconut Theology to the land of bananas, much Oceanic contextual theology has a playful aspect to it. The philosophy is always serious, but the expression is rarely ponderous. Her tale is lighthearted, but Kanongata'a was pointing to the difficulty of dialogue, a complex topic that is present in each of this book's chapters. In this concluding chapter, I reconsider dialogue and its possibilities one more time, asking about the potential for engagement between anthropology and theology.

Dialogues about Culture, God, and Otherness

In his bachelor of divinity thesis, Ama'amalele Tofaeono pointed to a matter confronting Samoan churches. "At present, ecumenism is a challenge to the life of the church in Samoa," he explained. "People's religiosity is confined to denominationalism and sectarianism. Ecumenical spirit is lacking. There is thus a great need to break down the barriers created by denominational rivalry and confess and proclaim Jesus Christ as the Lord, Savior and Owner of the whole Creation. Churches in Samoa need DIALOGUE!" (Tofaeono 1993, 115–116).

Church rivalry is just one issue that Christians in Oceania face.[1] Other pressing matters include local and national conflicts, the reconfiguration of indigenous identity in sovereign nation-states run by indigenous elites, liberal demands for freedom and equality in conservative societies, and the formulation of effective responses to climate change. As Tofaeono's statement makes clear, dialogue is the solution—or at least the first step. But the invocation of dialogue as an ideal, as this book suggests, must be examined critically for several reasons.

One reason is that not all speakers who insist on dialogue really want it to happen. Annelise Riles described the situation of nongovernmental organization (NGO) networks in Fiji who, as she put it, gain their effectiveness through self-description (2000). For example, NGO leaders see a necessary part of their work as engaging with the "grassroots"; but actually engaging with the grassroots—people outside of the network—would entail the promiscuous proliferation of ties that would undercut the role and position of NGO leaders. "Indeed, the problem for networkers," Riles noted, "was not so much how to expand connections as how to keep connections from expanding sui generis; how to stop the flow of information, resources, and commitments; and how to close the circle when all of their public rhetoric centered around 'keeping in touch,' 'soliciting your views,' or 'reaching out.'" Or, as one Fijian woman put it bluntly, "I don't believe in diplomacy if the facts need to be shared" (Riles 2000, 55). In a less amusing way, Fiji's coup-installed government of the mid- and late-2000s called for dialogue even as it was evident that dialogue was precisely what it wanted to shut down (Tomlinson 2014b, 92–117; 2017; see also Tomlinson and Millie 2017).

Another reason why calls for dialogue must be scrutinized critically is that the meaning of "dialogue" is not always clear. "Dialogue," like "culture," can slip and shift into many positions, and it often seems to serve primarily as an index of group values. In her analysis of neoliberal discourse, Bonnie Urciuoli examined such terms as "communication," "teamwork," and "leadership" and noted that they are "strategically deployable shifters," terms with vague denotational meaning that display "their users' alignment with corporate values" (2008, 213; see Silverstein 1976 for the classic argument about shifters). Similarly, invocations of dialogue sometimes seem mainly to indicate a topic's importance for theologians and each author's desire to be heard addressing it.

I do not mean to present a cynical view of dialogue in general. I only mean to suggest that calls for dialogue can function in many ways, just one of which is the actual initiation of a give-and-take, back-and-forth conversation in which people take up each other's words and ideas. In the case of my research on contextual theology, the theologians I met were more than willing to have conversations with me, and I was invited to explain my research at each of my field sites, so there was genuinely collaborative engagement. This book could not have taken shape without it. And because I have looked so intensely at contextual theologians' writings, including their theses and dissertations, the obvious point must be made that most acts of writing are invitations to respond, whether or not that invitation is taken up.

In concluding this book, therefore, I want to keep the focus on dialogue. As I suggest in the preceding chapters, it is a method, value, and ideal all at once, but how it really works in any specific context is a complicated question. Simply on a human-to-human level, there can seem to be a "miraculous co-ordination of perspectives...required for satisfactory communication" (Gumperz and Levinson 1996, 11). Add contextual theology into this mix, and the question gains new dimensions. How should humans speak and listen to other humans about God when their human differences are vividly apparent and God, semiotically speaking, is the ultimate moving target? What does it mean to say that God speaks, and how should this claim be understood in relation to claims that God reveals and inspires? (Wolterstorff 1995). These can be anthropological and historical questions as well as theological and philosophical ones, and to answer them satisfactorily, scholars from any field should clarify the terms—not only what we mean by "God" and what we mean by "human" but also what we mean by "dialogue."

I argue in this book that culture is the key concept with which Pacific contextual theologians have grounded their calls for dialogue. As the other chapters show, contextual theologians have established a distinct intellectual space by arguing that God's omnipresence works through culture's specificity. The Bible must be made more Samoan. Polynesian women should weave their wisdom against patriarchal cloth. The Pacific Way is the way of storytelling, mana, and kava ceremonies, and relationships with the ocean define Pacific Islanders' history and identity while connecting the islands with all of humanity.

It might seem obvious that the topic of culture can be a firm basis for dialogue between anthropologists and theologians. But a problem immediately presents itself: the models and definitions of culture that contextual theologians have worked with, as I observe in the introduction, are often structural functionalist and cognitivist. They describe location, stability, integrity, and reliable transmission. Few anthropologists are likely to accept these characterizations of culture anymore. Indeed, many anthropologists have ceased to see the culture concept as firm enough to explain anything or to resist dissolution in modern conditions. In other words, although some anthropologists (myself included) still think that culture is worth theorizing critically, others see it as a dead category—anthropology's vampire, sucking the life out of serious analysis.

The fact that anthropologists disagree profoundly on how to think about culture but would largely be united in disagreeing with contextual theologians' treatment of it is, of course, no reason to avoid dialogue about it. Indeed, spaces of shared difference can spark new insights about what goes unsaid and what has to be articulated explicitly. In her analysis of how Samoan migrants in the United States and New Zealand are turned into "culture bearers," Ilana Gershon effectively flipped the expectations of an older school of culture theory: rather than culture being a totalizing ground of difference, she argued, people's own reflexive social analysis identifies differences as "cultural" in particular contexts, such as when government bureaucrats see their policies as part of an acultural system and Samoan migrants' practices as cultural deviations (2012). Her work, and the work of contextual theologians who have critically acknowledged the problems of treating culture as a stable object or pure and unified thing, such as Jione Havea, Ama'amalele Tofaeono, and Nāsili Vaka'uta, can motivate fresh dialogues on topics such as "how the acultural is constructed" and what the consequences of such constructions are (Gershon 2012, 167).

Within recent anthropological scholarship, the most influential attempt to engage with theology has been that of Joel Robbins (see especially Robbins 2006, 2013a, 2013b). Robbins has been developing the argument that anthropologists can gain insight and motivation from theological approaches to otherness—to alterity, to grounding our investigations and analyses in the warrant that social difference is deep and real and worth thinking about critically (Robbins 2006; compare Tuwere 2002, 193–194). In anthropology's heyday of influence in the 1960s and 1970s, Robbins observed, the idea of difference was persuasive and attractive, as reflected in David Schneider's aphorism from 1967 that "one of the fundamental fantasies of anthropology is that somewhere there must be a life really worth living" (Schneider quoted in Robbins 2006, 292). Most Christian theologians, obviously, share a commitment to fundamental otherness at the level of religious faith: the Christian must be different from the non-Christian in order for Christian theology to make sense. If theology is "God-talk," then this is a conversation that some will join and others will not. But to a significant extent, anthropology has lost its certainty that otherness matters. Witness the death of the culture concept as a locus of theory as at least partial evidence of this loss, and new writings on ontology as attempts at partial recuperation.[2]

Robbins described how in the 1980s and 1990s, the longstanding anthropological engagement with the figure of the other shifted toward an engagement with the "suffering subject," the human on whom violence is inflicted. Trauma was identified as a key element of what it means to be human. Scholars could connect with peoples they studied through the practice of empathy rather than the concept of culture. As Robbins put it, "When trauma became universal, when it came to define a humanity without borders . . . anthropologists found a foundation for their science that allowed them to dispense with the notion of the other completely" (2013a, 454). If the verb "othering" had existed in the 1960s and 1970s, it would have been aspirational (groovy, man!), but by the 1980s and 1990s there was no dirtier word in anthropology, and attending to suffering seemed, ironically, to be the way forward for a more vibrant anthropology.

For Robbins, recapturing anthropology's commitment to otherness will help anthropologists avoid being reduced to "serving as witnesses to the horror of the world" (2006, 292) and inspire new research on topics such as value, morality, well-being, care, change, and hope (2013a)—topics of universal importance that call for a fresh appreciation of the depth of cultural diversity, a robust understanding of otherness that neither demonizes it nor refuses it with soft ethnocentrism. Such a constellation of projects, Robbins wrote, would constitute an "anthropology of the good" (2013a). I hope this book will be seen as an attempt at such a venture.[3]

Bringing together questions of dialogue and difference can, of course, bring one back to questions of culture. For example, Greg Urban has observed how older models of culture as something acquired are monologic in the sense that they portray a group consensus being transmitted smoothly over the years (2017). More recent understandings of culture are dialogic in M M Bakhtin's sense, with culture configured as something people respond to with multiple and often discordant voices. Urban urged a rapprochement between these views, a new vision of culture as something whose replication has both monologic and dialogic aspects.

Any understanding of otherness, difference, and dialogue can benefit by engagement with Bakhtin's writings on dialogism (especially Bakhtin 1981, 1984). For Bakhtin, discourse is a heteroglossic thing, the product of multiple voices and positions being present in any single utterance. When you speak, you do so in response to what you have heard in the past and in expectation of how others will respond in the future. His analytical and philosophical vision went further than discourse alone, as he saw dialogism as the mechanism of self-formation, the foundationally interactive relationship by which any human becomes a subject (Holquist 1990). But Bakhtin's writings have appealed especially to scholars examining the composition of texts, whether those scholars are anthropologists studying ritual language or biblical scholars analyzing scripture. Indeed, Tongan Methodist theologian Vaka'uta, whose work I discuss in chapter 1, originally planned to write his dissertation in theology with Bakhtin as a main referent, and several years before his doctoral research he had already published a Bakhtinian article in the *Pacific Journal of Theology* (Vaka'uta 1998).[4] In graduate school he was encouraged to change his focus and develop an explicitly Tongan hermeneutic, and did so, but in a nicely Bakhtinian touch, Vaka'uta's early use of Bakhtin has in turn been taken up and cited by at least two other Pacific theologians (Mariota 2012; Tupu 2012).

Scholarship on dialogism, I suggest, is sharpened and clarified to the extent that it includes critical appreciation of the practicalities of dialogue—in the context of this book, *talanoa* or conversation. The very fact that contextual theologians, and many anthropologists, insist on the value of dialogue means it is worth paying close attention to. An urgent task of any interdisciplinary engagement is to begin by asking what we mean by dialogue, who we expect to engage in it, and what kinds of consequences we allow, expect, and try to produce.

When God-Talk Talks Back

Here, crucially, we come to a question that has murmured in these pages but not yet found full voice: the question of religious faith and anthropology's perceived secularism. In arguing that anthropology can transform itself by drawing on theological appreciation of otherness, Robbins added that this need not involve religious faith: anthropologists ought "to recommit ourselves to finding real otherness in the world, not to commit ourselves to Christianity" (2006, 292). Some anthropologists have argued, however, that religious identity does and should generate its own theoretical insights (eg, Howell 2007; Priest 2000, 2001; see also Luhrmann 2012). For the record, I was baptized Catholic and am not an atheist, but I have never regularly attended Christian churches except during fieldwork. When asked during research about my religious identity, I admitted that I struggled with faith. This answer always received a positive and generous reply from the Christian theologians I was hanging out with, who were, after all, comfortable with the idea of doubt, the force of intellectual passion, and the conviction that whether or not I knew it, God was part of my project. Indeed, Brian Howell has pointed out that even an avowedly secular anthropologist writing in a secular vein on Christianity might be read by Christians as having produced a text that reveals God working in the world (pers comm, Nov 2016).

Matthew Engelke has argued for a specifically secular anthropological viewpoint—"I don't want to do Christian anthropology, not me," he emphasized—and he did so in order to underscore the point that dialogue can create new incommensurabilities: "The irreducible difference between anthropology and theology, between their distinct descriptive and normative workings, has value because it prevents the collapse of registers. The human sciences are better off with others. I'm not sure if this amounts to letting a thousand flowers bloom, but it does suggest that the point of dialogues or exchanges or shared projects between theologians and anthropologists might be most useful when they don't entirely work" (Engelke 2014, 6–7).

Similarly, Jon Bialecki suggested that although engagement between anthropology and theology might transform each discipline, it would not turn one into the other, and it might even reveal ways "to use incommensurability productively" (Bialecki in press; see also Keane 2013). Observing that anthropology and theology have their own ontological groundings, he pointed out that any really transformative interchange must make use of a third term. As a third term for an engagement between anthropology and theology, he proposed "people engaging in religion," something "with which [the disciplines] have a shared relation" articulated with "second-order relation[s] with things such as God, ritual, and ethics" (Bialecki 2018, 165) Following Bialecki's approach, the approach I have taken in the previous chapters could be recast as the argument that engagement itself is the generative problem we share (see also Bialecki 2012, 2017).

The arguments of Robbins, Engelke, and Bialecki add another dimension to a critical investigation of dialogue. Not only is dialogue difficult to start and sustain, not only do some calls for dialogue mask monologic intentions, and not only is the meaning of "dialogue" often opaque; in addition to all of this, dialogue can clarify difference and perhaps motivate projects of difference making rather than unification. In some ways, the pairing of anthropology and theology—unlike, say, anthropology and history or theology and philosophy—is a deliberately uncomfortable and "awkward" one (Robbins 2006, 2013b). As Stephen D Glazier put it, "Bringing theology and anthropology together might be compared to gift wrapping an elephant. No matter how much paper one uses, it still looks like an elephant. To make matters even more difficult, elephants are not fond of being gift wrapped and are able to put up considerable resistance" (2000, 423). His point, amusingly phrased as it is, is its own elephant in the room: we are, of course, talking not about elephants but about God. (I am bracketing the question of Ganesh here.)

Who wants to talk with God? Among many possible answers: Christians do. Theologians do. Some anthropologists do because of their personal faith, Christian or otherwise, or the faith of those they study. But the argument that anthropology is a project of understanding God will founder unless one configures anthropology as a necessarily religious project—something many anthropologists would decisively resist. This kind of configuration, needless to say, is automatic for most theologians, who see their field (in the words of St Anselm) as "faith seeking understanding" and understanding as a product of dialogue.[5] Moreli Niuatoa, writing about Jesus, said, "Every time I read my Samoan Bible I can hear him speaking back to me in Samoan" (2018, 30).

Contextual theology, according to Tevita T M Puloka, is ultimately a dialogue with God: "Contextualization[,] as a theological methodology, is a natural growth that takes both the gospel and the context into the process of announcing the reign of God and the response of the people. It is thus a responsive dialogue between God and God's people" (2005, 16). Again, the nature of this dialogue must be analyzed. As Engelke pointed out, "Theologians are often writing about how people *should* live; anthropologists write about how people *do* live" (2014; emphases in original; see also Fountain, Hynd, and Tan 2018; Tomlinson 2015a). If, following Puloka, God's reign is announced, what is the range of possible responses that people can make, and to whom—to God, to other Tongans, to other people of Oceania? To nosy anthropologists? To all of humanity?

My own understanding is that most contextual theologians want to speak with people about God so that God can speak to people. Whether this shift from *speaking with* to *speaking to* constitutes a shift from dialogue to monologue is an open question. What makes contextual theology different from other kinds of theology is that its practitioners do this by speaking in idioms marked as cultural—as indigenous, as Fijian, Samoan, Tongan, Oceanian, and so forth. Many anthropologists would embrace the idea that speaking in idioms marked as cultural—or at least marked as socially different, as something that could have been otherwise—is a key part of our method. When it comes to religious commitment, one can argue plausibly that becoming Christian is at least partly a matter of learning the language and narratives of faith, sacrifice, and destiny (Harding 2000). My point, however, is that although anthropological dialogues can become complicated—we want to speak with our field interlocutors, our fellow anthropologists, and scholars across disciplines—in contextual theology there is always another partner in the conversation.

The literary critic James Wood wrote that "theology is always striving to be an ultimacy" (2015, 94), which seems to be another way of saying that when you include God in dialogue, the dialogue becomes complete. This claim, perhaps, underpins the confidence that Robbins observed in theological treatments of otherness. But isn't anthropology, in its own way, striving to be an ultimacy? When we try to understand others on their own terms and thereby develop new understandings of ourselves, don't we achieve a wholeness that we realize is lacking in most nonanthropological treatments of social action?

*   *   *

Whenever I think of my original fieldwork in Kadavu, Fiji, one moment always returns to me as an especially resonant and uplifting one. It took place at a kava session, which might not be surprising because so many things take place at kava sessions and kava sessions take place every day. But this moment was at the end of a session. At such times, all of the people seated near the bowl, including the mixer and cupbearer, clap together in a five-pulse rhythm. In Fiji, you clap with your hands cupped crosswise, producing a deep and resonant sound. And if you have spent decades farming and fishing as many Kadavuans have, you can produce an especially impressive clap. This was a night like any other, but for some reason, this is the instant I will always remember, with bodies sitting cross-legged on the mat, all of us together in the late hours in a small house whose corrugated iron walls added extra resonance to handclaps that took on the weight of cannon shots. Five claps and finished: the kava was empty, the night was over, and we were all together in a way that could borrow a page from social theory but was turned toward something bigger—human, divine—in a moment that had everything to do with both culture and ultimacy.

Notes

Introduction

1. In his 1992 textbook, Bevans offered five models for practicing contextual theology. He called them "translation" (identifying a Christian concept that transcends culture and figuring out how to make it meaningful in local cultural terms); "anthropological" (valuing a particular cultural identity as divinely contoured and seeking ways to develop people's spirituality by drawing primarily on local traditions); "praxis" (taking action as part of social transformation); "synthetic" (dialectically bringing together parts of these models); and "transcendental" (practicing intensified self-reflection in order to discover a subjectively true reality). Besides being cited by numerous scholars, Bevans's book was the main text for two undergraduate courses during my research: Theology 100 ("Beginning Theology in Aotearoa New Zealand"), coordinated by Helen Bergin at the University of Auckland in 2013, and Theology and Ethics 401 ("Contextual Theology in Oceania"), run by Uesile Tupu at Piula in 2015. The Auckland course had more than thirty students, including students from South Africa, Japan, France, Tonga, and Fiji as well as New Zealand. All nine students in the Piula course (required for fourth-year students) were Samoans.

2. The first use of the term "contextualization" for theology is generally attributed to Shoki Coe (Chang Hui Hwang), a Taiwanese theologian, who delivered a paper on the topic at a World Council of Churches meeting in 1972 (Wheeler 2002; see also Chang 2018).

3. Volker Küster grouped contextual theologies of the "Third World" (a term, he noted, adopted by the Ecumenical Association of Third World Theologians) into two main schools, one oriented toward liberation and the other toward "inculturation and dialogue" (2010, 1n3, 4–5). His distinction is overdrawn, ignoring the fuzzed and repeatedly crossed boundaries between these categories, but it serves nonetheless as a useful starting point for classifying the theologies Te Paa mentioned. For Küster, liberationist theologies included such movements as liberation theology proper (a Marx-inflected movement for social justice associated most strongly with the Peruvian Catholic Gustavo Gutiérrez); Black theology as developed by South Africans and African Americans; *dalit* theology focused on India's "untouchable" caste; and Korea's similarly subaltern *minjung* theology. He did not discuss theologies informed by queerness, but presumably they would be included in this group. He characterized inculturation and dialogue-focused theologies as intentionally inclusive: "Inculturation theologies give Christian faith a local shape

and partly integrate elements of other religions as well, whereas dialogue theologies involve them in conversation" (Küster 2010, 5). Māori, African, coconut, and water buffalo theologies (the last of these a creation of the Japanese theologian Kosuke Koyama based on his experiences as a missionary in Thailand) would be counted as both inculturationist and dialogic by these criteria.

4. I have gathered Boseto's biographical details from Forman 2005, 116; Swain and Trompf 1995, 213; and National Parliament of Solomon Islands 2007.

5. Havea and Tuilovoni, as well as Lalomilo Kamu from Sāmoa, received their BD degrees from Drew University in New Jersey in the 1950s and 1960s (all three were Methodists, and Drew was originally established as a Methodist seminary)—a considerable distinction at a time when few scholars from Oceania studied overseas. Tuilovoni received his BD degree in 1950, Havea in 1955, and Kamu in 1963. My thanks to the staff of the Drew University Archives for providing this information. Tuilovoni went on to obtain a master of sacred theology degree from Union Theological Seminary in 1962.

6. In an interview, he mentioned another of the coconut's characteristics: "When it falls, it rolls to the lowest level; it doesn't stop where it falls, it goes to the lowest level, and that's what you call evangelism" (S Havea quoted in Ernst 1994, 286).

7. For the early development of Havea's ideas for a Pacific-focused theology, see S Havea 1977, 1982; *Mission Review* 1985. See also Havea's contribution to a "theological consultation" held in Suva in 1985 (S Havea 1986). At that event, his paper was read by one of his sons, Tevita K Havea, who would later be the general manager of PTC while I was there. One of its points was that the Good News of Christ came to all the world in Jesus, not only the lands he was in; thus "this Good News was already present before missionaries came to the Pacific" (S Havea 1986, 22). Another point was that "the coconut is more relevant than the bread and wine" for Holy Communion in Oceania, a suggestion I return to in chapter 3. A plenary discussion followed, with various speakers offering comments on Havea's theology. Some were lighthearted: Itubwa Amram from Nauru noted that eating coconuts is "very bad for diabetics"; Oka Fauolo, principal of Malua Theological College in Sāmoa, wrote that "Dr Havea is not wanting us to 'over-coconut' Christian theology, but just to 'coconut' it enough." Others had more critical gravity: Helmut Horndash from the Melanesian Association of Theological Schools in Lae, Papua New Guinea, criticized the idea that the Good News reached Oceania before the missionaries arrived, and Etuale Lealofi from American Sāmoa commented, "Deep down I have an uneasy feeling.... It is all very well to say 'If Christ had been born in the Pacific he would have done so and so.' The fact is, he was not. He was born into a certain culture at a certain time in history. The bread and wine belong to that tradition, and we cannot do away with this part of our heritage. The coconut is a beautiful illustration, but we cannot really use it as a substitute" (PCC, PTC, and SPATS 1986, 25–27; italics deleted).

Another criticism of Coconut Theology is that it is a symbol rather than a fully developed theology—a metaphor stuck at the level of metaphor. One author who has made this criticism, Randall Prior, has also faulted Coconut Theology for not having a political dimension. Or rather, if Coconut Theology has a political dimension, he noted, it is a top-heavy one: "So far, Coconut theology has emerged from a small minority of chiefly figures in the Pacific churches"; it has not "arisen from the struggles of the people in their own hope for the Kingdom" of God, and it "has done little to touch the wider church at the parish level or to address itself to the pressing social issues facing the Pacific" (Prior 1993, 39). Prior's criticisms are valid, but the key question about Coconut Theology, I suggest, is not whether it is fully developed or whether Oceanic discourse and politics should be expected to follow a pre-set pattern of liberation (however defined), but rather what it accomplished in establishing a new field of scholarship. The symbol can be critiqued, but its establishment meant that later scholars had a recognized field in which to begin developing more complex work (Uriam 1999, 145–161; see also Uriam and Gardner 2018).

8. Contextual theology is a close cousin of studies of "inculturation," a term used by many Catholic theologians (see Angrosino 1994). Bevans, himself a Catholic, argued that "contextualization" is a better term than "inculturation" (as well as "indigenization" and "incarnation of the gospel") for making "culture…understood in more dynamic, flexible ways and…not as closed and self-contained, but as open and able to be enriched by an encounter with other cultures and movements" (1992, 21–22). Lucien Legrand, who endorsed "inculturation" as a cultural-theological process, criticized the term for (among other reasons) the way it ironically thwarts dialogue with anthropology, which does not include "inculturation" within its "word stock" (2000, xi–xvii, xii). On "indigenization" in Pacific theology, note Sione 'Amanaki Havea's criticism: "Contextualisation is a term that goes beyond indigenisation. Indigenisation refers to cultures, history and customs, that grow out of the local soil. Contextualisation refers to that which grows out of the local soil *and* also to current sociological, political, and environmental events of the past, present and even of the future" (1986, 21).

9. He went on to suggest that *fa'asāmoa* might be understood in terms of Paul Tillich's "ultimate concern" (Tillich 1959).

10. Kamu, explaining "why the Samoan people are so tenaciously sensitive about their culture," argued that it is because culture is seen as divinely given: "While the general concepts of culture are attributed to human endeavour, the Samoans insist that their culture is of divine origin. This concept is consistent with their belief in God as their Creator. According to the people, their culture is not exclusively a human achievement because its origin was from god Tagaloa; it was he who gave them direction for organising and living life." Kamu's own understanding was nuanced: "The Gospel is not culture and culture is not the Gospel. However…one can conclude that the Gospel is culturally presented and it is culturally received" (1996, 36, 179).

11. Mataolemu is the peak of a volcano on Savai'i, Sāmoa's largest island (Efi 2014, 38).

12. Those who speak on behalf of chiefs are differently positioned in each national tradition. In Fiji, those who speak for chiefs are called *matanivanua*, which is often translated as "herald" (see, eg, Arno 1990, 254), and can also be called a "*vanua*'s representative," with *vanua* meaning both the people within a chiefdom and the chiefdom's territory. The *matanivanua* fills a mediating position between chiefs and the people of the chiefdom, which is why Tuwere has argued that Jesus, as the mediator between God and humanity, is the "supreme *matanivanua*" (2002, 106). In Sāmoa, orators *(tulāfale)* are titleholders along with high chiefs (*ali'i;* the term for both kinds of titleholder is *matai,* often translated as "chiefs"; see Tcherkézoff 2000 for a historical analysis of the terminology). In Tonga, the titles of orators, *matāpule* (sometimes called "ceremonial attendants" in English; see, eg, Marcus 1980b, 442),

"have never been considered of chiefly status...but they are a means by which individuals, unmarked by any claims to *'eiki* [chiefly] status, can be integrated indirectly into the chiefly system" (Marcus 1980a, 58–59).

These clarifications bypass the larger issue of what makes a chief a chief in modern Oceania; a good starting point for addressing this complex topic is the collection of essays in White and Lindstrom 1997.

13. The BD program was not run between 2006 and 2009 because of low demand. When the master of theology degree program was established in 1987, it was only for Church history, but concentrations were soon added in biblical studies (1989) and ministry and theology (1992). The PhD program began in 2004 as a partnership with Charles Sturt University of Australia but was dissolved in 2008, after which PTC began its own PhD program. On these developments, as well as PTC's programs in distance learning and women's fellowship development, the mission program called God's Pacific People, and the sociologist Manfred Ernst's Institute for Research and Social Analysis at PTC, see Nokise 2015, 33–54.

14. The master's degree program included specializations in biblical studies, Christian thought and history, moral and practical theology, practical theology, and theology proper. For these statistics, I gratefully acknowledge the registrar of the University of Auckland, Adrienne Cleland.

15. Independent Sāmoa (formerly Western Sāmoa) and American Sāmoa are historically, culturally, and linguistically unified, although they are politically separate. Sāmoa gained its independence from New Zealand in 1962. Many Samoans migrate to New Zealand for work and education. American Sāmoa, a short distance to the southeast, is a territory of the United States like Puerto Rico or Guam. The islands are separated by the international dateline, so today in Sāmoa is yesterday in American Sāmoa. Sāmoa has its own currency, drives on the left-hand side of the road, and is mad about rugby; American Sāmoa uses the US dollar, drives on the right-hand side of the road, and enjoys rugby but shows more interest in American football, with cars and pickup trucks emblazoned with team logos, especially those of the San Francisco 49ers and Seattle Seahawks. In both places, the usual language of daily interaction is Samoan.

16. This history is published on the school's website (Kanana Fou Theological Seminary 2014). The diploma of theology has been replaced by a certificate in theological study (Kanana Fou Theological Seminary 2016).

17. The Methodists had established a training institution at Satupaitea on Savai'i four years earlier, but war forced a move, and the present site next to Lufilufi was chosen partly because of its political importance (Fa'alafi 1994, 2005; Garrett 1982, 129).

18. Kanana Fou also has *'auā'iga*, and there the English term "parish" is used as an equivalent. Rather than work together every day, the *'auā'iga* at Kanana Fou were generally scheduled to meet on Wednesday afternoons and occasionally for Sunday lunches after church *(to'ona'i)*. As at Piula, those at Kanana Fou are meant to be pastoral groups as well as working units, so if a student or student's spouse has a problem, he or she should be able to go to the mother and father (the faculty member and his wife) leading the *'auā'iga*.

19. For a historical analysis of physical labor at Pacific theological schools, see Uriam 2005.

20. At Piula, promising students are chosen by the faculty to go on to the BD program after completing the four-year diploma. A student cannot simply choose to pursue the BD degree on his own. The credential that a student receives after

four years of study at Piula is called a certificate if his grade point average is below 65 and a diploma if it is above 65. Only diploma students can go on for the BD degree, which requires two additional years of study, although the fourth year of the diploma counts as the first year of BD study. Piula established its BD program in September 1998 (M Maliko 2009, 86). At Kanana Fou, in comparison, the diploma program was abolished several years ago, and all students, including women, now receive BD degrees.

At higher degree levels, too, students from Pacific churches can be sent for further study even if they were not hoping to be selected. For example, the Piula lecturer whose pastoral family I joined, Solaese, had been working as the youth coordinator for the Samoan Methodist Church's New South Wales (Australia) synod in 2009 when he was told that he would be sent to PTC to get his master's degree—something he had not sought or planned. The answer to the question of how people become theologians, then, is that sometimes that their elders tell them they have to do it.

In a plenary discussion at a "theological consultation" in Suva in 1985, Russell Chandran of PTC said, "It is important that the [master's degree] candidates [at PTC] come not because of their own personal interest, even though that is an important factor.... It would be important that the candidates are chosen and sponsored by their colleges or their churches. In admitting the candidates PTC should certainly give priority to candidates who are sponsored and sent by churches rather than those who come on their own" (Chandran quoted in PCC, PTC, and SPATS 1986, 136).

Chapter 1: Writing Back at the Bible

1. Kava is not alcoholic, and being "drunk" on kava involves none of the skewed perceptions or emotional fluctuations of alcohol consumption. See Lebot, Merlin, and Lindstrom 1992; Aporosa 2011; and Aporosa and Tomlinson 2014.

2. In this quote, I have eliminated, without adding ellipses, Havea's citations of several scholars: himself on the "sea of stories" and diasporic communities; Daniel Boyarin on Midrash (1990); Danna Nolan Fewell on intertextuality (1992); and Kathleen P Rushton (2014), Judith E McKinlay (2014), and Jeanette Mathews on counterpoint readings (2014).

3. In a classic analysis, Donald Brenneis observed that for Indo-Fijians (citizens of Indian descent in Fiji), *talanoa* is understood to be talk "about the less-than-worthy doings of absent others," leading him to translate *talanoa* as "gossip" (1984, 493). See also Silverstein 2013 for a reanalysis of Brenneis's data in service of a general theory of culture.

4. "An–other" is Vaka'uta's spelling.

5. A revised version of this piece was published as Filemoni-Tofaeono 2003. Filemoni-Tofaeono was enrolled as a PhD candidate at the University of Auckland under the supervision of Elaine Wainwright during the period of my research, but we did not meet.

6. She referred here to a source—Paterson 1999, 101–104—that is omitted from her bibliography and that I have been unable to track down.

7. The "Mead-Freeman controversy" in anthropology focused in part on whether *taupou*-as-virgins enabled sexual license for other unmarried females (Margaret Mead's position) or served as a model for all unmarried females to follow (Derek

Freeman's position). Useful evaluative summaries of the issues, facts, and interpretations at stake include Tcherkézoff 2008 and Shankman 2009.

8. In reading Numbers 30, Havea favored the Hebrew version known as the Masoretic Text because he considered it "the least harmonized of the ancient versions.... I prefer the [Masoretic Text] rendering for transoceanic reasons...: disharmonies open the text for interpretation and hold back readers' control" (J Havea 2003, 16, 18).

9. Vaka'uta's argument that Rahab is not a prostitute, but rather a woman slurred for misogynistic and ultimately genocidal reasons, is such a fundamental challenge that Old Testament scholar David M Gunn more or less avoided it in his commentary on Vaka'uta's chapter. Gunn deftly raised several questions, including whether taking a Canaanite's point of view means we should see Rahab as a traitor and whether it is fair to charge the Israelites with imperialism when they were fleeing slavery. He countered Vaka'uta's certainty with strategic ambiguity: "It is perhaps not so clear to me who is alienating whom within the story world" (Gunn 2014, 253). But he bypassed Vaka'uta's central claim that Rahab should not be considered a prostitute, simply noting that in the rhetoric of Deuteronomy, "foreign women are harlots," categorically (Gunn 2014, 252). Gunn noted that Osage author Robert Allen Warrior also "takes a Canaanite perspective" on the story of Rahab (Gunn 2014, 252) but did not mention Warrior's conclusion that the Exodus story is not a good general model for conquered indigenous peoples, who would do better to "listen to ourselves" rather than accept the "alien gods" of Judaism and Christianity (Warrior 1989, 264–265).

10. Quoted material is from my transcription of this portion of Vaka'uta's lecture and the student's response.

11. Sugirtharajah was Ma'ilo Fuaiva'a's dissertation supervisor at the University of Birmingham.

12. In the Samoan version, "O Aperaamo o le tama o Isaako, o Isaako o le tama o Iakopo, o Iakopo foi o le tama lea o Iuta ma ona uso." In quoting Ma'ilo Fuaiva'a, I have eliminated the underlining he uses to keep track of key terms and phrases.

13. In the Samoan version, "Na usu Aperaamo ia Sara le afafine o Tara faaee le gafa o Isaako; usu Isaako ia Repeka le afafine o Petueli faaee le gafa o Iakopo; usu Iakopo ia Lea le afafine matua o Lapana faaee le gafa o Iuta ma ona uso."

14. As another example, Day changed Wilson's use of 'ulu (breadfruit) for "bread" in Matthew 7:9—"Or what man of you, if his son asks him for bread, will give him a stone?"—to areto, the transliteration of artos, a Greek term for "bread" (Ma'ilo Fuaiva'a 2008, 273).

15. Another resolution adopted at the same meeting was that "a whole chapter of the Bible should always be read in connection with every preaching service." The reason given was that "Some of the native preachers were in the habit of maiming a narrative and mangling a lesson by reading to the middle of a paragraph and abruptly concluding there" (Dyson 1875, 92).

Chapter 2: Weavers, Servants, and Prophets

1. The book was not designed for a specific course but rather was envisioned as a basis for individual study or for use in classes at member colleges of the South Pacific

Association of Theological Schools. It is described as "appropriate for any level of the curriculum" for those with adequate English skills (Weavers 2006, 6), and it is available for free download at https://www.otago.ac.nz/ctpi/otago614621.pdf.

2. This claim—that women can and should reshape theology—is the reason I refer to these authors as feminist. As Rosemary Radford Ruether argued, women's life experiences do tend to have differences from men's, and yet church tradition fully and firmly identifies male experience as the normative ground:

> It is precisely women's experience that has been shut out of hermeneutics and theological reflection in the past. This has been done by forbidding women to study and then to teach and preach the theological tradition. Women have not been able to bring their own experience into the public formulation of the tradition. Not only have women been excluded from shaping and interpreting the tradition from their own experience, but the tradition has been shaped and interpreted against them. The tradition has been shaped to justify their exclusion. The traces of their presence have been suppressed and lost from the public memory of the community. The androcentric bias of the male interpreters of the tradition, who regard maleness as normative humanity, not only erase women's presence in the past history of the community but silence even the questions about their absence. One is not even able to remark upon or notice women's absence, since women's silence and absence is the norm. (Ruether 1985, 112–113)

Not all male interpreters have an androcentric bias, to be sure, just as not all women writing theology are feminists. And, as contextual theologians have argued vigorously, feminist scholarship must not ignore, of all things, culture: a feminism that reinscribes Eurocentric convictions substitutes one error for another. For a useful history of the development of self-described "Third World" feminist theology, see King 1994.

3. The Western feminist theologian mentioned most often in *Weavings* is Letty M Russell, whose work is cited by Lydia Johnson, Tamara Wete, Joan Alleluia Filemoni-Tofaeono, Ilisapeci Meo, and 'Asinate F Samate.

4. Note that Fijian Methodism, Meo's denomination, does ordain women, but this does not mean they are treated the same way as male ministers. See Tomlinson 2015a for a discussion and Malogne-Fer 2016 for an account of how women have come to be ordained in the Maohi Protestant Church of French Polynesia.

5. Fa'alafi reported that in 1967 the Samoan Methodist Church's president, Kamu Tagaolo, allowed women to become lay preachers, but a decade and a half later, while "many women lay-preachers are officially approved by the Church...practically, very few of them are preaching. This depends very much on the Ministers, whether they accept to make use of them or not" (1982, 81). The current principal of Piula, Ma'ilo Fuaiva'a, argued in his bachelor of divinity thesis that male ministers and their wives should be ordained as a team (Ma'ilo Fuaiva'a 2001, 54; see also Nofoaiga 2006). In *Weavings*, Siera Tion Bird, the wife of Solomon Islands theologian Cliff Bird, described her work with her husband as "partnership ministry" that involves "collaborating in our overall ministry, but [each partner] concentrating on specific areas" (Tion Bird 2003, 195).

Of my four main field sites, the University of Auckland was the school with the most impressive female leadership, with Elaine Wainwright serving as the head of the School of Theology for the duration of its existence from 2002 to 2014. PTC did not have female faculty teaching in the degree programs during my time there, but since 1980 it has run a study program specifically for women, which currently awards a certificate for completion (Pacific Theological College 2015, 102–105).

6. To develop this theology, Vaai extended the meaning of *fa'aaloalo*. Drawing partly on the definition of the root *alo* as a polite term for "face (in the direction of)" (see Milner 1993, 15), he defined *fa'aaloalo* primarily as "relationship" and included in its field of meaning "mutuality, love, honouring, sharing, inclusiveness, reciprocity, complementary, communal way of life, receptiveness" (Vaai 2006, 283).

7. In 2006, a Congregationalist church in Solosolo, Upolu, Sāmoa, got into a dispute with its minister, with each side accusing the other of misusing funds. The real problem, however, was that the minister then warned his congregation that "misusing the funds would result in harm to either them, or their children"—a threat the congregation interpreted as his pronouncing a curse on them (Ah Mu 2006, 2). He was removed from his position and later renounced Christianity. In April 2015, I attended a seminar this former minister gave at the National University of Samoa. In it, he referred to himself as a theologian and declared that his goal was to "revisit, rekindle, and resurrect the ancestral gods of Samoa."

8. The phrase gets translated in various ways but always with the same core meaning that one needs to serve first in order to lead later. Here, I am using the translation offered by Tofaeono (1993, 121n44). Serge Tcherkézoff translated the saying as "service is the way to power [i.e., being a chief]" (2015, 170; brackets in original).

9. The emphasis on service-in-leadership extends to elected politicians. "As qualified voters, my wife and I have received campaign letters from the candidates running for the [American Samoa] House of Representatives and the US Congress in the coming election (6 November, 1990)," wrote Gustav Allen. "In the letters, the candidates mention their qualifications and years of government service. They stress the word *tautua* as their motto for serving the people. One candidate's motto is *tautua alofa* (service with love).... Other candidates... all emphasize the concept of service" (Allen 1990, 92–93). In addition, there is a political party in independent Sāmoa named the Tautua Samoa Party.

10. Tofaeono cautioned that mana "belongs to those terms that cannot be clearly explained in words, but must be experienced" (2000, 168; see also my discussion in chapter 3). *Tapu* is "taboo," and *tapui* (which Tofaeono also used) can be glossed as "be tabooed" (see Milner 1993, 243). Articulating the relationship between them, Tofaeono explained that "while *mana* connotes the energetic aspects of divine objects, *tapui/tapu* emphasizes the consecrated dimension.... When a chief is known to possess *mana*, he/she and the villagers will observe the *tapui* in case difficulties might arise" (2000, 170). Pulling this all together, then, Jesus—who is "the *mana* of God" (251)—is the ultimate mediator, a *tautua* whose service is to unite people with each other in families and with all of existence. Conceiving Christ's functions as *tautua mana e tapu* then consolidates the conviction that ecological life is a creative process founded on an ever-living energy or a mediating agent. "And it is through this mediating agent that everything there in creation [was] recognized as conscious and animate, as all are rooted and linked to this life-giving energy, the Logos of Christ or Life" (Tofaeono 2000, 252; he referred at this point to the Bible verse John 1:4 ["In him was life, and the life was the light of men"]).

11. Amituana'i, who was the principal of Piula in 1990–1991, developed a sur-

prising interpretation of the Samoan ritual practice of *tāpua'i*, which means to "be in thought and sympathy at the time [someone] is undergoing a test or ordeal (in the belief that this will bring about the success desired)" (the nominal form *tāpua'iga* is translated as "act of worship, church service"; definitions from Milner 1993, 243). He argued that because titleholders *(matai)* were the ones who traditionally gathered in thoughtful and sympathetic ritual support for ongoing activities, this was a kind of service by the more powerful to the less powerful. It was chiefs serving people. But because chiefs "were regarded as gods" (Amituana'i 1979, 69), this was actually a case of gods serving people. This idea led Amituana'i to argue that *tāpua'iga* is not a good term for Christian worship. Rather, *tautua* is a better term because of its emphasis on "total commitment," selflessness, and willingness (Amituana'i 1979, 75–76)—and, I suspect, although Amituana'i did not actually say it, because it emphasizes a low-to-high dynamic rather than a high-to-low one. For him, service and worship are thus the same thing.

12. Cluny Macpherson and La'avasa Macpherson described chiefs as "sponsors and protectors" of missionaries and ministers, adding: "Despite their religious authority, and the secular influence and respect accorded them, pastors serve at the pleasure of the village polity and cannot survive without the political patronage of the chiefs of a village" (2010, 107). They also described the situation of people who have sought to establish new religious denominations in villages and met resistance from village councils (Macpherson and Macpherson 2010, 132). Brian T Alofaituli, in his comments on my manuscript for this book (4 May 2018), pointed out that "*matai* or chiefs maintain the sanctity of the institution of the Christian Church. Theologians and pastors may have ideas about understanding religion and its practices based on exposure from their theological training outside of the islands, but *matais* play a major role in the implementation of these ideas."

13. Meleiseā contextualized the story of the Nafanua prophecy by observing three key facts and events associated with it. First, before John Williams's arrival, varieties of Christianity were already known in Sāmoa due to Samoans' contact with Tongans, the rise of a local religious movement sometimes called the "Siovili cult" (Freeman 1959), and the vernacular teachings of foreign beachcombers. Second, Williams was led to Sapapali'i by Fauea, a supporter of Malietoa who traveled with the British missionary from Tonga to Sāmoa. Third, Malietoa saw the political opportunity that the arrival of the missionaries offered, and, of the eight Polynesian evangelists Williams left in 1830, kept four of them for himself and gave four to his brother. "It seems likely," Meleiseā observed, "that Malietoa intended to monopolise this new source of sacred power, and hence kept the mission teachers to himself" (1992, 20; see also Latai 2016, 34–36; Niuatoa 2018, 42–43).

14. As R A Knox put it, "All chiliastic [millenarian] movements outlive the nonfulfilment of their prophecies" (1950, 137)—some with more vigor than others. See also Festinger, Riecken, and Schacter 1956.

15. For example, two memorial tributes to Catholic Bishop Patelisio Finau referred to him in terms of being prophetic (Barr 1994; Helu 1994). In addition, one honorific term applied to Samoan ministers is *perofeta* (see Tofaeono 2000, 136n20). There are many honorific Samoan terms for ministers (see especially Setefano 2008; Tuivanu 2013; Niuatoa 2018, 19n24).

16. Thorogood later became the general secretary for the Council for World Mission, the successor to the London Missionary Society. He was a notably productive

contributor to *PJT*, publishing ten articles and many Bible-study pieces therein, with the first article in 1964 and the last in 1995.

17. In one case, a student wrote frankly that his topic—why members were leaving the Congregational Christian Church of American Samoa—was something that 60 percent of the church's ministers had considered unimportant when they were surveyed several years earlier (Faleali'i 2002, 6).

Chapter 3: Coconut Theology and the Cultivation of a Pacific Way

1. Several statements by Sitiveni Halapua about his organization of the "talanoa process" for political reconciliation can be found online; see, eg, S Halapua 2013, 2015. The online site for the *talanoa*-based academic conferences is talanoaoceania. net, and various papers from these events, published in the edited collections by Jione Havea (2010) and Nāsili Vaka'uta (2011), are discussed in this chapter and elsewhere in this book.

2. His brother, economist and political moderator Sitiveni Halapua—whose work Winston discusses at length (W Halapua 2008b, 56–61)—characterized *talanoa* more fancifully as "engaging in dialogue with or telling stories to each other absent concealment of the inner feelings and experiences that resonate in our hearts and minds" (S Halapua 2015, 1). Conversely, Jione Havea (who, like the Halapua brothers, is of Tongan heritage) suggested that it can mean one is bullshitting: "To muse is to talk about nothing, to bullshit. Such do[es] happen in talanoa circles (when hyphenated, *tala-noa* means 'tell nothing')" (J Havea 2013, 157; but see his other statements on *talanoa* in this chapter).

3. Mawyer related the case of a man born on Pitcairn Island and living on Mangareva in French Polynesia. The man, Warren, struggled to gain legal recognition as a citizen because he did not possess a birth certificate. Without legal recognition, he could not establish his right to use particular portions of land on Mangareva. When Mawyer was preparing to sail for Pitcairn, Warren asked him to have a birth certificate made for him there. Their conversation, Mawyer recalled,

> revolved around one term. Surprisingly, he used a singular conceptual frame to cover all of the different qualities of the object, cause, effect, event and the various tasks involved. Warren used *mana* and its causative form *'akamana* to refer to what the Pitcairn authorities needed to do for this document—that is, to empower it, to legitimately authorise Warren's claims, in some sense his (legal) existence. At the same time, he referred to the document as *mana* and to *mana* as a character or quality of the incipient document. *"Na koe i 'akamana 'ia toku kaie, toku* [*birth*] *certificat"* ("You will have made-mana (stamped, authorised) my paper, my birth certificate") he repeated while gesturing the action of stamping, with his hand serving as a virtual stamp. (Mawyer 2016, 224)

4. Tuwere's analysis of mana comprises a three-chapter section of his monograph (Tuwere 2002, 134–169); for an analysis of his work in comparison with that of other Fijian Methodist theologians, see Tomlinson and Bigitibau 2016.

5. In contrast to these authors, Māori Catholic theologian Henare Arekatera Tate tried to describe mana with linguistic precision. He offered a 113-word defini-

tion that is centered on *tapu* (colloquially, "taboo," although Tate's definition of *tapu* is far wider than this); indeed, the center of his own definition of mana is that "*mana* is *tapu* centred" (Tate 2010, 84).

6. Timothy Jenkins mentioned substances such as millet and corn being used for the wheat in bread, and palm wine and banana wine being used instead of wine from grapes (2007, 134). The "Baptism, Eucharist and Ministry" paper produced by the World Council of Churches in 1982 hedges its bets on the theological appropriateness of using indigenous substances in Holy Communion:

> Since New Testament days, the Church has attached the greatest importance to the continued use of the elements of bread and wine which Jesus used at the Last Supper. In certain parts of the world, where bread and wine are not customary or obtainable, it is now sometimes held that local food and drink serve better to anchor the eucharist in everyday life. Further study is required concerning the question of which features of the Lord's Supper were unchangeably instituted by Jesus, and which features remain within the Church's competence to decide. (World Council of Churches 1982, 17; see also Garrett and Mavor 1973)

7. London Missionary Society (LMS) evangelist George Turner wrote that in the early days of Christianity in Sāmoa, local chiefs believed that any white man could serve as a Christian "high-priest." And, Turner added, some gladly took up the role. He told of an unnamed Englishman who went through the motions of worship (reading, singing, praying) and then, on one occasion, took an extra step: "There was a special religious service, which was no doubt meant to be the observance of the Lord's Supper. Only the chiefs and heads of families and their wives were admitted to this. They knew not what it meant, but, from their description of little bits of taro, and a sip of cocoa-nut water, it is evident that it was an attempt at the holy communion" (Turner 1861, 103, 105–106; see also Goodall 1954, 362). Turner, not surprisingly, did not approve of these faux church ministers, but theologian Tofaeono commented approvingly on the way their actions shared nature's blessings and cultivated fellowship (2000, 76). Indeed, Tofaeono argued that the use of "foreign elements" like wine and bread in Samoan Christianity is actually "an act of desacralization of the local and indigenous gifts of God's creation" (2000, 154).

A century after Turner, another LMS missionary, Bernard Thorogood, recalled of his service in Aitutaki in the Cook Islands:

> One adaptation which would rile the purists is our change from wine to coconut water. Wine is foreign, and has no significance here beyond booze, whereas the juice of the coconut is an everyday drink, not made by hand, but coming straight from the fruit. There are times in the outer islands when flour is impossible to obtain and so bread cannot be used. The substitute is often *uto*, the solid, cake-like centre of a sprouting coconut, which can be cut up into squares and eaten raw. What matters, surely, is that we receive the proper significance from these symbols. When Jesus said "Do this," are we to take it as a command to imitate that first meal? If so, then not only should we use wine and special unleavened bread, but we should also recline in groups of twelve around the celebrant. How literal can you get? (Thorogood 1960, 12)

8. Malogne-Fer explained why most churches on Moʻorea were receptive to the use of indigenous elements in Communion (2016, 46–47). First, some of the leaders of the Evangelical Church of French Polynesia (now Maohi Protestant Church) Theological Commission proposing the change were from Moʻorea and thus could persuade locals. Second, many English-speaking tourists visit Moʻorea, so the church tends to appoint English-speaking ministers there—and these ministers tend to have been trained at PTC in Suva, where they learn contextual theology.

9. Maʻafu Palu referred to a case in which leaders of the Free Wesleyan Church of Tonga rejected the suggestion by Sione ʻAmanaki Havea, advocate of Coconut Theology, for an indigenized communion. At the church's general conference in 1984, "Dr. Havea, the then President of the Church and Chairperson of the Conference, proposed that coconut flesh and juice be used instead of the traditional elements of the Lord's Supper. It did not take long for the meeting to agree that such a proposition was highly impractical and thus was unacceptable to the majority of the church members who consisted mostly of lay people" (M Palu 2003, 55n22).

10. Arguing that the "use of local elements for the sacraments is a priority," Tofaeono suggested that Christian baptisms might be conducted in the sea (2000, 282).

11. Many (but not all) teachers at Piula enjoyed casual kava-drinking sessions, especially on weekends, which I believe is somewhat unusual for Sāmoa. This may have been partly due to the fact that all of the teachers at Piula during my fieldwork had attended PTC in kava-soaked Fiji.

12. The teacher offered two other stories. A filmmaker wanted to film a Samoan woman at the pool in a lavalava with her leg tattoo exposed—a taboo thing. The filmmaker did not tell anyone at the college what he was going to do. Down at the pool, he asked everyone in the pool to get out so he could get his shot. Everyone cleared out, and he filmed. Later—the next day, I believe—he returned and complained that when he had checked his images, there were kids jumping into the pool in the background. The teacher also referred to an older story in which photos taken of the pool showed up as blanks with red x's when developed.

13. On Samoan spirits (aitu) and Christianity, see also Macpherson and Macpherson 2010, 106–107.

14. Stephanie Lawson pointed out that although Ratu Mara might have introduced the term, his vision of the Pacific Way was an aristocratic one at odds with the anticolonial model the term was soon felt to offer (Lawson 2010).

15. In choosing to focus on the Pacific Way and PJT, I do not mean to marginalize the related and influential discourse about the Melanesian Way (per Narokobi 1980). Melanesia as its own site, category, and focus in theology deserves its own treatment; one key resource is the Melanesian Journal of Theology.

16. The publication of PJT by the South Pacific Association of Theological Schools has been supported by grants from overseas institutions. I have not found any complete history of funding, but a snapshot from 1994 gives a sense of how far-flung the financial sources have been. That year, the World Council of Churches and organizations from Germany, Denmark, the Netherlands, Canada, the United States, and the United Kingdom were thanked for giving money either to the journal or to SPATS general funds, which "make the publication of this Journal possible" (PJT 1994).

17. In both series 1 and series 2, the editors of earlier issues were of European heritage and those of later issues have been of indigenous heritage. For series 1,

John Bradshaw (Malua Theological College's principal at the time) edited the first six issues and was followed by John Wilton and Clarence E Norwood, with Lopeti Taufa then taking over and editing issues 19 through 34, the conclusion of series 1. For series 2, Bruce J Deverell edited the first three issues, followed by Kerry Prendeville, Lydia Johnson-Hill, and Carrie Walker-Jones. Since issue 13, every issue has had a guest editor. Guest editors have included leaders of the Methodist Church in Fiji (Ilaitia Sevati Tuwere, Tevita Banivanua); school faculties, their principals, or both (Piula and Malua in Sāmoa and Sia'atoutai Theological College in Tonga); the women's theological collective Weavers, as represented by Tilisi Bryce and Virginia Fornasa; and individual scholars including Tevita K Havea, Kafoa Solomone, Ama'amalele Tofaeono, and Kambati Uriam. No editors were named for issues 42 through 45. *PJT* has had an editorial board since its inception, and the board has presumably shaped the journal's direction. Since issue 13 of series 2, Tessa Mackenzie has served continuously as chair of the editorial board as well as guest editor for issues 17, 23, and 31.

18. Of the 277 BD theses and project reports (long research papers equivalent to bachelor's theses) written at the college between 1968 and 2007, the greatest number, 83, focused on Sāmoa; in comparison, 46 or 47 focused on Fiji (depending on whether one includes a work on Solomon Islanders in Fiji; please note that the Fiji category includes Rotuma and Rabi). Similarly, of the 125 master of theology theses between 1988 and 2007 that I tallied, Sāmoa was the focus of 31, and Fiji was the focus of 14. Tonga was the focus of 22 BD theses and project reports and 18 master of theology theses. For Papua New Guinea (including Bougainville), there were 4 BD theses and project reports and 22 master of theology theses.

19. I did not find any master of theology theses that took Oceania as their focus, although several theses were missing from the library, so one might exist. Of the 227 BD theses and project reports, I noted only 3 that took the whole of Oceania as their area.

20. Deciding what counted as an article's geographical focus was sometimes difficult; my decisions about listing social and geographical foci for articles were judgment calls based on each article's overall context, and I tried to err on the side of inclusivity. My summary of the research is presented in Tomlinson 2015b, on which much of this section is based. That article contains an error in endnote 9 on page 66, where I wrote that the most cited article published in *PJT*, one by Leslie Boseto, is not cited in other articles in *PJT*. Yet I overlooked the fact that Google Scholar, my source for citations, does not index *PJT* itself.

21. On these developments, see, respectively, Germon 1964; Germon 1965; Carter 1966a; and [Carter 1966b]. See also Forman 1986 and Garrett 1997 for useful overviews of the era.

22. See *PJT* issues 13 (1995); 17 (1997); 27 and 28 (2002); and 33 (2005), which focuses on Melanesian contextual theology.

Chapter 4: Sea and Earth

1. In response to this current of thought, one of the several declarations offered by Pacific leaders on the topic of climate change, the Otin Tai (or Otin Taai) Declaration made in Kiribati in 2004, includes this statement: "We would like to say a

word about God's promise to Noah not to flood the earth again. Some Christians view this covenant as a guarantee that they are not at risk of flooding from climate change. But the sea level is rising and threatening Pacific Islands with flooding from high tides and storm surges. This is not an act of God. It is a result of human economic and consumer activities that pollute the atmosphere and lead to climate change" (World Council of Churches 2004).

2. Halapua explicitly discussed Hauʻofa's influence on his own work, but he then seemed to forget Hauʻofa's point when he wrote of the Pacific's "tiny…scattered islands" and Niuatoputapu as "tiny" and "remote" (W Halapua 2008b, 8–9, 18, 29).

3. In June 2013, PhD student Terry Pouono gave a seminar in Auckland at which a student from India commented on the gendered aspects of land-based theology. The student, Jekheli Kibami Singh, identified herself as being from a "tribal background" (Sümi/Sema Naga heritage, from northeastern India). She observed that indigenous theologians from her region have argued that "land should be a starting point for developing tribal theology." She described her concerns with this line of argument, saying, "Even if I was there in Nagaland, I don't have a right to inheritance [of land] because I am a woman. So in that way… the proposition itself becomes very exclusive." My thanks to Singh for allowing me to quote her comment from the seminar.

4. Near the end of the book, quoting verses from Leviticus, Amos, and Job, Tuwere declared, "Human beings are called neither to worship nor to abuse nature but to live creatively and productively with their fellow creatures. Peace on earth does not merely entail the absence of war but also sustainable ecological peace, peace among the different creatures and our natural environment" (Tuwere 2002, 204). But Joseph Bush, who taught at PTC in the 1990s, described how the entanglement of Fijian land and people led to less of an environmentalist emphasis than he had expected: "I was very excited when I moved to Fiji because the paradigm of the *vanua,* the land, is already in place here. I was expecting that this emphasis on society's dependence on nature would result in a clear environmental ethic. However, I discovered that the paradigm of *vanua* is connected with various structures of traditional authority and relations between peoples that might have very little to do with environmental issues *per se*" (1997, 69).

5. There were six students in the class. I got the sense that two of them resisted Tofaeono's general argument about the Gospel being inherent to pre-Christian Samoan culture. But one of them explicitly agreed—had indeed said, two weeks earlier in the same class, on the subject of the arrival of the European missionaries in Sāmoa, "We already had a Gospel, which was our connection with the environment." I do not know whether this student had read Tofaeono's work, but he expressed Tofaeono's point well.

6. Augustin Krämer described connections between forms of the deity: "Without beginning was the existence of the highest god Tagaloa. As in the Christian religion, this highest god (atua) has numerous other names, thus The Creator, faʻatupunuʻu, The Immeasurable One, nimonimo, The Worker of Miracles, le mana, etc. which epithets Samoans look upon less as such rather than as brothers, sons or descendants of the god of heaven Tagaloaalagi, all of whom they combine in the Satagaloa, the 'Tagaloa family,' not unlike the Titans" (1994, 24). Different Samoan authors spell the god's full name with minor variations. Tui Atua Tamasese Efi, Sāmoa's former head of state, wrote the full name as Tagaloaalelagi (Efi 2014, 15); Amaʻamalele

Tofaeono, as Tagaloalagi (Tofaeono 2000); and Mālama Meleiseā, as Tagaloa-a-lagi (Meleiseā 1987b, 6, 8; see also Freeman 1959, 196). Here, I stick with the short form of the inclusive name that most authors agree on, Tagaloa.

7. The English translation here is by Mark Ashley. The German original is: "Der Ungebundene, Unbeschränkte in Raum und Zeit, daher der Allmächtige, der Absolute, der Souveräne, der Höchste, der Herr über alles, weil er nicht gebunden ist durch irgend ein Tabu" (Tofaeono 2000, 164n47).

8. Tofaeono used both short and long forms of the deity's name (Tagaloa, Tagaloalagi) and italicized them, but in the quoted excerpts I change the long form to the short form and do not italicize. I also de-italicize the name of the octopus god, Fee (Fe'e). For the eastern versions of creation stories, Tofaeono referred to the work of John Fraser, Mālama Meleiseā, Hans Nevermann, Franz Reinecke, and John Stair as well as his interviews with people from Manu'a. For the western versions, he referred to the work of Werner von Bülow, W T Prichard, George Turner, and Stair.

9. Tofaeono identified *tuli* as a "species of plover" (2000, 177). G B Milner indicated that the term can be used for several species of bird, including kinds of curlew, godwit, tattler, "and perhaps also the turnstone" (1993, 286).

10. This sentence, as phrased, makes it sounds like Tagaloa and God are separate, which is clearly not the case in Tofaeono's theology. I believe the sentence was constructed this way simply to avoid excessive repetition of the name Tagaloa, which can result from Tofaeono's avoidance of gender-marked pronouns for divinity. See also note 14.

11. The origin story of Manu'a describes how their paramount chiefs descend from Satagaloa, the "family" of high gods, whereas "the common people come forth from rotten creepers, which change into maggots (ilo), and ... Tagaloa's messengers draw limbs out of the bodies of these maggots and bring them a soul (agaga)" (Krämer 1994, 24; see also Krämer 1994, 539–544). Comparing the story of Tagaloa's role in cosmic generation to the scientific model of the Big Bang, Sāmoa's former head of state translated *ilo* as "germs" (Efi 2009c, 191–192).

12. Jione Havea, whose work I discuss in chapter 1, also cast a critical eye on discourse about climate change, but for a different reason: such discourse turns the ocean into a threat, something seen "as enemy rather than as context, home and who we are" (2010a, 352–353).

13. Agreeing with Wilhelm Lütgert's assertion that "in theology since the beginning of the nineteenth century the doctrine of creation has taken second place to the doctrine of redemption" (1934, 27), Pelikan ascribed this imbalance to "reasons ... ranging from the impact of modern science to the 'Jesus-centered' piety of the evangelical movements" (1963, 8–9).

14. Invoking the canonical model of the Trinity while also flagging his disagreement with it, Tofaeono wrote:

An affirmation of the Trinity of God as Father (sic), Son, and Holy Spirit ... is ... an acknowledgment of the oneness and communal nature of the Godhead. The triune God is a community in partnership. Though diverse in nature, the Trinity co-exists, co-eternal, united, and infinite. The co-existential partnership and the subordination of personal qualities of the Trinity in an unconditional fellowship is maintained. It is in this divine fellowship that the genesis and the existence of the whole universe is being created. As God's house and household, therefore, creation which is made up of living beings, matter, energy, bodies, and forces exists in permanent interactive relations to one another and to the Godhead. (2000, 237–238; "(sic)" in original)

In the trinitarian model informed by Tofaeono's reading of Samoan myth, then, God is not just a Father. The Godhead is associated with Tagaloa. Yet Tofaeono endorsed a trinitarian model of divinity because it "plainly embraces God at the centre of all life," allows for recognition of divinity's immanence and transcendence alike, and conveys an understanding of God as "relational and communicative" (2000, 239–240, 244, 264; see also Tofaeono 2010).

In the passage where Tofaeono mentions God's "relational and communicative" nature, he referred to God with a gendered pronoun—"She" (2000, 264). He usually avoided gendered language for God, however, making his theological vision as expansive and inclusive as possible. For Tofaeono, God is a mystery, and humans cannot apprehend God but can experience the unfolding of the mystery. In my interview with him on 2 May 2016, he referred to Tagaloa as a "principle" rather than a "person" and said that the Trinity should be understood as communion, not as a "mathematical" thing (ie, three-in-one; see also the claim made directly by Sāmoa's former head of state: "Tagaloa is both male and female" [Efi 2009b, 105]).

Tofaeono's understanding of the Trinity put him at odds with Kanana Fou's president, Niuatoa, who endorsed the canonical model based on God the Father. Niuatoa urged students to invoke this gendered Trinity during their sermons in the sermon class that all students take in their second year and are required to pass in order to be allowed to preach. The disagreement between the two top staff members caused concern and confusion among both faculty and students. A practical focus of this concern was on how students should prepare to deliver their sermons for sermon class when they were getting conflicting advice from the seminary's two top authorities.

15. In that same class, on 9 March 2016, I asked Tofaeono whether we could speak of "the Gospel according to Tagaloa." He agreed; hence this section's title.

16. Tuwere was more cautious, arguing that although Fijian deities like Degei and Dakuwaqa have "a place in the overarching tradition in Christ," nonetheless "in Christ, their significance is broken and opened up for new possibilities of Christian experience." Yet he also suggested that the ancestral fertility deity Ratumaibulu is "part of this 'salvation history'" wherein "the trinitarian God is continually at work" (Tuwere 2002, 155, 179). See also Tomlinson 2014a; 2016, 18–19.

Conclusion: Culture, Dialogue, and the Divine

1. Courtney Handman has argued that it is analytically productive to see Protestant schism in terms of critique rather than breakdown. Denominationalism, she argued, is its own productive form of sociality, for even when continually splitting off from their old churches, disaffected Protestants have a "desire...to be separate together with others, as the church militant and not simply the subject militant" (Handman 2015, 14; emphasis in original).

2. Note, however, that one of the most influential works of anthropology in the 1990s, Arjun Appadurai's *Modernity at Large*, includes the claim that "the most valu-

able feature of the concept of culture is the concept of difference, a contrastive rather than a substantive property of certain things" (1996, 12).

3. Robbins's writings on anthropology, Christianity, and theology have motivated many other scholars to work in these intersecting zones. Indeed, he has often been a participant in and commentator on these projects (see Engelke and Robbins 2010; Fountain and Lau 2013; Robbins 2013c; Meneses and others 2014; Robbins and Haynes 2014).

4. He wrote in the conclusion to his article, "The Bible is dialogic. Meaning is to be approached dialogically. Biblical hermeneutics should be a dialogical task. It must be a reflection of our multicultural co-existence and interactions, which could potentially form a harmonious chorus of response to the continued intervention of God, in Christ, and through the Holy Spirit, here in the unfinished present, and there in the unexpected future" (Vaka'uta 1998, 50).

5. For a brief and accessible discussion of this phrase's shades of meaning, and St Anselm's particular understanding of it, see Migliore 2014, 2–7.

References

Adams, Emma H
 1890 *Jottings from the Pacific: Life and Incidents in the Fijian and Samoan Islands.* Oakland: Pacific Press Publishing Company.

Adams, Walter Randolph, and Frank A Salamone, editors
 2000 *Anthropology and Theology: God, Icons, and God-Talk.* Lanham, MD: University Press of America.

Ah Mu, Alan
 2006 Pastor Denies Money Claims. *Sunday Samoan,* 26 Nov, 1–2.

Ah Siu-Maliko, Mercy, editor
 2010 *Women's Stories in Pastoral Counselling.* Apia: Piula Theological College.

Allen, Gustav
 1990 Patterns of Authority in Samoa: An Assessment of Their Practice in the Society and in the Church from a Christian Perspective. BD project paper (equivalent to a thesis), Pacific Theological College, Suva.

Amituana'i, Tevita
 1979 A Survey of Christian Worship in Relation to Samoan Concepts of "Tapuaiga" and "Tautua." BD project paper (equivalent to a thesis), Pacific Theological College, Suva.

Amosa, Saneterini
 1991 A Historical Analysis of the Schism between [the] Congregational Christian Church in Samoa and the Congregational Christian Church in American Samoa. BD project paper (equivalent to a thesis), Pacific Theological College, Suva.

Anae, Melani
 2010 Teu Le Va: Toward a Native Anthropology. *Pacific Studies* 33 (2–3): 222–240.

Angrosino, Michael V
 1994 The Culture Concept and the Mission of the Roman Catholic Church. *American Anthropologist* 96 (4): 824–832.

Aporosa, S "Apo"
 2011 Is Kava Alcohol? The Myths and the Facts. *Pacific Health Dialog* 17 (1): 157–164.
 2015 The New Kava User: Diasporic Identity Formation in Reverse. *New Zealand Sociology* 30 (4): 58–77.

Aporosa, S "Apo," and Matt Tomlinson
 2014 Kava Hangover and Gold-Standard Science. *Anthropologica* 56 (1): 163–175.

Appadurai, Arjun
1996   *Modernity at Large: Cultural Dimensions of Globalization.* Minneapolis: University of Minnesota Press.

Arno, Andrew
1985   Impressive Speeches and Persuasive Talk: Traditional Patterns of Political Communication in Fiji's Lau Group from the Perspective of Pacific Ideal Types. *Oceania* 56 (2): 124–137.

1990   Disentangling Indirectly: The Joking Debate in Fijian Social Control. In *Disentangling: Conflict Discourse in Pacific Societies,* edited by Karen Ann Watson-Gegeo and Geoffrey M White, 241–289. Stanford: Stanford University Press.

Bach, Richard
1970   *Jonathan Livingston Seagull.* New York: Macmillan.

Bakhtin, M M
1981   *The Dialogic Imagination: Four Essays.* Edited by Michael Holquist. Translated by Caryl Emerson and Michael Holquist. Austin: University of Texas Press.

1984   *Problems of Dostoevsky's Poetics.* Edited and translated by Caryl Emerson. Minneapolis: University of Minnesota Press.

Bargatzky, Thomas
1997   "The Kava Ceremony Is a Prophecy": An Interpretation of the Transition to Christianity in Samoa. In *European Impact and Pacific Influence: British and German Colonial Policy in the Pacific Islands and the Indigenous Response,* edited by Hermann J Hiery and John M MacKenzie, 82–99. London: I B Tauris.

Barr, Kevin J
1994   Prophetic Priest or Political Activist? *Pacific Journal of Theology* (series 2) 11:35–48.

Besnier, Niko
1995   *Literacy, Emotion, and Authority: Reading and Writing on a Polynesian Atoll.* Cambridge: Cambridge University Press.

Bevans, Stephen B
1992   *Models of Contextual Theology.* Maryknoll, NY: Orbis Books.

Bialecki, Jon
2012   Virtual Christianity in an Age of Nominalist Anthropology. *Anthropological Theory* 12 (3): 295–319.

2017   *A Diagram for Fire: Miracles and Variation in an American Charismatic Movement.* Berkeley: University of California Press.

2018   Anthropology, Theology, and the Problem of Incommensurability. In *Theologically Engaged Anthropology,* edited by J Derrick Lemons, 156–178. Oxford: Oxford University Press.

Bielo, James S
2009   Introduction: Encountering Biblicism. In *The Social Life of Scriptures: Cross-Cultural Perspectives on Biblicism,* edited by James S Bielo, 1–9. New Brunswick, NJ: Rutgers University Press.

Birch, L Charles
1965   *Nature and God.* London: SCM Press.

Bird, Cliff
    2009   Re-Conceptualising Salvation: Some Insights from a Solomon Islands Cul-
           ture towards a Relevant Theology of Salvation for Today. *Pacific Journal of*
           Theology (series 2) 42:23–39.

Bloch, Maurice
    1975   Introduction. In *Political Language and Oratory in Traditional Society,* edited
           by Maurice Bloch, 1–28. London: Academic Press.

Boseto, Leslie
    1995   Do Not Separate Us from Our Land and Sea. *Pacific Journal of Theology*
           (series 2) 13:69–72.

Boyarin, Jonathan
    1990   *Intertextuality and the Reading of Midrash.* Bloomington: Indiana University
           Press.

Brenneis, Donald
    1984   Grog and Gossip in Bhatgaon: Style and Substance in Fiji Indian Conver-
           sation. *American Ethnologist* 11 (3): 487–506.

Brown, Terry
    2005   Christian Contextual Theology–A Pacific Example. *Pacific Journal of Theol-*
           ogy (series 2) 33:5–35.

Brueggemann, Walter
    1977   *The Land: Place as Gift, Promise, and Challenge in Biblical Faith.* Philadelphia:
           Fortress Press.

Bush, Joseph
    1997   Response to Haraka Gaudi. *Pacific Journal of Theology* (series 2) 17:65–71.

Callick, Rowan
    1977   Appendix: An Account of a Theologian's Workshop. In *Christ in Melanesia:*
           Exploring Theological Issues, 256–261. Biannual edition of *Point.* Goroka:
           Melanesian Institute for Pastoral and Socio-Economic Service.

Caputo, John D
    1993   *Demythologizing Heidegger.* Bloomington: Indiana University Press.

Carroll, Seforosa
    2008   Out of the Womb: Reflections on Women and Theology from the Pacific and
           Pacific Diaspora. Presentation at Talanoa Oceania conference, Sydney, 30
           Sept; notes online at https://docs.google.com/viewer?a=v&pid=sites&srcid
           =bm9tb2EuY29tfHRhbGFub2F8Z3g6NGRkZTFmNzBlMmQ2YzhjMQ
           [accessed 30 Aug 2016]
    2010a Stranded... *Pacific Journal of Theology* (series 2) 43:16–43.
    2010b Homemaking in the Diaspora: A Theological Framework for Homing as a
           Niu Local. *Pacific Journal of Theology* (series 2) 44:16–29.

Carson, Rachel
    1962   *Silent Spring.* Boston: Houghton Mifflin.

Carter, G G
    1966a The Dedication of the Pacific Theological College. *Pacific Journal of Theol-*
           ogy 19–20: 65–67.

[Carter, G G]
    1966b Further Celebrations at the Opening of the Pacific Theological College.
           Pacific Journal of Theology 19–20: 68–69.

Casimira, Aisake
  2008   *Who Do You Say I Am? Interaction between Bible and Culture.* Suva: Ecumenical Centre for Research, Education and Advocacy.

Chang, Ying-Cheng
  2018   Interdisciplinary Engagement: The Contextuality of Two "Indigenous" Christians in Taiwan. *St Mark's Review* 244:100–113.

Churchward, C Maxwell
  1959   *Tongan Dictionary: Tongan-English and English-Tongan.* Nuku'alofa: Government of Tonga.

Clery, Tui Nicola
  2014   Extending the Talanoa: Weaving Pacific and Performative Methods for Peace Research in Contemporary Fiji. In *Talanoa: Building a Pasifika Research Culture,* edited by Peggy Fairbairn-Dunlop and Eve Coxon, 105–127. Auckland: Dunmore Publishing.

Coleman, Simon
  2006   When Silence Isn't Golden: Charismatic Speech and the Limits of Literalism. In *The Limits of Meaning: Case Studies in the Anthropology of Christianity,* edited by Matthew Engelke and Matt Tomlinson, 39–61. New York: Berghahn.

Crapanzano, Vincent
  2000   *Serving the Word: Literalism in America from the Pulpit to the Bench.* New York: New Press.

Culbertson, Philip, and Susan Smith
  2010   Conclusion: Opening Up Conversations. In *Spirit Possession, Theology, and Identity: A Pacific Exploration,* edited by Elaine M Wainwright, Philip Culbertson, and Susan Smith, 271–293. Hindmarsh, South Australia: ATF Press.

Deverell, Bruce J
  1966   The Church and Custom. *Pacific Journal of Theology* 19–20: 57–65.
  1986   Models in Theological Education: The Role of the Christian Educator at the Pacific Theological College, Suva. DMin dissertation, Pacific School of Religion, Berkeley.

Doom, John
  1983   The Protest by Churches to Nuclear Testing in the Pacific. In *Before It's Too Late: The Challenge of Nuclear Disarmament,* edited by Paul Abrecht and Ninan Koshy, 353–354. Geneva: World Council of Churches.

Duranti, Alessandro
  1984   Lāuga and Talanoaga: Two Speech Genres in a Samoan Political Event. In *Dangerous Words: Language and Politics in the Pacific,* edited by Donald L Brenneis and Fred R Myers, 217–242. New York: New York University Press.
  1994   *From Grammar to Politics: Linguistic Anthropology in a Western Samoan Village.* Berkeley: University of California Press.
  1997   Indexical Speech Across Samoan Communities. *American Anthropologist* 99 (2): 342–354.

Dyson, Martin
  1875   *My Story of Samoan Methodism; Or, a Brief History of the Wesleyan Methodist Mission in Samoa.* Melbourne: Fergusson and Moore.

Efi, Tui Atua Tupua Tamasese Ta'isi

2009a Faasamoa Speaks to My Heart and My Soul. In *Su'esu'e Manogi: In Search of Fragrance; Tui Atua Tupua Tamasese Ta'isi and the Samoan Indigenous Reference*, edited by Tamasailau M Suaalii-Sauni, I'uogafa Tuagalu, Tofilau Nina Kirifi-Alai, and Naomi Fuamatu, 52–60. Lepapaigalagala, Sāmoa: Centre for Samoan Studies, National University of Samoa. First presented in 2000 as a keynote address to the Pasifika Medical Association Conference, Auckland.

2009b In Search of Harmony: Peace in the Samoan Indigenous Religion. In *Su'esu'e Manogi: In Search of Fragrance; Tui Atua Tupua Tamasese Ta'isi and the Samoan Indigenous Reference*, edited by Tamasailau M Suaalii-Sauni, I'uogafa Tuagalu, Tofilau Nina Kirifi-Alai, and Naomi Fuamatu, 104–114. Lepapaigalagala, Sāmoa: Centre for Samoan Studies, National University of Samoa. First presented in 2005 as a paper at "Resources for Peace in Traditional Religions: Acts of the Colloquium," Vatican City, Rome, 12–15 January.

2009c In Search of Tagaloa: Pulemelei, Samoan Mythology and Science. In *Su'esu'e Manogi: In Search of Fragrance; Tui Atua Tupua Tamasese Ta'isi and the Samoan Indigenous Reference*, edited by Tamasailau M Suaalii-Sauni, I'uogafa Tuagalu, Tofilau Nina Kirifi-Alai, and Naomi Fuamatu, 189–198. Lepapaigalagala, Sāmoa: Centre for Samoan Studies, National University of Samoa. First presented in 2004 as a keynote address at the Kon-Tiki Museum's Samoan Exhibition, Oslo, 16 April.

2014 Whispers and Vanities in Samoan Indigenous Religious Culture. In *Whispers and Vanities: Samoan Indigenous Knowledge and Religion*, edited by Tamasailau M Suaalii-Sauni, Maualaivao Albert Wendt, Vitolia Mo'a, Naomi Fuamatu, Upolu Lumā Va'ai, Reina Whaitiri, and Stephen L Filipo, 11–41. Wellington: Huia.

Ehrman, Bart D

2005 *Misquoting Jesus: The Story Behind Who Changed the Bible and Why*. New York: HarperSanFrancisco.

Elisaia, Elisaia

2008 The Significance of Wesley's Sermon on "The Use of Money" in Relation to the Samoan Concept of *Fa'asoa* and Its Existence in the Samoan Methodist Church. BD thesis, Piula Theological College, Sāmoa.

Engelke, Matthew

2014 Exchanging Words: Anthropology and Theology. Association of Social Anthropologists conference plenary presentation, Edinburgh, June.

Engelke, Matthew, and Joel Robbins, editors

2010 *Global Christianity, Global Critique*. Special issue of *South Atlantic Quarterly* 109 (4).

Ernst, Manfred

1994 *Winds of Change: Rapidly Growing Religious Groups in the Pacific Islands*. Suva: Pacific Conference of Churches.

Ernst, Manfred, editor

2006 *Globalization and the Re-Shaping of Christianity in the Pacific Islands*. Suva: Pacific Theological College.

Ete-Lima, Michiko

2003 A Theology of the Feagaiga: A Samoan Theology of God. In *Weavings: Women Doing Theology in Oceania*, edited by Lydia Johnson and Joan

Alleluia Filemoni-Tofaeono, 24–31. Suva: Weavers/SPATS and Institute of Pacific Studies, University of the South Pacific.

2013   The Martha and Mary in Me the Faletua! *Malua Journal* 1:87–103.

Ewins, Rory

1998   *Changing Their Minds: Tradition and Politics in Contemporary Fiji and Tonga.* Christchurch, NZ: Macmillan Brown Centre for Pacific Studies.

Fa'aeafaleupolu, Hemisemidemiquaver

2004   The Relevancy of EFKS Worship Today. BD thesis, Malua Theological College, Sāmoa.

Fa'alafi, Fineaso T S

1982   An Historical Survey of the Changing Role and Status of Samoan Women. BD thesis, Pacific Theological College, Suva.

1994   A Century in the Making of the Samoan Church: 1828–1928. ThD dissertation, Melbourne College of Divinity.

2005   *Carrying the Faith: Samoan Methodism: 1828–1928.* Apia: Piula Theological College.

Fa'asi'i, Urima

1993   Gospel and Culture in the Ava Ceremony. *Pacific Journal of Theology* (series 2) 10:61–63.

Faitala, Hariesa

2003   Journey to a Forbidden Land: My Life in God's Service. In *Weavings: Women Doing Theology in Oceania,* edited by Lydia Johnson and Joan Alleluia Filemoni-Tofaeono, 200–203. Suva: Weavers/SPATS and Institute of Pacific Studies, University of the South Pacific.

Faleali'i, Nafatali

2002   The Congregational Christian Church in American Samoa as a Liberated Mission Church: A Theological Approach to the Problem of Church Defection. BD thesis, Kanana Fou Theological Seminary.

Faleali'i, Tele'a Logoleo V

1998   God in the Ava Ceremony: A Theological Reflection from One Polynesian Context. Master's thesis, Pacific Theological College, Suva.

Festinger, Leon, Henry W Riecken, and Stanley Schacter

1956   *When Prophecy Fails.* Minneapolis: University of Minnesota Press.

Fewell, Danna Nolan, editor

1992   *Reading between Texts: Intertextuality and the Hebrew Bible.* Louisville: Westminster/John Knox Press.

Fiji Bureau of Statistics

2016   Population by Religion and by Race—1996 Census of Population. http:// www.statsfiji.gov.fj/statistics/social-statistics/religion [accessed 26 July 2016]

Filemoni-Tofaeono, Joan Alleluia

2002   Marthya: Her Meneutic of His Story, A Reflection on Luke 10:38–42. *Pacific Journal of Theology* (series 2) 28:73–88.

2003   A Reflection on Luke 10:38–42, Marthya: Her Meneutic of His Story. In *Weavings: Women Doing Theology in Oceania,* edited by Lydia Johnson and Joan Alleluia Filemoni-Tofaeono, 108–132. Suva: Weavers/SPATS and Institute of Pacific Studies, University of the South Pacific.

Filemoni-Tofaeono, Joan Alleluia, and Lydia Johnson
  2006   *Reweaving the Relational Mat: A Christian Response to Violence against Women from Oceania.* London: Equinox.
Finau, Sitaleki 'Ata'ata, Si'ata Tavite, 'Eseta Finau, and Daleki Fole Finau
  2010   Fakaui of the Pacific Peoples: "United We Stand Divided We Fall." In *Talanoa Rhythms: Voices from Oceania,* edited by Nāsili Vaka'uta, 137–168. Palmerston North, NZ: Pasifika@Massey.
Fonoti, Ioane Vito
  2011   *Faafaaipoipoga o le Faakerisiano ma le Aganuu Faasamoa.* Auckland: privately published.
Forman, Charles W
  1986   *The Voice of Many Waters.* Suva: Lotu Pasifika Productions.
  2005   Finding Our Own Voice: The Reinterpreting of Christianity by Oceanian Theologians. *International Bulletin of Missionary Research* 29 (3): 115–122.
Fountain, Philip, and Sin Wen Lau, editors
  2013   *Anthropological Theologies: Engagements and Encounters.* Special issue of *The Australian Journal of Anthropology* 24 (3).
Fountain, Philip, Douglas Hynd, and Tobias Tan
  2018   Theology, Anthropology, and the Invocation to Be Otherwise. *St Mark's Review* 244:9–21.
Freeman, J D
  1959   The Joe Gimlet or Siovili Cult: An Episode in the Religious History of Early Samoa. In *Anthropology in the South Seas: Essays Presented to H.D. Skinner,* edited by J D Freeman and W R Geddes, 185–200. New Plymouth, NZ: Thomas Avery & Sons.
Freud, Sigmund
  1961   *Civilization and Its Discontents.* Edited and translated by James Strachey. New York: W W Norton. First published in 1930 as *Das Unbehagen in der Kultur* (Vienna: Internationaler Psychoanalytischer Verlag).
Fugui, Leslie
  1986   Melanesian Sacrifice and Christianity. In *Christ in South Pacific Cultures,* edited by Cliff Wright and Leslie Fugui, 36–41. Suva: Lotu Pasifika Productions.
Fuka-Tu'itupou, Lynette Mo'unga
  2001   Introduction. In *Tonga—Women and Theological Impact,* edited by Lynette Mo'unga Fuka-Tu'itupou, 9–13. Alexander, NC: Mountain Church.
Fuka-Tu'itupou, Lynette Mo'unga, editor
  2001   *Tonga—Women and Theological Impact.* Alexander, NC: Mountain Church.
Fusi, Teatu
  2005   Tuvalu: A Sinking Nation. BD thesis, Malua Theological College, Sāmoa.
Garner, Stephen
  2011   Morningside for Life! Contextual Theology Meets Animated Television in bro'Town. *Studies in World Christianity* 17 (2): 156–174.
Garrett, John
  1982   *To Live Among the Stars: Christian Origins in Oceania.* Geneva: World Council of Churches; Suva: Institute of Pacific Studies, University of the South Pacific.

1997   *Where Nets Were Cast: Christianity in Oceania Since World War II.* Suva: Institute of Pacific Studies at the University of the South Pacific; Geneva: World Council of Churches.

Garrett, John, and John Mavor
1973   *Worship, the Pacific Way.* Suva: Lotu Pasifika Productions.

Geertz, Clifford
1974   Religion as a Cultural System. In *The Interpretation of Cultures: Selected Essays,* 87–125. New York: Basic Books. First published in 1966 in *Anthropological Approaches to the Study of Religion,* edited by Michael Banton (London: Tavistock), 1–46.

Gell, Alfred
1995   Closure and Multiplication: An Essay on Polynesian Cosmology and Ritual. In *Cosmos and Society in Oceania,* edited by Daniel de Coppet and André Iteanu, 21–56. Oxford: Berg.

Germon, Cyril
1963   What Can the Pacific Contribute to the [*sic*] Theology? *Pacific Journal of Theology* 7:5–7.
1964   Pacific Theological College: Adventure in Theological Training. *Pacific Journal of Theology* 12:26–27.
1965   The Laying of the Foundation Stone of the Pacific Theological College. *Pacific Journal of Theology* 14:22–23.
2001   Planning the Pacific Theological College (PTC): The Idea of a Central Theological College for the Pacific. *South Pacific Journal of Mission Studies* 25:24–28.

Gershon, Ilana
2006   Converting Meanings and the Meanings of Conversion in Samoan Moral Economies. In *The Limits of Meaning: Case Studies in the Anthropology of Christianity,* edited by Matthew Engelke and Matt Tomlinson, 147–163. New York: Berghahn.
2012   *No Family Is an Island: Cultural Expertise among Samoans in Diaspora.* Ithaca, NY: Cornell University Press.

Gibbs, Philip
2010   Emerging Indigenous Theologies in Oceania. *Concilium* 2010 (5): 34–44.

Glazier, Stephen D
2000   Anthropology and Theology: The Legacy of a Link. In *Anthropology and Theology: God, Icons, and God-Talk,* edited by Walter Randolph Adams and Frank A Salamone, 407–423. Lanham, MD: University Press of America.

Golub, Alex, and Jon Peterson
2016   How Mana Left the Pacific and Became a Video Game Mechanic. In *New Mana: Transformations in a Classic Concept in Pacific Languages and Cultures,* edited by Matt Tomlinson and Ty P Kāwika Tengan, 309–347. Canberra: ANU Press.

Goodall, Norman
1954   *A History of the London Missionary Society, 1895–1945.* London: Oxford University Press.

Goodman, Richard A
1971   Some Aitu Beliefs of Modern Samoans. *Journal of the Polynesian Society* 80 (4): 463–479.

Goundar, Shiu Nathan
    2005   Talanoa: The Way Forward for Peace, Unity and Reconciliation in Fiji. Master's thesis, University of Auckland.

Gumperz, John J, and Stephen C Levinson
    1996   Introduction: Linguistic Relativity Re-Examined. In *Rethinking Linguistic Relativity,* edited by John J Gumperz and Stephen C Levinson, 1–18. Cambridge, UK: Cambridge University Press.

Gunn, David M
    2014   Breaking Bible Boundaries. In *Bible, Borders, Belonging(s): Engaging Readings from Oceania,* edited by Jione Havea, David J Neville, and Elaine M Wainwright, 249–257. Atlanta: Society of Biblical Literature.

Gutiérrez, Gustavo
    1974   *A Theology of Liberation: History, Politics and Salvation.* Translated by Caridad Inda and John Eagleson. London: SCM Press.

Hage, Ghassan
    2005   A Not So Multi-Sited Ethnography of a Not So Imagined Community. *Anthropological Theory* 5 (4): 463–475.

Halapua, Sitiveni
    2013   Talanoa in Building Democracy and Governance. Paper presented at "Future Leaders of the Pacific" conference, Pago Pago, American Sāmoa, February. http://talanoa.org/Home_files/Talanoa%20in%20Building%20Democracy%20and%20Governance.pdf [accessed 19 Dec 2015]
    2015   Talanoa Process: The Case of Fiji. http://unpan1.un.org/intradoc/groups/public/documents/un/unpan022610.pdf [accessed 19 Dec 2015]

Halapua, Winston
    1998   Fakakakato: Symbols in a Pacific Context. *Pacific Journal of Theology* (series 2) 20:21–32.
    2003   *Tradition, Lotu and Militarism in Fiji.* Lautoka: Fiji Institute of Applied Studies.
    2008a Moana Methodology: A Way of Promoting Dynamic Leadership. Address at the Talanoa Oceania conference, Sydney, 30 Sept. https://sites.google.com/a/nomoa.com/talanoa/Home/papers-presentations/halapua—moana [accessed 6 Nov 2014]
    2008b *Waves of God's Embrace: Sacred Perspectives from the Ocean.* London: Canterbury Press Norwich.

Handman, Courtney
    2015   *Critical Christianity: Translation and Denominational Conflict in Papua New Guinea.* Berkeley: University of California Press.

Hardin, Jessica
    2015   Christianity, Fat Talk, and Samoan Pastors: Rethinking the Fat-Positive-Fat-Stigma Framework. *Fat Studies* 4 (2): 178–196.
    2016   "God Is Your Health": Healing Metabolic Disorders in Samoa. In *Christianity, Conflict, and Renewal in Australia and the Pacific,* edited by Fiona Magowan and Carolyn Schwarz, 183–204. Leiden: Brill.

Harding, Susan Friend
    2000   *The Book of Jerry Falwell: Fundamentalist Language and Politics.* Princeton: Princeton University Press.

Hau'ofa, Epeli
   1993a A Beginning. In *A New Oceania: Rediscovering Our Sea of Islands,* edited by
           Eric Waddell, Vijay Naidu, and Epeli Hau'ofa, 126–139. Suva: School of
           Social and Economic Development, University of the South Pacific.
   1993b Our Sea of Islands. In *A New Oceania: Rediscovering Our Sea of Islands,* edited
           by Eric Waddell, Vijay Naidu, and Epeli Hau'ofa, 2–16. Suva: School of
           Social and Economic Development, University of the South Pacific.
Havea, Jione
   1998 "Tau Lave!" (Let's Talk). *Pacific Journal of Theology* (series 2) 20:63–73.
   2003 *Elusions of Control: Biblical Law on the Words of Women.* Leiden: Brill.
   2004a Numbers. In *Global Bible Commentary,* edited by Daniel Patte, 43–51. Nash-
           ville: Abingdon Press.
   2004b Would the Real Native Please Sit Down! In *Faith in a Hyphen: Cross-Cultural
           Theologies Down Under,* edited by Clive Pearson, 199–210. Adelaide, South
           Australia: Openbook Publishers and UTC Publications.
   2010a The Politics of Climate Change: A Talanoa from Oceania. *International
           Journal of Public Theology* 4 (3): 345–355.
   2010b Sea of Talanoa: Gift and Gifting. In *Talanoa Ripples: Across Borders, Cultures,
           Disciplines,* edited by Jione Havea, 180–192. Palmerston North: Pasifika@
           Massey; Auckland: Masilamea Press.
   2010c Welcome to Talanoa. In *Talanoa Ripples: Across Borders, Cultures, Disciplines,*
           edited by Jione Havea, 11–22. Palmerston North: Pasifika@Massey; Auck-
           land: Masilamea Press.
   2011 The Cons of Contextuality...Kontextuality. In *Contextual Theology for the
           Twenty-First Century,* edited by Stephen B Bevans and Katalina Tahaafe-
           Williams, 38–52. Eugene, OR: Pickwick Publications.
   2012 Kautaha in Island Hermeneutics, Governance and Leadership. *Pacific
           Journal of Theology* (series 2) 47:3–13.
   2013 Death Roots: Musings of a Pacific Island Native. In *Pacific Identities and
           Well-Being,* edited by Margaret Nelson Agee, Tracey McIntosh, Philip Cul-
           bertson, and Cabrini 'Ofa Makasiale, 157–168. New York: Routledge.
   2014a Bare Feet Welcome: Redeemer Xs Moses @ Enaim. In *Bible, Borders,
           Belonging(s): Engaging Readings from Oceania,* edited by Jione Havea, David
           J Neville, and Elaine M Wainwright, 209–222. Atlanta: Society of Biblical
           Literature.
   2014b Engaging Scriptures from Oceania. In *Bible, Borders, Belonging(s): Engaging
           Readings from Oceania,* edited by Jione Havea, David J Neville, and Elaine
           M Wainwright, 3–19. Atlanta: Society of Biblical Literature.
Havea, Jione, editor
   2010 *Talanoa Ripples: Across Borders, Cultures, Disciplines.* Palmerston North:
           Pasifika@Massey; Auckland: Masilamea Press.
Havea, John A [Sione 'Amanaki Havea]
   1956 Church Unity in the South Pacific. *The Ecumenical Review* 8 (2): 197–200.
Havea, Sione 'Amanaki
   1977 The Pacificness of Theology. *Mission Review* 2 (Dec): 3–4.
   1982 Moving Towards a Pacific Theology. *Mission Review* 19 (April–June):
           4–5.

1986   Pacific Theology. In *Towards a Relevant Pacific Theology: Theological Consulta-
         tion, Bergengren House, Suva, 8–12 July 1985,* 21–24. Suva: Lotu Pasifika.
1987   Christianity in the Pacific Context. In *South Pacific Theology: Papers from the
         Consultation on Pacific Theology, Papua New Guinea, January 1986,* 11–15. Par-
         ramatta: World Vision International South Pacific; Oxford: Regnum Books.

Helu, 'I Futa [misspelled as M F Halu]
1994   The Prophet. *Pacific Journal of Theology* (series 2) 11:17–19.

Hezel, Francis X
1992   The Cruel Dilemma: Money Economies in the Pacific. *Pacific Journal of
         Theology* (series 2) 8:11–21.

Hobsbawm, Eric
1983   Introduction: Inventing Traditions. In *The Invention of Tradition,* edited by
         Eric Hobsbawm and Terence Ranger, 1–14. Cambridge, UK: Cambridge
         University Press.

Hocart, A M
1929   *Lau Islands, Fiji.* Honolulu: Bernice P Bishop Museum.

Hoiore, Here J
2011   A Devotion. *Pacific Journal of Theology* (series 2) 45:44–49.

Holquist, Michael
1990   *Dialogism: Bakhtin and His World.* London: Routledge.

Howell, Brian M
2007   The Repugnant Cultural Other Speaks Back: Christian Identity as Ethno-
         graphic "Standpoint." *Anthropological Theory* 7 (4): 371–391.

Ieremia, Lale
1967   The Indigenisation of Worship: The Use of Traditional Ceremonies.
         Pacific Journal of Theology 25:22–26.

Inoue, Miyako
2006   *Vicarious Language: Gender and Linguistic Modernity in Japan.* Berkeley: Uni-
         versity of California Press.

Jenkins, Timothy
2007   The Next Christendom: The Coming of Global Christianity. Revised and
         expanded edition. New York: Oxford University Press.

Johnson, Lydia
2003   Introduction: "Weaving the Mat" of Pacific Women's Theology: A Case
         Study in Women's Theological Method. In *Weavings: Women Doing Theology
         in Oceania,* edited by Lydia Johnson and Joan Alleluia Filemoni-Tofaeono,
         10–22. Suva: Weavers/SPATS and Institute of Pacific Studies, University of
         the South Pacific.

Johnson, Todd M, and Gina A Zurlo, editors
2007   *World Christian Database.* Leiden: Brill.

Kamu, Lalomilo
1996   *The Samoan Culture and the Christian Gospel.* Apia: Donna Lou Kamu.

Kanana Fou Theological Seminary
2014   Our History. http://www.kftseminary.org/History.html [accessed 5 Feb
         2016]
2016   *Handbook, 2015–2017.* Revised edition. Tafuna, American Sāmoa: Kanana
         Fou Theological Seminary.

Kanongata'a, Keiti Ann
　　1992　A Pacific Women's Theology of Birthing and Liberation. *Pacific Journal of Theology* (series 2) 7:3–11.
　　2002　Why Contextual? *Pacific Journal of Theology* (series 2) 27:21–40.
Keane, Webb
　　1997　*Signs of Recognition: Powers and Hazards of Representation in an Indonesian Society.* Berkeley: University of California Press.
　　2013　Reflections on Political Theology in the Pacific. In *Christian Politics in Oceania,* edited by Matt Tomlinson and Debra McDougall, 211–223. New York: Berghahn.
Keesing, Felix M
　　1934　*Modern Samoa: Its Government and Changing Life.* London: George Allen & Unwin.
Keesing, Felix M, and Marie M Keesing
　　1956　*Elite Communication in Samoa: A Study of Leadership.* Stanford: Stanford University Press.
Khan, Chantelle
　　2003　Looking for God with New Eyes. In *Weavings: Women Doing Theology in Oceania,* edited by Lydia Johnson and Joan Alleluia Filemoni-Tofaeono, 186–191. Suva: Weavers/SPATS and Institute of Pacific Studies, University of the South Pacific.
King, Ursula
　　1994　Introduction. In *Feminist Theology from the Third World: A Reader,* edited by Ursula King. London: Society for Promoting Christian Knowledge; New York: Orbis Press.
Knox, R A
　　1950　*Enthusiasm: A Chapter in the History of Religion.* Oxford: Clarendon Press.
Knuth, Anton
　　2012　Second response to keynote address. *Pacific Journal of Theology* (series 2) 47:59–66.
Koria, Paulo
　　1999　Moving Toward a Pacific Theology: Theologising with Concepts. *Pacific Journal of Theology* (series 2) 22:3–14.
Krämer, Augustin
　　1994　*The Samoa Islands.* Vol 1. Translated by Theodore Verhaaren. Auckland: Polynesian Press. First published in 1902–1903 as *Die Samoa-inseln* (Stuttgart: E Schweizerbart).
Kupa, Samasoni
　　2006　Jesus Christ: The Revelation of "Fa'aaloalo." BD thesis, Malua Theological College, Sāmoa.
Küster, Volker
　　2010　*A Protestant Theology of Passion: Korean Minjung Theology Revisited.* Leiden: Brill.
Lamb, Marie
　　1964　The Role of Women. *Pacific Journal of Theology* 12:8–9.
Larsen, Timothy
　　2014　*The Slain God: Anthropologists and the Christian Faith.* Oxford: Oxford University Press.

Latai, Latu
   2015   Changing Covenants in Samoa? From Brothers and Sisters to Husbands and Wives? *Oceania* 85 (1): 92–104.
   2016   Covenant Keepers: A History of Samoan (LMS) Missionary Wives in the Western Pacific from 1839 to 1979. PhD dissertation, Australian National University.

Lawson, Stephanie
   2010   "The Pacific Way" as Postcolonial Discourse. *Journal of Pacific History* 45 (3): 297–314.

Leach, Edmund
   1972   The Structure of Symbolism. In *The Interpretation of Ritual: Essays in Honour of A. I. Richards,* edited by J S La Fontaine, 239–275. London: Tavistock.

Leaupepe, Malutafa
   2013   Nafanua: A Prophetess of God: The Congregational Christian Church Samoa and Hermeneutics. *Malua Journal* 1:39–47.

Lebot, Vincent, Mark Merlin, and Lamont Lindstrom
   1992   *Kava: The Pacific Drug.* New Haven: Yale University Press.

Legrand, Lucien
   2000   *The Bible on Culture: Belonging or Dissenting?* Maryknoll, NY: Orbis.

Lévi-Strauss, Claude
   1987   *Introduction to the Work of Marcel Mauss.* Translated by Felicity Baker. London: Routledge & Kegan Paul. First published in 1950 as *Introduction à l'oeuvre de Marcel Mauss* (Paris: Presses Universitaires de France).

Lima, Peletisala
   2012   Performing a Remigrant Theology: Sons and Daughters Improvising on the Return Home. PhD dissertation, Charles Sturt University, Australia.

Lindstrom, Lamont
   1982   Grog Blong Yumi: Alcohol and Kava on Tanna, Vanuatu. In *Through a Glass Darkly: Beer and Modernization in Papua New Guinea,* edited by Mac Marshall, 421–432. Boroko, PNG: Institute of Applied Social and Economic Research.

Linnekin, Jocelyn
   1990   The Politics of Culture in the Pacific. In *Cultural Identity and Ethnicity in the Pacific,* edited by Jocelyn Linnekin and Lin Poyer, 149–173. Honolulu: University of Hawai'i Press.

Liuaana, Featuna'i Ben
   2004   *Samoa Tula'i: Ecclesiastical and Political Face of Samoa's Independence, 1900–1962.* Malua, Sāmoa: Malua Printing Press.

Luhrmann, T M
   2012   *When God Talks Back: Understanding the American Evangelical Relationship with God.* New York: Alfred A Knopf.

Lütgert, Wilhelm
   1934   *Schöpfung und Offenbarung: Eine Theologie des ersten Artikels.* Gütersloh, Germany: C Bertelsmann.

Macpherson, Cluny, and La'avasa Macpherson
   2010   *The Warm Winds of Change: Globalization in Contemporary Samoa.* Auckland: Auckland University Press.

Mageo, Jeanette
  1998   *Theorizing Self in Samoa: Emotions, Genders, and Sexualities.* Ann Arbor: University of Michigan Press.
Maʻilo Fuaivaʻa, Mosese
  2001   Jesus' Attitude Towards Women in the Gospel According to John (2:1–11; 20:11–18). BD thesis, Piula Theological College, Sāmoa.
  2008   The Politics of Bible Translation in Early 19th Century Polynesia: Re-Examining the Construction of the Samoan Bible Translation in the Light of Contemporary Postcolonial Concerns. PhD dissertation, University of Birmingham.
  2011   The Challenge and Contribution of Postcolonial Theory to Theological Hermeneutics in Oceania. *Pacific Journal of Theology* (series 2) 46:34–54.
  2013   Celebrating Hybridity in Island Bibles: Jesus, From Tamaalepo (Son of the Dark) into Tamaʻaiga (Son with Many Families) in Mataio 1:18–26. *Pacific Journal of Theology* (series 2) 50:48–60.
  2015   Celebrating Hybridity in Island Bibles: Jesus, the Tamaalepō (Child of the Dark) in Mataio 1:18–26. In *Islands, Islanders, and the Bible: RumInations,* edited by Jione Havea, Margaret Aymer, and Steed Vernyl Davidson, 65–76. Atlanta: SBL Press.
  2016   *Bible-ing My Samoan.* Apia: Piula Theological College.
Maliko, Mercy
  2009   Piula Theological College Theses and Projects Report, 2001–2008. *Pacific Journal of Theology* (series 2) 41:86–99.
Maliko, Tavita
  2012   O Le Sogaʻimiti: An Embodiment of God in the Samoan Male Body. PhD dissertation, University of Auckland.
Malley, Brian
  2009   Understanding the Bible's Influence. In *The Social Life of Scriptures: Cross-Cultural Perspectives on Biblicism,* edited by James S Bielo, 194–204. New Brunswick, NJ: Rutgers University Press.
Malogne-Fer, Gwendoline
  2016   A Dispute at the Lord's Supper: Theology and Culture in the Māʻohi Protestant Church (French Polynesia). In *Christianity, Conflict, and Renewal in Australia and the Pacific,* edited by Fiona Magowan and Carolyn Schwarz, 35–58. Leiden: Brill.
Mara, Ratu Sir Kamisese
  1997   *The Pacific Way: A Memoir.* Honolulu: University of Hawaiʻi Press.
Marcus, George E
  1980a   *The Nobility and the Chiefly Tradition in the Modern Kingdom of Tonga.* Wellington: The Polynesian Society.
  1980b   Role Distance in Conversations between Tongan Nobles and Their "People." *Journal of the Polynesian Society* 89 (4): 435–453.
Mariota, Martin Wilson
  2012   A Samoan Palagi Reading of Exodus 2–3. Master's thesis, University of Auckland.
Mathews, Jeanette
  2014   Deuteronomy 30: Faithfulness in the Refugee Camps of Moab, Babylonia, and Beyond. In *Bible, Borders, Belonging(s): Engaging Readings from Oceania,*

edited by Jione Havea, David J Neville, and Elaine M Wainwright, 157–170. Atlanta: Society of Biblical Literature.

Mawyer, Alexander
  2016 The State of Mana, the Mana of the State. In *New Mana: Transformations in a Classic Concept in Pacific Languages and Cultures,* edited by Matt Tomlinson and Ty P Kāwika Tengan, 203–236. Canberra: ANU Press.

McClintock, Anne
  1995 *Imperial Leather: Race, Gender, and Sexuality in the Colonial Contest.* London: Routledge.

McFague, Sallie
  1987 *Models of God: Theology for an Ecological, Nuclear Age.* Philadelphia: Fortress Press.

McKinlay, Judith E
  2014 Slipping Across Borders and Bordering on Conquest: A Contrapuntal Reading of Numbers 13. In *Bible, Borders, Belonging(s): Engaging Readings from Oceania,* edited by Jione Havea, David J Neville, and Elaine M Wainwright, 125–142. Atlanta: Society of Biblical Literature.

Meleiseā, Mālama
  1980 We Want the Forest, yet Fear the Spirits: Culture and Change in Western Samoa. *Pacific Perspective* 9 (1): 21–29.
  1987a Ideology in Pacific Studies: A Personal View. In *Class and Culture in the South Pacific,* edited by Antony Hooper, Steve Britton, Ron Crocombe, Judith Huntsman, and Cluny Macpherson, 140–152. Auckland: Centre for Pacific Studies at the University of Auckland; Suva: Institute of Pacific Studies, University of the South Pacific.
  1987b *The Making of Modern Samoa: Traditional Authority and Colonial Administration in the Modern History of Western Samoa.* Suva: Institute of Pacific Studies, University of the South Pacific.
  1992 *Change and Adaptations in Western Samoa.* Christchurch: Macmillan Brown Centre for Pacific Studies, University of Canterbury.

Meneses, Eloise, Lindy Backues, David Bronkema, Eric Flett, and Benjamin L Hartley
  2014 Engaging the Religiously Committed Other: Anthropologists and Theologians in Dialogue. *Current Anthropology* 55 (1): 82–104.

Meo, Ilisapeci
  1990 Why Do Women Remain Silent in Meetings and Discussions with Men? *Pacific Journal of Theology* (series 2) 3:45–47.
  1992 Empowerment for Participation. *Pacific Journal of Theology* (series 2) 7:39–44.
  1994 A Woman's Response to Winds of Change: A Critical Analysis of a Culture-Oriented Church. *Pacific Journal of Theology* (series 2) 12:63–67.
  1996 Feminist Theologies, Pacific Island. In *Dictionary of Feminist Theologies,* edited by Letty M Russell and J Shannon Clarkson, 108–110. London: Mowbray.
  1997 Response to Rev. Marie Ropeti. *Pacific Journal of Theology* (series 2) 17:42–44.
  2003 Asserting Women's Dignity in a Patriarchal World. In *Weavings: Women Doing Theology in Oceania,* edited by Lydia Johnson and Joan Alleluia

Filemoni-Tofaeono, 150–160. Suva: Weavers/SPATS and Institute of Pacific Studies, University of the South Pacific.

2012   Women and Theological Education[:] Its Significance in the 21th [*sic*] Century and Beyond. *Pacific Journal of Theology* (series 2) 47:42–51.

Meo, Jovili, Dorothy A Dale, and Alfred S Dale

1985   *Plant Today for Tomorrow: A Self Study Report of [the] Methodist Church in Fiji and Rotuma*. Suva: Lotu Pasifika Productions.

Meylan, Nicolas

2017   *Mana: A History of a Western Category*. Leiden: Brill.

Migliore, Daniel L

2014   *Faith Seeking Understanding: An Introduction to Christian Theology*. Third edition. Grand Rapids, MI: William B Eerdmans.

Milner, G B

1993   *Samoan Dictionary*. Auckland: Polynesian Press. First published in 1966.

1967   *Fijian Grammar*. Second edition. Suva: Government Printing Department.

Mission Review

1985   Coconut Theology. *Mission Review* 31 (April–June): 7.

Moltmann, Jürgen

1985   *God in Creation: An Ecological Doctrine of Creation*. London: SCM Press.

Morgain, Rachel

2016   Mana for a New Age. In *New Mana: Transformations in a Classic Concept in Pacific Languages and Cultures*, edited by Matt Tomlinson and Ty P Kāwika Tengan, 285–307. Canberra: ANU Press.

Mortreux, Colette, and Jon Barnett

2009   Climate Change, Migration and Adaptation in Funafuti, Tuvalu. *Global Environmental Change* 19 (1): 105–112.

Muir, John

1911   *My First Summer in the Sierra*. Boston: Houghton Mifflin.

Narayan, Kirin

2007   *My Family and Other Saints*. Chicago: University of Chicago Press.

Narokobi, Bernard

1980   *The Melanesian Way: Total Cosmic Vision of Life*. Boroko, PNG: Institute of Papua New Guinea Studies. First published in 1976–1978 as articles in the *Papua New Guinea Post-Courier*.

National Parliament of Solomon Islands

2007   Hon. Rev. Leslie Boseto. http://www.parliament.gov.sb/index.php?q =node/153 [accessed 18 Jan 2016]

Nepo, Gataivai

1990   A Theological Study of "Tautua" (Service) in the Light of the Christian Faith, with Special Reference to the Ministry of the Congregational Christian Church in Samoa. BD project paper (equivalent to a thesis), Pacific Theological College, Suva.

Niebuhr, H Richard

2001   *Christ and Culture*. New edition. New York: HarperOne. First published in 1951 (New York: Harper).

Niuatoa, Moreli

2007   Faʻa-Samoa—The Epistemology of Samoan Spirituality: A Theological and Psychological Exploration for Religious Education of Spiritual Formation. PhD dissertation, Claremont School of Theology.

2009   The "September 29" Event: A Religious (Not Religiosity) Perspective. Manuscript in author's files.

2018   *We Really Lost Jesus in Hermeneutics: Fashion Me a Theology of a "Samoan–Jesus."* Tafuna, American Sāmoa: Kanana Fou Theological Seminary.

Niukula, Paula

1994   *The Three Pillars: The Triple Aspect of Fijian Society.* Suva: Christian Writing Project.

Nofoaiga, Vaitusi Lealaiauloto

2006   Crowds as Jesus' Disciples in the Matthean Gospel. Master's thesis, University of Auckland.

Nokise, Feleterika

1978   A History of the Pacific Islanders' Congregational Church in New Zealand, 1943–1969. Master's thesis, University of Otago.

2011   Ecumenism and Its Hermeneutical Experience in Oceania. *Pacific Journal of Theology* (series 2) 46:95–127.

2015   Navigating the Ecumenical Dream: A Brief History of PTC's First 50 Years. In *Oceanic Voyages in Theology and Theological Education: Reflections and Reminiscences in Celebration of the 50th Anniversary of the Pacific Theological College,* edited by Feleterika Nokise and Holger Szesnat, 7–70. Suva: Pacific Theological College.

Oroi, Aram

2016   "Press the Button, Mama!" Mana and Christianity on Makira, Solomon Islands. In *New Mana: Transformations in a Classic Concept in Pacific Languages and Cultures,* edited by Matt Tomlinson and Ty P Kāwika Tengan, 183–201. Canberra: ANU Press.

Ortner, Sherry B

1973   On Key Symbols. *American Anthropologist* 75 (5): 1338–1346.

Pacific Theological College

2015   *Handbook 2016.* http://ptc.ac.fj/wp/wp-content/uploads/2013/10/Handbk-2016-A5__20151205-FINAL.pdf [accessed 28 Jan 2016]

Palu, Ma'afu

2002   Pacific Theology. *Pacific Journal of Theology* (series 2) 28:21–53.

2003   Pacific Theology: A Reconsideration of Its Methodology. *Pacific Journal of Theology* (series 2) 29:30–58.

2005   Contextualisation as Bridging the Hermeneutical Gap: Some Biblical Paradigms. *Pacific Journal of Theology* (series 2) 34:2–43.

2006   Contextualisation within the Parameters of the Biblical Narrative "World": AIDS as a Test Case. *Pacific Journal of Theology* (series 2) 36:12–25.

2012   Dr Sione 'Amanaki Havea of Tonga: The Architect of Pacific Theology. *Melanesian Journal of Theology* 28 (2): 67–81.

2016   Eaters of the Soil: Holiness for Tongan Wesleyans. World Methodist Evangelism blog post. https://www.worldmethodist.org/kimberly-reisman/maafu-palu-eaters-of-the-soil/ [accessed 17 March 2017]

2017   *Pacific Theology: Problems and Proposals.* Nuku'alofa, Tonga: Ichtus.

Palu, Valamotu

2003   Tapa Making in Tonga: A Metaphor for God's Care. In *Weavings: Women Doing Theology in Oceania,* edited by Lydia Johnson and Joan Alleluia Filemoni-Tofaeono, 62–71. Suva: Weavers/SPATS and Institute of Pacific Studies, University of the South Pacific.

2010   Crossing Over—Peace and Harmony. In *Voices of Tongan Women: Theo-logical Reflections,* edited by Marlene Wilkinson, 35–43. No listed publisher.

Pase, Mine
2003   Gospel and Culture: Samoan Style. In *Weavings: Women Doing Theology in Oceania,* edited by Lydia Johnson and Joan Alleluia Filemoni-Tofaeono, 72–78. Suva: Weavers/SPATS and Institute of Pacific Studies, University of the South Pacific.

Patte, Daniel
2004   Introduction. In *Global Bible Commentary,* edited by Daniel Patte, J Sev-erino Croatto, Nicole Wilkinson Duran, Teresa Okure, and Archie Chi Chung Lee, xxi–xxxiii. Nashville: Abingdon Press.

PCC, PTC, and SPATS; Pacific Conference of Churches, Pacific Theological College, and the South Pacific Association of Theological Schools
1986   Plenary Discussion. In *Towards a Relevant Pacific Theology: Theological Con-sultation, Bergengren House, Suva, 8–12 July 1985.* Suva: Lotu Pasifika.

Pelikan, Jaroslav
1963   The Functions of Theology. In *Theology in the Life of the Church,* edited by R W Bertram, 3–21. Philadelphia: Fortress Press.
1985   *Jesus through the Centuries: His Place in the History of Culture.* New Haven: Yale University Press.

Perelini, Otele
1999   The Emancipation of Church Women: A Biblical Reflection—Luke 13:10–17. *Pacific Journal of Theology* (series 2) 22:15–18.

Peters, John Durham
1999   *Speaking into the Air: A History of the Idea of Communication.* Chicago: Univer-sity of Chicago Press.

PJT, Pacific Journal of Theology
1994   Gratitude. *Pacific Journal of Theology* (series 2) 11:76.

Portola Institute
1972   *The Last Whole Earth Catalog: Access to Tools.* Menlo Park, CA: Portola Institute.

Pouono, Terry
2013   *Teu le Va:* The Samoan Cosmic-Community in *Aotearoa;* Preserving Harmo-nious Relationships...Where Is the Harmony? *Pacific Journal of Theology* (series 2) 50:88–103.

Pratt, George
1862   *A Samoan Dictionary: English and Samoan, and Samoan and English; With a Short Grammar of the Samoan Dialect.* Sāmoa: London Missionary Society Press.

Priest, Robert J
2000   Christian Theology, Sin, and Anthropology. In *Anthropology and Theology: Gods, Icons, and God-talk,* edited by Walter Randolph Adams and Frank A Salamone, 59–75. Lanham, MD: University Press of America.
2001   Missionary Positions: Christian, Modernist, Postmodernist. *Current Anthro-pology* 42 (1): 29–46.

Prior, Randall
1993   I Am the Coconut of Life: An Evaluation of Coconut Theology. *Pacific Journal of Theology* (series 2) 10:31–40.

Puloka, Tevita Tonga Mohenoa
   1998   Evangelization: Culture and Communication. *Pacific Journal of Theology* (series 2) 19:42–54.
   2005   Freedom of Options (Choices) on Traditional Systems. *Pacific Journal of Theology* (series 2) 34:5–21.

Raitiqa, Lesila Taranatoba
   2000   Jesus: Healer of Vanua Sickness and Mana of the Vanua. Master's thesis, Pacific Theological College, Suva.

Ratuvili, Sitiveni
   1971   The Career and Thought of Irenaeus of Lyons, with Special Reference to the Bearing of His Teaching about Church, Scripture and Tradition on the Present Situation of Fiji Methodism. BD thesis, Pacific Theological College, Suva.

Raymond, Miner
   1877–   *Systematic Theology.* 3 volumes. Cincinnati: Hitchcock and Walden.
   1879

Riles, Annelise
   2000   *The Network Inside Out.* Ann Arbor: University of Michigan Press.

Robbins, Joel
   2006   Anthropology and Theology: An Awkward Relationship? *Anthropological Quarterly* 79 (2): 285–294.
   2013a Beyond the Suffering Subject: Toward an Anthropology of the Good. *Journal of the Royal Anthropological Institute* 19 (3): 447–462.
   2013b Let's Keep It Awkward: Anthropology, Theology, and Otherness. *The Australian Journal of Anthropology* 24 (3): 329–337.
   2013c Why Is There No Political Theology among the Urapmin? On Diarchy, Sects as Big as Society, and the Diversity of Pentecostal Politics. In *Christian Politics in Oceania,* edited by Matt Tomlinson and Debra McDougall, 198–210. New York: Berghahn.

Robbins, Joel, and Naomi Haynes, editors
   2014   *The Anthropology of Christianity: Unity, Diversity, New Directions.* Special issue of *Current Anthropology* 55 (S10).

Rogers, Muriel
   2008   To What Extent Does Theological Education in Oceania Perpetuate Violence against Women. *Pacific Journal of Theology* (series 2) 39:5–23.

Rokotuiviwa, Paula
   1975   *The Congregation of the Poor.* Suva: South Pacific Social Sciences Association.

Rubow, Cecilie, and Cliff Bird
   2016   Eco-Theological Responses to Climate Change in Oceania. *Worldviews* 20 (2): 150–168.

Ruether, Rosemary Radford
   1985   Feminist Interpretation: A Method of Correlation. In *Feminist Interpretation of the Bible,* edited by Letty M Russell, 111–124. Oxford: Basil Blackwell.

Rushton, Kathleen P
   2014   On the Crossroads between Life and Death: Reading Birth Imagery in John in the Earthquake-Changed Regions of Otautahi Christchurch. In *Bible, Borders, Belonging(s): Engaging Readings from Oceania,* edited by Jione Havea, David J Neville, and Elaine M Wainwright, 57–72. Atlanta: Society of Biblical Literature.

Ryle, Jacqueline
  2010   *My God, My Land: Interwoven Paths of Christianity and Tradition in Fiji.* Farn-
         ham, Surrey, UK: Ashgate.
Sahlins, Marshall
  1985   *Islands of History.* Chicago: University of Chicago Press.
Sakai, Pemerika
  2009   Ia So'o le Fau ma le Fau (Let the Arched-Purlin Be Connected with the
         Arched-Purlin): A Contextual Theology of Mission in the Samoan Con-
         text. *Pacific Journal of Theology* (series 2) 41:19–34.
Sala, Ulisese Elisara
  1980   A Theology of Samoan Christian Immigrants in the United States. DMin
         professional project, School of Theology at Claremont.
Samate, 'Asinate Fuakautu'u
  2003   The Challenge of a Call to Ministry: A Tongan Woman's Experience in a
         Patriarchal Setting. In *Weavings: Women Doing Theology in Oceania,* edited
         by Lydia Johnson and Joan Alleluia Filemoni-Tofaeono, 165–171. Suva:
         Weavers/SPATS and Institute of Pacific Studies, University of the South
         Pacific.
  2011   The Challenge and Contribution of Gender to Theological Hermeneu-
         tics in Oceania. *Pacific Journal of Theology* (series 2) 46:55–94.
Schoeffel, Penelope
  1995   The Samoan Concept of Feagaiga and Its Transformation. In *Tonga and
         Samoa: Images of Gender and Polity,* edited by Judith Huntsman, 85–106.
         Christchurch: Macmillan Brown Centre for Pacific Studies.
Schreiter, Robert J
  1985   *Constructing Local Theologies.* Maryknoll, NY: Orbis.
Setefano, Imoamaua [writing as Imoa Emanuel Cluny Moa]
  2008   O Le Faifeau—The Servant of God: Redefining the Faifeau Paradigm of
         the Congregational Christian Church of Samoa in Aotearoa New Zea-
         land. Master's thesis, University of Auckland.
Shankman, Paul
  2009   *The Trashing of Margaret Mead: Anatomy of an Anthropological Controversy.*
         Madison: University of Wisconsin Press.
Shore, Bradd
  1976   Incest Prohibitions and the Logic of Power in Samoa. *Journal of the Polyne-
         sian Society* 85 (2): 275–296.
  1982   *Sala'ilua: A Samoan Mystery.* New York: Columbia University Press.
Sila, Saunoa
  2012   Le Laau o le Sopoaga: A Plant for a Journey; Planting Samoan Methodism
         in New Zealand. PhD dissertation, University of Auckland.
Silverstein, Michael
  1976   Shifters, Verbal Categories, and Cultural Description. In *Meaning in
         Anthropology,* edited by Keith H Basso and Henry A Selby, 11–55. Albu-
         querque: University of New Mexico Press.
  2013   Discourse and the No-thing-ness of Culture. *Signs and Society* 1 (2): 327–366.
Simolea, Liusamoa
  2015   Reclaiming Fafine in Isaiah 7:14. Master's thesis, Graduate Theological
         Union, Berkeley.

Smith, Frank
  2010   The Johannine Jesus from a Samoan Perspective: Toward an Intercul-
          tural Reading of the Fourth Gospel. PhD dissertation, University of
          Auckland.
Solomone, Kafoa
  2000   Ecumenism in Oceania. *Pacific Journal of Theology* (series 2) 24:88–106.
Sugirtharajah, R S, editor
  2006   *Voices from the Margin: Interpreting the Bible in the Third World.* Third edition.
          Maryknoll, NY: Orbis Books.
Swain, Tony, and Garry Trompf
  1995   *The Religions of Oceania.* London: Routledge.
Szesnat, Holger
  2010   A Church-State Covenant on the Environment? *Pacific Journal of Theology*
          (series 2) 44:30–55.
Ta'avao, Iopu
  2003   The Theology of Fa'aaloalo: A Manifestation of God's Grace. BD thesis,
          Piula Theological College, Sāmoa.
Talapusi, Faitala
  1976   Jesus Christ in a Pacific World of Spirits. BD project paper (equivalent to
          a thesis), Pacific Theological College, Suva.
Tanaki, Pitasoni
  1964   Youth Bible Study Groups in Niue. *Pacific Journal of Theology* 10:23–24.
Taofinu'u, Pio
  1995   *O Le 'Ava O Se Pelofetaga: The Kava Ceremony Is a Prophecy.* Revised edition.
          Apia: Archdiocese of Western Samoa.
Taotua, Wesley Tulimanu
  2011   An Analysis on the Theological Education of Ministers and Its Relevance
          to the Expanding Ministry of the Methodist Church Samoa. Master's the-
          sis, Pacific Theological College, Suva.
Tapuai, Fa'atauva'a
  1972   A Comparative Study of the Samoan and the Hebrew Concepts of the
          Covenant. BD thesis, Pacific Theological College, Suva.
Tate, Henare Arekatera
  2010   Towards Some Foundations of a Systematic Māori Theology: He Tiro-
          hanga Anganui Ki Ētahi Kaupapa Hōhonu Mō Te Whakapono Māori.
          PhD dissertation, Melbourne College of Divinity.
Taule'ale'ausumai, Feiloaiga Janette
  1994   The Samoan Face of God. Master's thesis, Victoria University, Wellington,
          New Zealand.
Tcherkézoff, Serge
  2000   The Samoan Category Matai ("Chief"): A Singularity in Polynesia? Histor-
          ical and Etymological Comparative Queries. *Journal of the Polynesian Society*
          109 (2): 151–190.
  2008   *"First Contacts" in Polynesia: The Samoan Case (1722–1848); Western Misun-*
          derstandings about Sexuality and Divinity. New edition. Canberra: ANU E
          Press. First published in 2004 (Christchurch: Macmillan Brown Centre
          for Pacific Studies; Canberra: Journal of Pacific History).
  2015   "Sister or Wife, You've Got to Choose": A Solution to the Puzzle of Village

Exogamy in Samoa. In *Living Kinship in the Pacific,* edited by Christina Toren and Simonne Pauwels, 166–185. New York: Berghahn.

Te Paa, Jenny
    2007   Kia Rangona Te Reo o Te Wahine: Let the Voices of Women Be Heard. In *Pacific Indigenous Dialogue on Faith, Peace, Reconciliation and Good Governance,* edited by Tui Atua Tupua Tamasese Taisi Efi, Tamasailau M Suaalii-Sauni, Betsan Martin, Manuka Henare, Jenny Plane Te Paa, and Taimalieutu Kiwi Tamasese, 119–127. Le'auva'a, Sāmoa: Alafua Campus Continuing and Community Education Programme, University of the South Pacific.
    2011   Context, Controversy, and Contradiction in Contemporary Theological Education: Who Bene "Fits" and Who Just Simply Doesn't Fit? In *Contextual Theology for the Twenty-First Century,* edited by S B Bevans and K Tahaafe-Williams, 69–86. Eugene, OR: Pickwick Publications.

Thompson, Liona Le'i
    2007   Toward a Relational Theology of the Fa'a-Samoa. DMin professional project, Claremont School of Theology.

Thornley, Andrew
    2005   *A Shaking of the Land: William Cross and the Origins of Christianity in Fiji.* Suva: Institute of Pacific Studies, University of the South Pacific.

Thorogood, Bernard
    1960   *Not Quite Paradise.* London: London Missionary Society.
    1967   The Church as Establishment. *Pacific Journal of Theology* 23–24: 3–6.
    1995   After 200 Years—The LMS Legacy. *Pacific Journal of Theology* (series 2) 14:5–15.
    2014   *A Minister's Minutes.* Bloomington, IN: Xlibris.

Tillich, Paul
    1959   *Theology of Culture.* Edited by Robert C Kimball. Oxford: Oxford University Press.

Tion Bird, Siera
    2003   A Widening Road: My Story of Becoming. In *Weavings: Women Doing Theology in Oceania,* edited by Lydia Johnson and Joan Alleluia Filemoni-Tofaeono, 192–199. Suva: Weavers/SPATS and Institute of Pacific Studies, University of the South Pacific.

Titimaea, Titimaea Sini
    2014   *Tsunami: Punishment or Natural?* Apia: Donna Lou Kamu.

Toap, Wesis Porop
    1998   A Melanesian Pig Theology: An Anthropological/Theological Interpretation of a Pig Culture amongst the Woala Highlanders of Papua New Guinea. Master's thesis, Pacific Theological College, Suva.

Tofaeono, Ama'amalele
    1993   A Quest for a Samoan Theology of Creation. BD thesis, Pacific Theological College, Suva.
    2000   *Eco-Theology: Aiga—The Household of Life; A Perspective from Living Myths and Traditions of Samoa.* Erlangen: Erlanger Verlag für Mission und Ökumene.
    2005   Behold the Pig of God: Mystery of Christ's Sacrifice in the Context of Melanesia–Oceania. *Pacific Journal of Theology* (series 2) 33:82–102.

2010 The Moana Declaration—An Eco-Theological Debate. *Concilium* 2010 (5): 78–87.

Toma, Vavae
1961 Foreword. *Pacific Journal of Theology* 1:1.

Tomlinson, Matt
2009 *In God's Image: The Metaculture of Fijian Christianity.* Berkeley: University of California Press.
2013 The Generation of the Now: Denominational Politics in Fijian Christianity. In *Christian Politics in Oceania,* edited by Matt Tomlinson and Debra McDougall, 78–102. New York: Berghahn.
2014a Bringing Kierkegaard into Anthropology: Repetition, Absurdity, and Curses in Fiji. *American Ethnologist* 41 (1): 163–175.
2014b *Ritual Textuality: Pattern and Motion in Performance.* New York: Oxford University Press.
2015a Gender in a Land-Based Theology. *Oceania* 85 (1): 79–91.
2015b A Preliminary Historical Survey of the *Pacific Journal of Theology*. *Pacific Journal of Theology* (series 2) 53:51–66.
2016 Little People, Ghosts, and the Anthropology of the Good. *Journal of the Polynesian Society* 125 (1): 11–32.
2017 Imagining the Monologic. In *The Monologic Imagination,* edited by Matt Tomlinson and Julian Millie, 1–18. New York: Oxford University Press.

Tomlinson, Matt, and Sekove Bigitibau
2016 Theologies of Mana and Sau in Fiji. In *New Mana: Transformations in a Classic Concept in Pacific Languages and Cultures,* edited by Matt Tomlinson and Ty P Kāwika Tengan, 237–256. Canberra: ANU Press.

Tomlinson, Matt, and Miki Makihara
2009 New Paths in the Linguistic Anthropology of Oceania. *Annual Review of Anthropology* 38:17–31.

Tomlinson, Matt, and Debra McDougall, editors
2013 *Christian Politics in Oceania.* New York: Berghahn.

Tomlinson, Matt, and Julian Millie, editors
2017 *The Monologic Imagination.* New York: Oxford University Press.

Tomlinson, Matt, and Ty P Kāwika Tengan
2016 Introduction: Mana Anew. In *New Mana: Transformations of a Classic Concept in Pacific Languages and Cultures,* edited by Matt Tomlinson and Ty P Kāwika Tengan, 1–36. Canberra: ANU Press.

Tone, Peteru
1986 The Place of Women in the Church and Society in the Pacific. In *Towards a Relevant Pacific Theology: Theological Consultation, Bergengren House, Suva, 8–12 July 1985,* 59–67. Suva: Lotu Pasifika.

Toren, Christina
1988 Making the Present, Revealing the Past: The Mutability and Continuity of Tradition as Process. *Man* (ns) 23 (4): 696–717.

Trompf, Garry, editor
1977 *Prophets of Melanesia: Six Essays.* Port Moresby: Institute of Papua New Guinea Studies; Suva: Institute of Pacific Studies, University of the South Pacific.

Tuaiaufai, Koneferenisi
    2007   A Reverse Perspective of Honour and Shame: A Socio-Scientific Interpre-
            tation of Philippians 1:12–21. Master's thesis, Pacific Theological College,
            Suva.
Tuilovoni, S A
    1948   The Effect of the War on the Church in Fiji. *International Review of Missions*
            37 (145): 76–79.
Tuivanu, Tuivanu
    2013   Taufaleali'i: Reorienting Theology of Leadership towards Mission in the
            Methodist Church in Samoa. Master's thesis, Pacific Theological College,
            Suva.
Tupu, Uesile
    2010   Matthew 25:14–30: A Concise Analysis of Scholarly and Ordinary Inter-
            pretations. BD thesis, Piula Theological College, Sāmoa.
    2012   Mutually Indispensable? A Theological Exploration of Uto ma le Maene
            as an Expression of Gospel and Culture Relationship in the Methodist
            Church in Samoa. Master's thesis, Pacific Theological College, Suva.
Turner, George
    1861   *Nineteen Years in Polynesia: Missionary Life, Travels, and Researches in the
            Islands of the Pacific.* London: John Snow.
Turner, James W
    1986   "The Water of Life": Kava Ritual and the Logic of Sacrifice. *Ethnology* 25
            (3): 203–214.
Tutuila, Fereti
    2009   A Critical Analysis of the Meaning of Tautua (Service) in the Lives of
            Faife'au Samoa (Samoan Ministers): Congregational Christian Church of
            Samoa (CCCS). Master's thesis, University of Auckland.
Tuwere, Ilaitia Sevati
    1989   Justice and Peace in the Womb of the Pacific. *Pacific Journal of Theology*
            (series 2) 1:8–15.
    1990   He Began in Galilee and Now He Is Here: Thoughts for a Pacific Ocean
            Theology. *Pacific Journal of Theology* (series 2) 3:4–9.
    1991   Theological Reflection on the Contextualisation of Spiritual Formation.
            Pacific Journal of Theology (series 2) 5:8–14.
    1992   Emerging Themes for a Pacific Theology. *Pacific Journal of Theology* (series
            2) 7:49–55.
    1995   An Agenda for the Theological Task of the Church in Oceania. *Pacific
            Journal of Theology* (series 2) 13:5–12.
    2002   *Vanua: Towards a Fijian Theology of Place.* Suva: Institute of Pacific Studies
            at the University of the South Pacific; Auckland: College of St. John the
            Evangelist.
    2006   A Were-Kalou Response to Epistemology. In *Dreadlocks Vaka Vuku,* edited
            by Mohit Prasad, 24–29. Suva: Pacific Writing Forum, University of the
            South Pacific.
    2007   Land: A Fijian Perspective. *Concilium* 2007 (2): 79–86.
    2010   Jesus as Tui (King) and Turaga (Chief). In *Oceania and Indigenous The-
            ologies,* edited by Elaine Wainwright, Diego Irarrázaval, and Dennis Gira.
            Concilium 2010 (5): 51–59.

Uasike, Lousiale
2010 Women's Ministry in Both Contemplation and Service: A Paradigmatic Representation of "Active Discipleship" in the Martha-Mary Story. In *Voices of Tongan Women: Theological Reflections,* edited by Marlene Wilkinson, 24–34. No listed publisher.

Unasa, Uesifili
2009 The Borderlands: Relocating Samoan Identity. In *Suʻesuʻe Manogi: In Search of Fragrance; Tui Atua Tupua Tamasese Taʻisi and the Samoan Indigenous Reference,* edited by Tamasailau M Suaalii-Sauni, Iʻuogafa Tuagalu, Tofilau Nina Kirifi-Alai, and Naomi Fuamatu, 265–272. Lepapaigalagala, Sāmoa: Centre for Samoan Studies, National University of Samoa.

Urban, Greg
2017 Cultural Replication: The Source of Monological and Dialogical Models of Culture. In *The Monologic Imagination,* edited by Matt Tomlinson and Julian Millie, 19–46. New York: Oxford University Press.

Urciuoli, Bonnie
2008 Skills and Selves in the New Workplace. *American Ethnologist* 35 (2): 211–228.

Uriam, Kambati
1999 Theology and Practice in the Islands: Christianity and Island Communities in the New Pacific, 1947–1997. PhD dissertation, Australian National University.
2005 Doing Theology in the New Pacific. In *Vision and Reality in Pacific Religion: Essays in Honour of Niel Gunson,* edited by Phyllis Herda, Michael Reilly, and David Hilliard, 287–311. Christchurch: Macmillan Brown Centre for Pacific Studies; Canberra: Pandanus Books.

Uriam, Kambati, and Helen Gardner
2018 Coconuts and Fautasi: In Search of a Pacific Theology. *St Mark's Review* 244:57–76.

Vaai, Upolu Lumā
2001 Towards a Theology of Giving with Reference to the Methodist Church in Samoa. BD thesis, Piula Theological College, Sāmoa.
2006 Faaaloalo: A Theological Reinterpretation of the Doctrine of the Trinity from a Samoan Perspective. PhD dissertation, Griffith University, Brisbane.

Vaaimamao, Seresese T S
1990 Mana: An Inquiry for a True Pacific Spirituality. BD project paper (equivalent to a thesis), Pacific Theological College, Suva.
1998 Justice and Righteousness: A Comparative Study of the Word Pair in Amos with Its Application to the Life of Communalism in Samoa. Master's thesis, University of Otago, Dunedin.

Vakaʻuta, Nāsili
1991 Tongan Culture and Christian Faith: An Artist's Impression. *Pacific Journal of Theology* (series 2) 5:82–83.
1998 Relocating the Boundaries: An Alternative for Biblical Interpretation. *Pacific Journal of Theology* (series 2) 20:40–53.
2010a Lau Faka-Tuʻa: Reading the Bible Tuʻa-Wise. *Concilium* 2010 (5): 45–50.
2010b Tālanga: A Tongan Mode of Interpretation. In *Talanoa Ripples: Across Borders, Cultures, Disciplines,* edited by Jione Havea, 149–165. Palmerston

North: Pasifika@Massey; Auckland: Masilamea Press. First published in 2009 in *AlterNative* 5 (1): 126–139.

2011   *Reading Ezra 9–10 Tu'a-Wise: Rethinking Biblical Interpretation in Oceania.* Atlanta: Society of Biblical Literature.

2014   Border Crossing/Body Whoring: Rereading Rahab of Jericho with Native Women. In *Bible, Borders, Belonging(s): Engaging Readings from Oceania,* edited by Jione Havea, David J Neville, and Elaine M Wainwright, 143–155. Atlanta: Society of Biblical Literature.

2015   Island-Marking Texts: Engaging the Bible in Oceania. In *Islands, Islanders, and the Bible: RumInations,* edited by Jione Havea, Margaret Aymer, and Steed Vernyl Davidson, 57–64. Atlanta: SBL Press.

Vaka'uta, Nāsili, editor
2011   *Talanoa Rhythms: Voices from Oceania.* Palmerston North: Pasifika@Massey; Auckland: Masilamea Press.

Valeri, Valerio
1985   *Kingship and Sacrifice: Ritual and Society in Ancient Hawaii.* Translated by Paula Wissing. Chicago: University of Chicago Press.

Vuetanavanua, Savenaca
2009   Veibuli (Chiefly Installation): A Theological Exploration. Master's thesis, University of Auckland.

Wainwright, Elaine M
2003   Looking Both Ways or in Multiple Directions: Doing Theology in Context in the Twenty-First Century. Inaugural Lecture as Head of the School of Theology at the University of Auckland, 28 October. Sound recording (Cassette SC04-050), University of Auckland Library.

2005   Looking Both Ways or in Multiple Directions: Doing/Teaching Theology in Context into the Twenty-First Century. *Pacifica* 18 (2): 123–140.

2010   Introduction. In *Spirit Possession, Theology, and Identity: A Pacific Exploration,* edited by Elaine M Wainwright, Philip Culbertson, and Susan Smith, v–x. Hindmarsh, South Australia: ATF Press.

Wainwright, Elaine M, Philip Culbertson, and Susan Smith, editors
2010   *Spirit Possession, Theology, and Identity: A Pacific Exploration.* Hindmarsh, South Australia: ATF Press.

Walley, Christine J
1997   Searching for "Voices": Feminism, Anthropology, and the Global Debate over Female Genital Operations. *Cultural Anthropology* 12 (3): 405–438.

Warrior, Robert Allen
1989   Canaanites, Cowboys, and Indians: Deliverance, Conquest, and Liberation Theology Today. *Christianity and Crisis* 49 (12): 261–265.

Weavers, Women in Theological Education
2006   *The Church and Violence Against Women: A Theological Education Course.* Suva: Weavers/SPATS.

Weber, Max
1978   *Economy and Society: An Outline of Interpretive Sociology.* Edited by Guenther Roth and Claus Wittich. Berkeley: University of California Press.

Wendt, Albert
1976a   The Faa-Samoa is Perfect, They Sd. In *Inside Us the Dead: Poems 1961 to 1974,* 46–47. Auckland: Longman Paul.

1976b   Towards a New Oceania. *Mana Review* 1 (1): 49–60.

Wete, Tamara
   2003   Motherhood: Feminist, Cultural and Theological Perspectives. In *Weavings: Women Doing Theology in Oceania*, edited by Lydia Johnson and Joan Alleluia Filemoni-Tofaeono, 49–57. Suva: Weavers/SPATS and Institute of Pacific Studies, University of the South Pacific.
Wheeler, Ray
   2002   The Legacy of Shoki Coe. *International Bulletin of Missionary Research*, April, 77–80.
White, Geoffrey M, and Lamont Lindstrom, editors
   1997   *Chiefs Today: Traditional Pacific Leadership and the Postcolonial State.* Stanford: Stanford University Press.
White, Lynn, Jr
   1967   The Historical Roots of Our Ecologic Crisis. *Science* 155 (3767): 1203–1207.
Wilson, Samuel
   1837   O le Evagelia a Mataio (The Gospel of Matthew). Huahine: LMS Mission Press.
Wolterstorff, Nicholas
   1995   *Divine Discourse: Philosophical Reflections on the Claim that God Speaks.* Cambridge: Cambridge University Press.
Wood, James
   2015   The Uses of Oblivion. *The New Yorker,* 23 March, 92–94.
Wood-Ellem, Elizabeth
   2000   Untitled tribute to Sione 'Amanaki Havea. *Pacific Journal of Theology* (series 2) 24:119.
World Council of Churches
   1982   Baptism, Eucharist and Ministry. Faith and Order Paper 11. Geneva: World Council of Churches.
   2004   Otin Tai Declaration. https://www.oikoumene.org/en/resources/documents/wcc-programmes/justice-diakonia-and-responsibility-for-creation/climate-change-water/otin-tai-declaration [accessed 21 March 2017]
   2009   Pacific Church Leaders' Statement: Our Oikos—A New Consciousness on Climate Change and Our Call to Action. [The "Moana Declaration."] https://www.oikoumene.org/en/resources/documents/wcc-programmes/justice-diakonia-and-responsibility-for-creation/climate-change-water/pacific-church-leaders-statement [accessed 1 March 2017]
Wright, Cliff, and Leslie Fugui, editors
   1986   *Christ in South Pacific Cultures.* Suva: Lotu Pasifika Productions.

Index

Page numbers in **boldface** indicate illustrations.

About the Author

Matt Tomlinson is associate professor of anthropology in the Department of Social Anthropology at the University of Oslo and the College of Asia and the Pacific at the Australian National University. He has conducted research in the Pacific Islands since 1996 and received his PhD from the University of Pennsylvania in 2002. He is the author of two previous books, *In God's Image: The Metaculture of Fijian Christianity* (2009) and *Ritual Textuality: Pattern and Motion in Performance* (2014). In addition, he has coedited several volumes, including *The Limits of Meaning: Case Studies in the Anthropology of Christianity* (with Matthew Engelke, 2006); *Christian Politics in Oceania* (with Debra McDougall, 2012); *New Mana: Transformations in a Classic Concept in Pacific Languages and Cultures* (with Ty P Kāwika Tengan, 2016); and *The Monologic Imagination* (with Julian Millie, 2017).